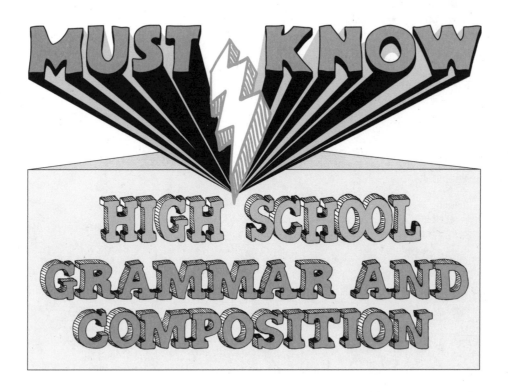

MUST KNOW

HIGH SCHOOL GRAMMAR AND COMPOSITION

Rosemary Scalera

Mc
Graw
Hill

New York Chicago San Francisco Athens London Madrid
Mexico City Milan New Delhi Singapore Sydney Toronto

1 2 3 4 5 6 7 8 9   LCR   28 27 26 25 24 23

ISBN   978-1-265-36962-0
MHID   1-265-36962-3

e-ISBN   978-1-265-37242-2
e-MHID   1-265-37242-X

Interior design by Steve Straus of Think Book Works.
Cover and letter art by Kate Rutter.

McGraw Hill books are available at special quantity discounts to use as premiums and sales promotions or for use in corporate training programs. To contact a representative, please visit the Contact Us pages at www.mhprofessional.com.

McGraw Hill is committed to making our products accessible to all learners. To learn more about the available support and accommodations we offer, please contact us at accessibility@mheducation.com. We also participate in the Access Text Network (www.accesstext.org), and ATN members may submit requests through ATN.

Contents

3 Colons and Semicolons   53

8 Sentence Structure and Variety 249

9 The Writing Process 287

Introduction

Welcome to your new Grammar and Composition book! Let us explain why we believe you have made the right choice. You may have found that a lot of books make promises about all the things you will be able to accomplish by the time you reach the end of a given chapter. In the process, those books can make you feel as though you missed out on the building blocks that you actually need in order to master those goals. You have probably also had your fill of books simply asking you to memorize several rules. This book has a different purpose. Although you are encouraged to memorize any or all the grammar rules, this book takes it a step further by helping you to understand the bigger picture and to transfer these skills into your everyday writing.

The *Must Know High School Grammar and Composition* book also has a unique and helpful format. At the start of every chapter, you will be introduced to one or more "Must Know" key ideas. These are the essential concepts that serve as the foundation of what you will learn throughout the chapter. To build on this foundation, you will find easy-to-follow rules of the topic at hand as well as comprehensive explanations, examples, and exercises—nearly 250 throughout the book—which will increase your ability to understand and remember the rules of grammar. Most chapters not only end with a set of review questions but also include an opportunity to incorporate your newly acquired skills in the context of writing.

This book has other features that will help you on your journey to learning grammar. It has a number of sidebars that will help provide helpful information or provide a quick break from your studies. The **BTW** sidebars ("by the way") point out important information and raise awareness regarding typical grammatical errors. Other times, an **IRL** sidebar ("in real life") will help you understand how what you are learning is connected to the real world. Other IRLs may just be interesting factoids.

In addition, this book is accompanied by a flashcard app that will give you the ability to test yourself at any time. The app includes 100 digital flashcards with a term, concept, or rule on one side and the answer on the other. Some readers choose to utilize the flashcards in isolation, while others prefer to attempt them after completing each chapter. To gain access to the app and learn how to use it, refer to the Flashcard App section below.

Before you get started, however, let us introduce you to your guide throughout this book. Rosemary Scalera has over 30 years of experience as an English Language Arts educator in all levels of middle school and high school. In addition, she is a sought-after college essay coach who has assisted hundreds of students in the college-application process by fostering their unique and sophisticated self-expression. Ms. Scalera understands what high school students need in a grammar and composition review book and has developed strategies to help you get there. Familiar with common errors and ongoing changes in the English language, Ms. Scalera will help you navigate these challenges by providing detailed explanations, varied examples, applicable exercises, and a practical writing section built into every chapter. We have great confidence in Ms. Scalera and are excited to leave you in her trustworthy hands as you expand your grammar and composition knowledge.

Before we leave you to the author's surefooted guidance, let us give you one piece of advice: While we know that saying something "is the *worst*" is a cliché, if anything *is* the worst in grammar, it is not knowing when to use "who" or "whom" or "affect" or "effect" when it matters most. Let Ms. Scalera clarify these uncertainties, so you will feel confident about your writing. Good luck with your studies!

The Editors at McGraw Hill

The Flashcard App

This book features a bonus flashcard app to help you test yourself on what you have learned. The app includes 100 grammar-related flashcards, featuring questions related to terms, concepts, or rules. Questions appear on the front of the card, and answers appear on the back. When you come to the end of each chapter, you will notice a QR code, which will link you directly to flashcards related to that particular unit of study. Although questions are organized according to chapter, you have the option to utilize flashcards at any point in your course of study.

To access the flashcard feature, follow these simple steps:

Search for the **Must Know High School** App from either Google Play or the App Store.

Download the app to your smartphone or tablet.

Once you have the app, use it in either of two ways:

Just open the app and you're ready to go.	Use your phone's QR code reader to scan any of the book's QR codes.
You can start at the beginning, or select any of the chapters listed.	You'll be taken directly to the flashcards that match the chapter you chose.

Be ready to test your grammar knowledge!

Capitalization

With the recent use of incorrect lowercase writing or the overuse of capitalization popular in texting and on social media posts, it is extremely important to understand that proper capitalization in academic and professional forums is not only recommended but required. Therefore, it is important to make the distinction between the two and know your audience.

Some of these rules may be a review for you, while others will be brand new. Either way, it is a good idea to practice capitalization skills.

Rule 1: Capitalizing the First Word of a Sentence, Salutation, and Closing

As you know, the *first word of a sentence* must be capitalized. This serves as a signal to the reader that a new complete thought is being introduced.

▶ To pursue her career as a film actress, Roma moved to Los Angeles.

The first word of the sentence—"To"—must be capitalized.

There is an *exception*, however. If you are connecting two related sentences with a *semicolon*, the first word of the sentence following the semicolon should *not* begin with a capital letter unless it is a word that must be capitalized such as the word "I" or a proper noun (like someone's name, the name of a specific place, etc.).

▶ Working on the weekends is not easy; everyone else has free time to socialize with their friends.

Since there is a semicolon preceding the word "everyone," and "everyone" is not a proper noun, it should not be capitalized.

When writing a letter, the first letter of the *salutation* and *closing* need to be capitalized.

> Dear Mrs. Rudolph,
>
> Thank you for hosting the club orientation meeting in your classroom. I look forward to working with you on several service projects this year.
>
> Sincerely,
> Joseph Bratstein
>
> *The word "Dear" is a salutation, and the word "Sincerely" is a closing in a letter, so the first letters of these words must be capitalized.*

Rule 2: Capitalizing the Pronoun "I"

In the English language, the word "I" is the only word that is capitalized no matter where it appears in a sentence (even though it is not a proper noun or proper adjective).

> Simeon and I love to waterski.
>
> *Even though "I" is not the first word of the sentence, it is always capitalized.*

Rule 3: Capitalizing Proper Nouns/Adjectives

As you know, a **noun** is a part of speech that represents a person, place, thing, or idea. There are two types of nouns: common nouns and proper nouns. **Common nouns** do not have a specific name (dogs, freedom) and are not capitalized. A **proper noun** is the *specific* name of a person, place, thing, or idea. Proper nouns are capitalized no matter where they fall in a sentence.

Proper nouns are never preceded by articles such as "a," "an," or "the" unless these words are part of a title or part of the name of a place or organization (*The Old Man and the Sea*, The Ohio State University, A Better Chance).

Proper nouns are not preceded by determiners such as "my" or "your" unless those words are part of a title, place, or organization (*My Antonia*, Your Heart on Art).

A common mistake made by students is that they capitalize the words "mother," "mom," "father," "dad," and other family members. The only time these words should be capitalized is if the student is addressing the person directly within dialogue format ("Mom, will you drive me to the party?"), if the word is followed by a proper name (Uncle Al, Grandma Mary), or if the word is used alone to replace a personal name (Did you see Mom at the grocery store?).

Students often make the mistake of capitalizing the words "high school." These words may only be capitalized if they are preceded by the name of the specific school (Green Oaks High School).

Smaller words within proper nouns are not capitalized unless they are the *first* word of the proper noun (*The Grapes of Wrath*, Joan of Arc).

The following chart will help you remember which nouns are proper nouns and will provide examples in each category for you. These categories need to be committed to memory, so you know whether to capitalize proper nouns when writing.

Categories of Proper Nouns

Names of people and pets	Examples
Geographical names such as	
• cities	Schenectady, NY
• towns	Carmel
• states	California
• sections of the country	the Northwest
• countries	Chile
• continents	Antarctica
• islands	Madagascar
• mountains/mountain ranges	Mount St. Helens/the Alps
• bodies of water	Great Salt Lake
• parks	Yellowstone National Park/Bronx Zoo
• streets	Nereid Avenue
• highways	Route 66
• provinces	Alberta
Special events, holidays, months, days of the week	Orange Bowl
	Memorial Day
	October
	Wednesday
Nationalities, tribes, religions, racial groups, languages	Japanese
	Inca
	Muslim
	Native American
	Farsi
Organizations, businesses, institutions, schools, government bodies, companies	the Salvation Army
	Olive Garden
	Vanderbilt University
	House of Representatives
	Google

(continued)

Categories of Proper Nouns, *continued*

Names of people and pets	Examples
Historical events and time periods	the American Revolution the Renaissance the Roaring Twenties the Great Depression the Civil Rights Movement
Brand names	Nike Abercrombie and Fitch Colgate
Title of a person when followed by a name	Aunt Celia Grandpa Frank Dean Black Pastor McDermott
Names of ships, planets, monuments, awards, aircrafts	*Lusitania* Venus Liberty Bell Pulitzer Prize *Concorde*

The *directional words* north, west, south, southeast, etc. are not capitalized when they simply refer to a direction and are not referring to a specific region of the country. Similarly, even though *planets* are capitalized, the words *sun, moon,* and *earth* are not capitalized when used by themselves. *Seasons* are not capitalized either.

EXAMPLES

> The roads to the east of Mill Highway were recently paved.
>
> *Since "east" does not refer to a specific region of a country, the word "east" should not be capitalized.*
>
> How soon will it be before citizens will be allowed to visit Mars?
>
> *Since Mars is a planet, it is capitalized.*

There are instances when adjectives are considered **proper adjectives**. This occurs when the noun form of that adjective is a proper noun and is normally capitalized (Canadian border, Christmas cards).

Did you know that there are standard correction marks or codes called **Proofreaders' Marks**? These symbols and abbreviations are used by editors and proofreaders. Perhaps you have seen these on some of the papers returned to you by teachers. If a letter is supposed to be capitalized but is not, you may see three short lines under that letter, indicating that letter should be a capital letter. You may also notice a slash through a letter. If you see that correction, it means that the letter should be lowercase.

The entire key to **Proofreaders' Marks** appears in Chapter 9.

Try using these marks while proofreading the sentences in the following exercises.

EXERCISE 1-1: Capitalization Rules 1–3

DIRECTIONS: The following sentences contain errors in capitalization.

- *Indicate that a letter should be capitalized by placing three small lines below that letter.*
- *Indicate that a capitalized letter should be lowercase by drawing a slash through that letter.*

1. I can't tell you why i am not going on our spring field trip out west to disney world in anaheim, california.

2. The newly elected President, abdullah shahid, addressed the united nations congregants in new york city.

3. do you know how quickly mars and venus rotate around the Sun?

4. *The Dublin merchant* was a ship that transported Irish emigrants from the city of cobh to Ellis island via the Atlantic ocean.

5. Does jivan celebrate hanukkah, kwanzaa, or Christmas?

6. calendars were developed in the bronze age by sumerians in Mesopotamia.

7. Do you prefer Band-aid bandages or Curad Bandages?

8. Early settlers in north America traveled West to explore the frontier.

9. The guest speaker shook the hand of principal Tomkins upon receiving the Most-valued Speaker award.

10. Fluffy, the siamese cat, runs faster than moxie, my german shepherd.

Rule 4: Capitalizing Abbreviations, Initialisms, and Acronyms

Abbreviations are shortened forms of actual words or phrases for the purpose of speeding up communication or using fewer symbols.

EXAMPLE

▶ After her back surgery, Harriet went to a rehab center to regain strength.

The abbreviation "rehab" is short for "rehabilitation." Notice that "rehab" is such a commonly known abbreviation that a period after the abbreviation is not even necessary.

An **initialism** is an abbreviation that shortens a term or phrase by representing it by using the first letters of the words. If the phrase or term has a small word within it (a, the, of), the first letters of those words are not usually included in the initialism.

Common initialisms seen in many different forms are those representing morning and afternoon. You have probably seen many different versions:

- 10:00 A.M.

- 10:00 AM

- 10:00 a.m.

- 10:00 am

So, which one is correct? The simple answer is that they are all used and acceptable. I tend to agree with the *Chicago Manual of Style* that lowercase "a.m." and "p.m." are best, since they are least commonly confused with other capitalized initialisms that use the same letters (AM for radio; PM for private message).

An **acronym** follows the same rules of capitalization as an initialism, so you may be wondering: What is the difference between them? The difference is in how the abbreviation is *pronounced*. If the abbreviation is read aloud letter by letter (DVR for "digital video recorder"), it is considered an initialism.

If the abbreviation is read aloud as one word (NASA for National Aeronautics and Space Administration), it is considered an acronym.

You may have noticed in the examples above that some initialisms and acronyms are formed from terms that are normally lowercase when spelled out (digital video recorder). That is because those terms are not proper nouns, but when they are shortened, capital letters are used to signify the abbreviation.

EXAMPLES

▶ It has been Moby's dream to work for the FBI.

> *"FBI" is an initialism, since we pronounce this abbreviation letter by letter: F-B-I.*

▶ To access the system, enter your PIN and password.

> *"PIN" stands for "personal identification number." It is an acronym because it is pronounced as a full word, "PIN," rather then letter-by-letter.*

A well-known example of a common noun that is capitalized when it is abbreviated is an *element* such as zinc or hydrogen. As you may know, the abbreviations for elements are capitalized: Z for zinc, H for hydrogen, etc.

Beware: Some element abbreviations begin with a different letter or different letters than the first letter of the element. This is often because the name of the element is derived from a word in Latin. For example, the abbreviation Fe is used for iron. This derives from the Latin word "ferrum," which means firmness.

If an *academic course* is referred to by an abbreviation, initialism, or acronym, it should be capitalized without periods (PE for physical education, APUSH for AP US History).

Although many abbreviations fall under the classification of either initialism or acronym, there are some abbreviations that do not fall under either category.

One type of abbreviation that *does not* fall under the category of initialism or acronym is the *shortening of a person's title.* The capitalization rule related to this is if the word would be capitalized in its full form, the abbreviation should begin with a capital letter (Doctor Smith = Dr. Smith). This only applies if the person's last name follows the abbreviation. If the sentence were rearranged with the word "doctor" elsewhere in the sentence, that word should not be abbreviated.

Incorrect: Roger Smith is a Dr.

Incorrect: Roger Smith is a dr.

BTW

Did you notice that periods are not used between the letters of initialisms and acronyms? In the past, it was customary to utilize periods between the letters of initialisms but not to use periods between the letters of acronyms, since acronyms were read as an entire word. However, nowadays, periods have been dropped between the letters of most initialisms as well. Exceptions are when initialisms can be confused with actual words in the English Language. P.O.W. stands for Prisoner of War but can also spell out the word "pow." The rules related to punctuating certain abbreviations vary by country. For example, in Great Britain, periods are not placed after abbreviated titles (Mr) or academic degrees (BA), whereas they are followed by a period in the United States.

EXAMPLE

▶ Roger Smith is a doctor.

The word doctor is separate from the last name "Smith." It should be spelled completely.

Other common abbreviations that require capitalization include *academic degrees* (Doctor of Philosophy = Ph.D. (The "h" is lowercase because it is part of the word "philosophy.")

One unusual set of abbreviations that does not follow the initialism or acronym format is the *US state postal code system.* This is because every state code is a two-letter code whether or not the state has two words. (MO = Missouri, MS = Mississippi, MI = Michigan, MN = Minnesota).

You may be wondering about the abbreviations popular in **text messaging**. Originally, text initialisms such as LOL and TTYL were capitalized. More recently, these expressions have become so well-known that capital letters have been eliminated. So, here is the best way to handle them.

When you are texting someone you know well, feel free to utilize either format.

However, if you refer to texting abbreviations in a formal setting or in a written paper, defer to the capital letters, as abbreviations in texts are technically considered initialisms and should, therefore, be capitalized.

Rule 5: Capitalizing Titles of Written Works, Pieces of Art, and Pieces of Music

When capitalizing *titles of stories*, *books*, *poems*, *speeches*, *plays*, *novels*, *memoirs*, *other publications*, *songs*, *operas*, *albums*, *symphonies*, *paintings*, and *sculptures*, always capitalize the first letter of the *first word*. Then, capitalize all words in that title except for:

- Articles (a, the)

- Coordinating conjunctions (and, or, but, yet, as, so, since, for)

- Short prepositions (at, from, for, in, of, to)

BTW

An exception is when the author/ artist uses all lowercase letters or all capital letters with intent. Here are some examples:

Poem title by e.e.cummings: "i carry your heart with me"

Song title by singer, Billie Eilish: "when the party's over"

Song title by rapper, Kendrick Lamar: "ELEMENT."

EXAMPLE

> *The Old Man and the Sea* is a famous novel by Ernest Hemingway.
>
> *Notice that the first "The" in the title is capitalized because it is the first word of the title. However, when the words "and" and "the" appear later in the title, they are lowercase.*

Rule 6: Capitalizing School Subjects and Courses

The names of *general school courses* should not be capitalized (math, science, social studies).

One exception is in the case of *language courses*, which should be capitalized (Chinese, American Sign Language).

If the title of a course is being provided, it should be capitalized (AP Chemistry, Social Studies 8, Writing 101).

NOTE: The capitalization and punctuation rules for courses presented as initialisms or acronyms are covered in the notes under Rule 3.

EXAMPLE

> Chelsea had trouble choosing an elective, since Chinese and cooking both interested her.
>
> *One course is a language (Chinese), so it must be capitalized, while the other course is general (cooking), so it does not require capitalization.*

The following exercises will help you practice distinguishing between the different types of capitalization rules discussed in the chapter.

EXERCISE 1-2: Capitalization Rules 4–6

DIRECTIONS: *Correct any words that are capitalized incorrectly or that need to be capitalized. Then, to the left of the question, write the letter of the rule that corresponds with your correction on the line provided.*

Rule Key
A: General Abbreviation Rule (unrelated to initialisms and acronyms)
B: Initialism Rule
C: Acronym Rule
D: Title of Work
E: Title of Course or School Subject

_____ 1. Dale decided to take math 202 in college even though he had never taken that course in high school.

_____ 2. Mr. Jones caught Bilal reading *The Fall Of The Roman Empire* in the hall right before the quiz.

_____ 3. Did you know that Dr. Phil does not have a Ph.d. or a D.P.C. degree?

_____ 4. It took Patty seven hours to drive from Baltimore, Md, to Raleigh, NC!

_____ 5. Etsy is known for its diy project ideas.

_____ 6. My grandmother has no idea what fomo means.

_____ 7. Zoe uses yolo and an emoji whenever she sends a meme to her cousin.

_____ 8. Although Mark was training to be a member of the Cia, he could not share this news with his family due to the confidential nature of the position.

_____ 9. Edgar traveled to Norway to see Edmund Munch's *the Scream* in person.

_____ 10. How did Guy do on the Foundations of Geology quiz?

EXERCISE 1-3: Writing with Capitalization

DIRECTIONS: In the space below, attempt to write a paragraph using all of the capitalization rules correctly. If you wish, you may use more than one capitalization rule within a sentence. Using parentheses after each sentence, write the number of the capitalization rule(s) you applied in that sentence.

PROMPT: You have decided to complete an application to take AP Art History as a senior in high school. As part of the application process, you must write a letter to your guidance counselor explaining why you qualify to be a student in that course.

Capitalization Rules

Rule 1: Capitalizing the First Word of a Sentence, Salutation, and Closing
Rule 2: Capitalizing the Pronoun "I"
Rule 3: Capitalizing Proper Nouns/Adjectives
Rule 4: Capitalizing Abbreviations, Initialisms, and Acronyms
Rule 5: Capitalizing Titles of Written Works, Pieces of Art, and Pieces of Music
Rule 6: Capitalizing School Subjects and Courses

_____

_____

_____

_____

Flashcard App

 # The Comma

MUST KNOW

 The comma is a very important punctuation mark that provides clarification and structure in a sentence.

 Commas help us understand what we are reading. They are so important that the entire meaning of a sentence can change based on a misplaced comma.

 Commas are also used to provide emphasis of certain words, phrases, and clauses.

What is the comma, and why does it "give us pause"? There are several comma rules to learn and even some exceptions to those rules. This chapter will help you have a better understanding of when and why to use a comma correctly. Try not to be overwhelmed with the number of comma rules in this chapter. Many will seem familiar to you. Others might include something you never knew. Either way, you will become a more sophisticated writer if you use the comma correctly.

Rule 1: Items in a Series

This is a rule that may be familiar to you. We insert a comma in a sentence when *listing more than two nouns, verbs, adverbs, or phrases.*

- The comma before the word "and" is also called the **Oxford** or **serial comma**.

- Some style guides such as *Chicago Manual of Style* use this comma, while others, including the *Associated Press (AP) Stylebook*, disagree with it.

NOTE: This rule *does not apply* when numerous *adjectives* appear in a sentence.

EXAMPLES

▶ Seth Rogen is a writer, a comedian, and a filmmaker.

Since we are listing more than two nouns, a comma belongs after "writer" and after "comedian" if we are including the Oxford comma.

▶ Cynthia crossed the path skillfully, carefully, and methodically.

Since we are listing more than two adverbs, a comma belongs after "skillfully" and after "carefully" if we are including the Oxford comma.

IRL In 2020, the Oxford comma was at the center of a $5 million class-action lawsuit filed by dairy drivers. A judge ruled in the drivers' favor, since the dairy's overtime policy was unclear due to the lack of an Oxford comma in a particular portion of the contract.

Rule 2: To Keep Numbers Clear

Most people know how to use commas to represent *place value* in numbers. Believe it or not, this varies by the country or language in which the number is being used, or even the context, such as in scientific writing. In certain countries, it is customary to punctuate numbers by using periods rather than commas.

Lately, in countries where English is spoken, commas may or may not be used in four-digit numbers. Perhaps this is because of how we read these numbers, like saying 2054 as "twenty fifty-four" rather than "two thousand fifty-four." Commas are always used in numbers over 10,000, and are placed every three digits from the right.

Some types of sentences, such as sentences that require **sequencing**, fall under Rule 2 (even though the sequential words may not include numbers at all). For introductory words to be classified as sequential, there must be multiple consecutive sentences beginning with introductory words that are listed in a *definite* order.

EXAMPLES

▶ Maxx received 12,476 demerits for chewing gum in class.

The comma is included after the 2 in the number 12,476 because you count three places backward from the right to indicate the thousands place.

> First, wake up. Then, eat breakfast. Next, take a shower. Finally, get dressed.
>
> *This is an example of sequencing. Even though there are no numbers in this sentence, the sentences must remain in sequential order, which falls under the umbrella of keeping numbers clear.*

Rule 3: In Dates and Addresses

When writing a date that includes the year, place a comma *between the day and the year*. Also, you must include a comma *between the city and state* or *between the city and country*. *Never* place a comma between the state and the zip code. In certain style guides such as *CMOS*, a comma is also placed *after* the year, state, or country if the sentence continues.

EXAMPLES

> Julia's birthday is September 25, 1996.
>
> *When writing the date, the comma belongs after the day and before the year.*

> Madame Therese travels to Paris, France every year.
>
> *The comma also belongs between a city and a country.*

BTW

There is something called an **Envelope Rule**. If you are writing out an address within a full sentence, you must place a comma after the word that would be the last word on the line of an addressed envelope. This is how the address looks on the envelope:

Jay Smith
Avian Middle School
26 Mill Road
Phoenix, Arizona 85003

Here is what it looks like in a sentence:

Please mail a replacement to Jay Smith, Avian Middle School, 26 Mill Road, Phoenix, Arizona 85003.

The comma goes after "Smith," "School," and "Road" because those are the last words that appear on each line of the envelope. Of course, you still need the comma between "Phoenix" and "Arizona" because of the city and state rule.

Rule 4: To Set Apart an Explanatory Phrase from a Direct Quotation

Commas are used to separate direct quotations from explanatory phrases. The term **direct quotation** refers to the *exact* words of a speaker. An **explanatory phrase** tells us who is speaking. This comma rule can only be applied if there are quotation marks in the sentence. The placement of the comma changes depending on whether the explanatory phrase is placed at the beginning, middle, or end of the sentence.

When a sentence ends in a quotation, *an ending comma or period must go inside the quotation mark.* An ending question mark or exclamation point goes inside the quotation mark if it is *part of the quotation* and outside the quotation mark if it is not.

▶ Ethan exclaimed, "The math exam was so easy!"

When the explanatory phrase is at the beginning of the sentence, only one comma is required. The comma goes after the explanatory phrase "Ethan exclaimed," and before the quotation mark. The ending exclamation point goes inside the quotation mark because it is part of the quotation.

▶ "What if," asked Jenny, "someone doesn't finish the test in the allotted time?"

When the explanatory phrase comes in the middle of a sentence, two commas are required—one before the first closing quotation mark (. . . if,") and one immediately after the explanatory phrase and before the next opening quotation mark (asked Jenny, "someone . . .).

▶ "I love Keith Urban," said Gina.

When the explanatory phrase comes at the end of the sentence, only one comma is required. The comma belongs BEFORE the closing quotation mark (. . . Urban,").

Rule 5: To Set Apart Interruptions

Interruptions are words or phrases that can be added to a sentence. They come after the first word of the sentence and before the last word of a sentence.

They *add no details* to a sentence, so they can't be someone's name or any other details.

The interruption can be removed from the sentence, and the sentence will still make sense.

Interruptions need to be *surrounded* by commas.

Common Interruptions

for example	therefore
I suppose	furthermore
I believe	thus
by the way	nevertheless
in any event	of course
in any case	in fact

The same words or sets of words can serve different functions in a sentence, depending upon their placement. Therefore, the words listed in the box above are not *always* considered interruptions.

EXAMPLES

▶ The giraffe, in fact, has no vocal cords.

The phrase "in fact" comes between the subject and the verb of the sentence. It adds no detail to the sentence. It can be removed from the sentence, and the sentence still makes sense. It needs to be surrounded by commas.

▶ There is, therefore, homework tonight.

The word "therefore" is in the middle of the sentence. It adds no detail to the sentence. It can be removed from the sentence, and the sentence still makes sense. It needs to be surrounded by commas.

Rule 6: Introductory Words

Introductory words or short phrases must be the *first* word/words of the sentence.

Often, introductory words end in "ly" (adverbs).

If more than one introductory word is connected by the word "and," the comma goes after the last introductory word.

Normally, **prepositions** (Rule 10) are *not* considered introductory words. Three exceptions to that rule are "for example," "for instance," and "of course," which count as introductory phrases and should be followed by a comma, despite their short length.

The introductory word/words *can* be removed from the sentence, and the sentence will still make sense.

EXAMPLES

▶ Clearly and concisely, the debater presented the closing argument.

The word "clearly" and the word "concisely" are adverbs that appear at the beginning of the sentence and are connected by the word "and." When two "ly" adverbs begin a sentence and are connected by the word "and," they are considered introductory words, and the comma should be placed after the second adverb. (NOTE: If there are three adverbs at the beginning of a sentence, follow Rule 1: Items in a Series.)

▶ Therefore, most high school students read Shakespeare's sonnets and plays.

In this sentence, the word "therefore" is at the beginning of a sentence, so it is considered an introductory word. It should be followed by a comma. If the word "therefore" were in the middle of the sentence, it would be an interruption (Rule 5).

▶ First, go to your Period 1 class.

> *Sequential words that come at the beginning of a sentence are usually considered introductory words. The exception is if they appear at the beginning of consecutive sentences that must be in a definite order. In that case, the comma placement remains the same, but the comma rule is Rule 2: To Keep Numbers Clear.*

Rule 7: When Directly Addressing a Person, Animal, or Group

The term **direct address** means when someone is addressing a person, animal, or group by their name.

The person's/animal's/group's name may come at the beginning, in the middle, or at the end of the sentence and must be set apart from the rest of the sentence by either one comma or two, depending on where it appears in the sentence.

When the name falls in the middle of the sentence, it needs to be *surrounded* by commas.

The name can be removed from the sentence, and the sentence will still make sense.

EXAMPLES

▶ Roberto, your hair looks great.

> *The speaker is talking directly to Roberto. Roberto's name can be taken out of the sentence, and there is still a complete sentence. Roberto's name must be followed by a comma. NOTE: Roberto is not an "introductory word." Rules 6 and 7 are not interchangeable.*

▶ Your talking, Rodney, has to stop.

The speaker is talking directly to Rodney, but Rodney's name is in the middle of the sentence, so his name needs to be SURROUNDED by commas. Rodney's name can be removed from the sentence, and it is still a complete sentence. NOTE: Rodney is not considered an "interruption" because Rodney adds information to the sentence.

▶ Thanks for the beautiful gift, Vivek.

Since the speaker is talking directly to Vivek and his name ends the sentence, a comma is necessary before Vivek's name. Vivek's name can be removed from the sentence, and there is still a complete sentence.

▶ Friends and family, I welcome you to our annual Thanksgiving celebration.

If the speaker addresses two people/animals or two sets of people/animals, the comma belongs after the second set. (If there are three people/animals or sets of people/animals at the beginning of a sentence, follow Rule 1: Items in a Series.)

Rule 8: To Set Apart Appositives from the Sentence

An **appositive** is a word or a group of words normally placed *after a noun or pronoun* to identify it further.

An appositive can *hardly ever* be the first word of a sentence. (You will see the exception in Chapter 8.)

When an appositive falls in the *middle* of the sentence, it needs to be *surrounded by commas.*

When an appositive falls at the *end* of the sentence, it should only be *preceded by a comma.*

An appositive can be removed from the sentence, and the sentence will still make sense.

▶ My brother, Fred, is flying here from Florida.

The name "Fred" is an appositive. It describes further the word "brother," which is a noun. The name "Fred" needs to be surrounded by commas, since it appears in the middle of the sentence. "Fred" can be removed from the sentence, and the sentence still makes sense.

▶ Dr. Dre, the cofounder of Death Row Records, mentored many rappers including Eminem.

The phrase "the cofounder of Death Row Records" is an appositive. It further describes "Dr. Dre," which is a proper noun. The phrase "the cofounder of Death Row Records" needs to be surrounded by commas, since it appears in the middle of the sentence. The phrase "the cofounder of Death Row Records" can be removed from the sentence, and the sentence still makes sense.

▶ Ms. Schwartz used to spend so much time with Buttercup, her tortoise, rather than with Chiquita, her iguana.

Some sentences have multiple appositives. In this sentence, "her tortoise" further describes the noun, "Buttercup." Since "her tortoise" is in the middle of the sentence, it is surrounded by commas. The phrase "her iguana" is also an appositive. It further describes "Chiquita." Since "her iguana" falls at the end of the sentence, it only requires one comma before "her." Both appositives can be removed from the sentence, and the sentence still makes sense.

Rule 9: To Connect Independent Clauses

This rule is also known as the **Run-on Rule**. A sentence is considered a **run-on** if it involves the connection of independent clauses without the use of proper punctuation or without the inclusion of connecting words called conjunctions.

The term **independent clause** means the same thing as **sentence**.

When you have *two* sentences that are connected by a **coordinating conjunction**, you need to place a comma before that conjunction. This is called a *compound sentence*.

Here are examples of the most common coordinating conjunctions:

and, or, but, yet, so, as (when meaning "since");
since (when meaning "because")

When you are reading a sentence that looks like it may be a compound sentence, find the coordinating conjunction, and conduct the following test:

- Read all the words before the conjunction. Do they make up a sentence all by themselves?

- If so, test all the words following the conjunction. Can they stand alone to make up a complete sentence?

- If they can, your coordinating conjunction requires a comma before it.

> **BTW**
> Even though the word **"because"** is a coordinating conjunction, you should **not** place a comma before it when it is connecting two sentences. It is the exception to this rule.

EXAMPLES

Will you pass science, or will you go to summer school?

Once you identify the coordinating conjunction in this sentence, which is "or," read what precedes it. Then, read what follows it. Since "Will you pass science" and "Will you go to summer school" are both complete sentences, a comma must be placed before the word "or."

▶ Angie studied so much, yet she thought the test was difficult.

If you look carefully, you will find the words "so" and "yet" in this sentence. However, that does not mean you will need to place commas before both of them. You need to conduct the test! When you isolate the word "so" and read what comes before it, you will find the sentence "Angie studied." So far, so good. Now, read what follows the word "so." Uh-oh, "much yet she thought . . . " is not a complete sentence. That means that "so" is not serving as a coordinating conjunction in this sentence. (It is serving as an adverb here!) You should not place a comma before "so." Now, let's look at the word "yet." Read what comes before it: "Angie studied so much" is a sentence. Read what comes after the word "yet." "She thought the test was difficult" is also a sentence. Therefore, you need to place a comma before the word "yet."

Here are two examples of sentences that seem like compound sentences but are not:

EXAMPLES

▶ Claire shopped and ate lunch at the mall.

The word "and" is not connecting two complete sentences.

▶ I want to go to Fordham University because that is the college my relatives attended.

The word "because" is a coordinating conjunction in this sentence, but it does not require a comma before it. It is the exception to the rule.

There is one more error associated with this rule. It is called the **comma splice**, which is a term that refers to a situation when two independent clauses are joined with only a comma, instead of with a comma and a coordinating conjunction. As you know, commas cannot connect two complete sentences.

Now that we have covered several comma rules, try your hand at inserting commas and identifying rules in the exercises that follow.

EXERCISE 2-1: Comma Rules 1–9

DIRECTIONS: Using the rule bank below, complete the following tasks:

- *Insert necessary commas in sentences. (Not all sentences require a comma.)*
- *Write the number of the rule to the left of the question, or if the sentence does not require a comma, write **NC** (for No Comma).*
- *Never replace a period with a comma.*

Comma Rules 1–9
Rule 1: Items in a Series
Rule 2: To Keep Numbers Clear
Rule 3: In Dates and Addresses
Rule 4: To Set Apart an Explanatory Phrase from a Direct Quotation
Rule 5: To Set Apart Interruptions
Rule 6: Introductory Words
Rule 7: When Directly Addressing a Person, Animal, or Group
Rule 8: To Set Apart Appositives from the Sentence
Rule 9: To Connect Independent Clauses

_____ 1. Please forward the books to Sheila Royden 684 Main Street Roslyn NY 11545.

_____ 2. Jody wrote a letter to Marissa her best friend from camp.

_____ 3. Patrick decided to study for his quiz since his grades in math were plummeting lately.

_____ 4. Jason said that he forgot his lunch today.

_____   5. The French students did not have the opportunity to travel to Quebec Canada.

_____   6. Nicole went to the bank to the post office and to CVS before returning home.

_____   7. Incidentally you are wearing two different sneakers.

_____   8. The grades therefore were lower than expected.

_____   9. Poppy enjoys going to the gym but hates working out.

_____   10. Go over to the door Matt.

_____   11. Catch the ball. Then run down the court. Next aim for the hoop. Finally shoot.

_____   12. "I have no more patience for you" said Nurse Monroe.

_____   13. Carefully and skillfully the spider crafted its web.

_____   14. Ms. Ramirez the most patient teacher accepts late assignments.

_____   15. You have no more pencils. Therefore you can't take the test.

_____   16. There are over 12642 students in the Fairlawn School District.

_____   17. Brian listens to rock country and jazz in his spare time.

_____   18. "The way to get there" exclaimed the tour guide "is quite simple."

_____   19. Irony and coincidence are terms confused often.

_____   20. Physics is a challenging course so you need to review your notes nightly so you are prepared for class each day.

Rule 10: When Prepositional Phrases Begin a Sentence

To master this rule, you need to be very familiar with words called prepositions.

Prepositions are words most often used to tell *when* and *where* things happen.

Common Prepositions

about	beneath	in	past
above	beside	inside	since (time)
across	between	into	through
after	beyond	like (similar)	to (not infinitive)
against	but (except)	near	toward
along	by	of	under
among	concerning	off	until
around	down	on	up
at	during	onto	upon
before	except	out	with
behind	for	outside	within
below	from	over	without

The comma rules for prepositions are only relevant if the preposition is the *first word of the sentence*.

Once you have identified a preposition as the first word of the sentence, identify the noun/pronoun that follows it. That noun or pronoun is called the **object of the preposition**. These words grouped together are considered a **prepositional phrase**. Remember, prepositions must be followed by nouns or pronouns called objects of the preposition. There are some instances when you might hear or read a preposition at the end of a sentence. In spoken language, it is becoming much more commonplace. In my opinion, however, in formal writing, it is better to avoid leaving the preposition at the end of a sentence by itself.

NOTE: What can also be confusing is that the words on the preposition list can sometimes serve as other parts of speech, such as adverbs. Before applying this comma rule, you need to ensure that the word is functioning as a preposition in the sentence.

When you are starting to learn about prepositional phrases, here are two tips to help you identify where a prepositional phrase begins and ends:

- Place a capital **P** above the preposition and the letters **OP** above the object of the preposition (noun or pronoun).

- A **prepositional phrase** begins with the preposition and ends with the object of the preposition. There can be words in between these two. Place the phrase in parentheses when you are considering whether a comma is required.

Follow these rules when you are determining whether to place commas after prepositional phrases:

Preposition Rule 1

Place a comma after a prepositional phrase if it appears at the *beginning* of the sentence (the preposition must be the first word of the sentence) and *contains more than two words*.

EXAMPLE

> **P   OP**
> ▶ (In the morning), I eat oatmeal for breakfast.
>
> *Since "in" is a preposition as the first word of the sentence and "morning" is the first noun that follows it, "In the morning" is considered a prepositional phrase. Because it is a three-word prepositional phrase, one must place a comma after morning (the OP). The word "I" (after "morning") is not a preposition, so there is only one three-word prepositional phrase at the beginning of the sentence.*

Preposition Rule 2

If two or more prepositional phrases in a row appear at the beginning of a sentence, place the comma *at the end of the final phrase in the series*.

> **P   OP   P   OP**
> ▶ (At the height) (of rush hour), there is a lot of traffic.
>
> *Since "at" is a preposition as the first word of the sentence and "height" is the first noun that follows it, "At the height "is a prepositional phrase. The word "of" is also a preposition, so we have to look for the noun that follows it, which is "hour." The word "there" is not a preposition. Therefore, we have two prepositional phrases in a row at the beginning of the sentence. We need to place a comma at the end of the final phrase, so the comma belongs after the word "hour."*

Preposition Rule 3

This part that tricks everyone: If a sentence begins with a prepositional phrase but there are *only two words in that phrase,* you should *not* place a comma there.

> **P   OP**
> ▶ (On Fridays) we have pizza for lunch in the cafeteria.
>
> *Since "On" is a preposition as the first word of the sentence and "Fridays" is the first noun that follows it, "On Fridays" is a prepositional phrase. We only have one two-word prepositional phrase at the beginning of the sentence, so we DO NOT place a comma after "Fridays."*

Preposition Rule 4

Of course, there is an exception to that rule! If you have *multiple* prepositional phrases at the beginning of a sentence, you should place a comma after the last phrase (*even if those phrases are only two words each*).

> **P OP   P   OP**
> ▶ (On top) (of spaghetti), I like a lot of cheese.
>
> *Since "On" is a preposition as the first word of the sentence and "top" is the noun that follows it, "On top" is a prepositional phrase. The word "of" is also a preposition, and the noun that follows it is "spaghetti." Multiple prepositional phrases at the beginning of a sentence, no matter how many words are in each phrase, require a comma after the last word of the last phrase (spaghetti).*

Remember: Three exceptions to this rule are "for example," "for instance," and "of course," which count as introductory phrases and should be followed by a comma despite the fact that they begin with a preposition and are only two words in length.

Preposition Rule 5

One more thing! If you have multiple prepositional phrases at the beginning of a sentence and they are connected by the word "*and*," treat them like they are directly next to each other and place the comma *after* the last phrase.

EXAMPLE

>   P   OP   P   OP
> ▶ (Over the river) and (beyond the trees), you will find a stream.
>
> *Since "Over" is a preposition as the first word of the sentence and "river" is the first noun to follow it, "Over the river" is a prepositional phrase. Even though the word "and" is not a preposition, the rule is if multiple prepositional phrases appear at the beginning of the sentence and are connected by conjunctions, the comma goes after the final consecutive phrase. After the word "and" (which is a conjunction), the word "beyond" is a preposition, and the word "trees" is the noun that follows it, meaning "beyond the trees" is an additional prepositional phrase. The word "you" (after "trees") is not a preposition. Therefore, we have two prepositional phrases in a row at the beginning of a sentence, and they are connected by the word "and," so the comma goes after the last object of the final phrase, which is "trees."*

Rule 11: To Separate Adjectives That Modify Equally

An **adjective** is a part of speech that tells us more about a noun or pronoun. Adjectives can tell us many things, including how many, which one, and what type.

Once you identify *multiple adjectives* in a sentence, you may need to place a comma between them. However, you don't need to have three or more adjectives to consider placing a comma in the sentence.

NOTE: Be sure that the sentence is not listing nouns, verbs, adverbs, or phrases. Then, you would be applying Rule 1 (Items in a Series).

There is a particular *order* in which adjectives need to be placed. If you have more than one adjective that fits into the same category (as listed below) you need a comma between them because their order in the sentence can be switched, and the sentence will still make sense. However, if you have multiple adjectives that fit *different* categories below, you *do not* need a comma between them.

Adjective Placement Order in Sentences

Order	Type of Adjective	Examples
First	determiner or article	a, an, the (articles) this, that, those, my, mine, your, yours, him, his, her, hers, their, theirs, some, our, several (determiners)
Second	number	two, four, few, couple
Third	quality or opinion	pretty, challenging
Fourth	size	tall, short, big, small
Fifth	age	young, old, new
Sixth	shape	round, oblong, irregular
Seventh	color/shade	blue, tan, dark, pale
Eighth	origin/ethnicity	Greek, Native American
Ninth	material	plastic, steel
Tenth	qualifier/other type of descriptor	*rush* hour, *after-school* activities,

This takes a lot of practice and is something that needs to be committed to memory. Native English speakers seem to know the order of adjectives in a sentence naturally, but many may not know whether a comma needs to be placed when writing a sentence that includes various types of adjectives.

NOTE: If the same types of adjectives are connected by the word "and" (in a series of more than two adjectives), a comma should be placed before the word "and," since the two adjectives joined by "and" can have the reverse order of word placement in the sentence.

Similar to what we did with prepositions, it is sometimes helpful to identify all the adjectives in a sentence by placing an **A** above them.

      A   **A**   **A**

▶ Jay is intelligent, kind, and athletic.

The reason why we need a comma between "intelligent" and "kind" is because they are the same TYPE of adjective, and their order can be switched, since the sentence will still make sense. The reason why we need a comma between "kind' and "and" is because the order of "kind" and "athletic" can be switched, since they are the same TYPE of adjective. In other words, we can say Jay is kind, intelligent, and athletic. We can also say Jay is intelligent, athletic, and kind.

    A **A**   **A**

▶ The tired, sweaty dog limped down the street.

There are three adjectives in a row here. We cannot switch the order of "The" and "tired," since they are different TYPES of adjectives (article and qualifier). However, we do need a comma between "tired" and "sweaty," since they are the same TYPE of adjective (qualifier), and their order in the sentence can be flipped and still make sense.

    A A **A**

▶ A big red truck was parked in the back of the building.

There are three adjectives in a row here. We cannot switch the order of "A" and "big," since they are different TYPES of adjectives (article and size). We also DO NOT need a comma between "big" and "red," since they are different TYPES of adjectives (size and color).

A   A   A   A   A   A   A

▶ Two large old blue, white, and green steel ships sailed away from the harbor.

> *There are five adjectives in a row here. We cannot switch the order of "Two" and "large," since they are different TYPES of adjectives (number and size). We also DO NOT need a comma between "large" and "old," since they are different TYPES of adjectives (size and age). We do not need a comma between "old" and "blue" because they are different TYPES of adjectives (age and color). However, we DO need commas after "blue" and after "white," since "blue," "white," and "green" are all the same TYPE of adjectives, and their order can be switched around (white, blue, and green; blue, green, and white). There is no comma between "green" and "steel," since they are different TYPES of adjectives (color and material).*

   A A   A   A   A

▶ The three creative, intelligent British men spoke at the conference.

> *There are five adjectives in a row here. We cannot switch the order of "The" and "three," since they are different TYPES of adjectives (article and number). We also DO NOT need a comma between "three" and "creative," since they are different TYPES of adjectives (number and quality). We DO need a comma between "creative" and "intelligent" because they are BOTH qualities, and their order in the sentence can be reversed, and the sentence will still make sense. We DO NOT need a comma between "intelligent" and "British," since they are different TYPES of adjectives (quality and origin).*

Congratulations, you have covered two of the most perplexing comma rules in the English language. Before moving forward with the rest of the comma rules, it might be helpful to practice Rules 10 and 11, since those require a great deal of concentration.

EXERCISE 2-2: Comma Rules 10 and 11

DIRECTIONS: Using the rule bank below, complete the following tasks:

- *Refer to the list of prepositions provided for you in this chapter. If the first word of the sentence appears on the preposition list, write **P** above the preposition and **OP** above the noun that follows it. Then, determine whether to place a comma. If the sentence requires a comma, write a **10** on the line provided. If the sentence does not require a comma (based on the preposition rules for commas), write **NC** (no comma) on the line provided.*

- *If the first word of the sentence is **not** a preposition, then you will be examining that sentence for adjectives that modify equally. Write an **A** above the adjectives that are in a sequence. Use the Adjective Placement Order chart (provided earlier in the chapter) to determine whether adjectives next to each other need a comma between them. If you place at least ONE comma between adjectives, write an **11** on the line provided. If you do not place any commas between sequential adjectives, write **NC** on the line provided.*

Comma Rules 10–11
Rule 10: When Prepositional Phrases Begin a Sentence **Rule 11:** To Separate Adjectives that Modify Equally

_____ 1. By the way the pollen index is 10 today.

_____ 2. Two big brown bears approached the campsite.

_____ 3. Under desks there are footrests.

_____ 4. The animals in the petting zoo were gentle friendly and playful.

_____ 5. On top of mountains there is a lot of snow.

_____ 6. Tennis players get a good night's sleep before participating in competitive arduous British tournaments such as Wimbledon.

_____ 7. Environmentalists are determined to save the environment by recycling old plastic water bottles.

_____ 8. After the prom and before graduation seniors take final exams.

_____ 9. The talented attractive actress received a bit part in the new _Star Wars_ movie.

_____ 10. The blue white and red French flag could be seen all over Paris on Bastille Day.

Rule 12: To Set Apart Nonrestrictive Clauses from the Sentence

Nonrestrictive clauses are groups of words that add information to a sentence.

They are like appositives (Rule 8) except they *must* begin with the words *who* or *which*.

They refer to a noun or pronoun that *precedes* them. This means that nonrestrictive clauses can *never* begin the sentence.

Nonrestrictive clauses can be taken out of a sentence, and the sentence will still make sense.

Nonrestrictive clauses are surrounded by commas when they fall in the middle of a sentence. They only require a comma before the clause if they appear at the end of the sentence.

The reason this type of clause is called **nonrestrictive** is because the clause, by itself, can form a complete question. It is *not dependent* upon the sentence's other words in order to be a complete thought.

EXAMPLES

▶ Sean Combs, who is the CEO of Bad Boy Records, has changed his name several times.

Locate the word "who" in the sentence. Notice that it is not the first word of the sentence. As you read from the word "who" forward, form the question to which the answer will be "Sean Combs." Those steps will help you identify the nonrestrictive clause. In this sentence, the nonrestrictive clause is "who is the CEO of Bad Boy Records" since Sean Combs (which precedes the word WHO) is the answer to that question. Since that nonrestrictive clause falls in the middle of the sentence, it needs to be surrounded by commas. Therefore, the commas belong before the word "who" and after the word "Records." To be certain you have placed commas correctly, remove the nonrestrictive clause from the sentence. You should still have a complete sentence remaining. "Sean Combs has changed his name several times" is a complete sentence in and of itself.

▶ Two periods per school day should be allocated for English Language Arts, which is such an important subject.

> *Identify the word "which" in the sentence. Notice that it is not the first word of the sentence. As you read from the word "which" forward, form the question for which the answer will be "English Language Arts." Those steps will help you identify the nonrestrictive clause. In this sentence, the nonrestrictive clause is "which is such an important subject" since English Language Arts (which precedes the word WHICH) is the answer to that question. Since that nonrestrictive clause falls at the end of the sentence, it needs only one comma before the word "which." To be certain you have placed commas correctly, remove the nonrestrictive clause from the sentence. You should still have a complete sentence remaining. "Two periods per school day should be allocated for English Language Arts" is a complete sentence in and of itself.*

Side note: I had to give a shout-out to English Language Arts somewhere in the book.

Rule 13: After Salutations (in Friendly Letters) and Closings (in All Letters)

This rule is associated with letter writing. You may remember the terms **salutation** and **closing** from Chapter 1 (Capitalization).

A **salutation** is also known as a *greeting*. It is at the beginning of a letter, where you address the person before writing the body of the letter. If it is a *friendly letter* (meaning you know the person well and you are not writing to a person of authority), the salutation ends in a comma. If it is a *business letter*, which is more formal (such as a letter to your school principal or a company president), the salutation ends with a colon (:).

After the body of a letter, it is customary to include a **closing** (also called a **complimentary closing**) before signing or typing your name. Closings are *always* followed by a comma (never a colon).

 IRL In today's world, we often communicate with others via emails, text messages, or social media platforms. Salutations and closings are not used in these situations.

"Thank you" is not considered an appropriate closing. If a writer wishes to give thanks to the letter's recipient, that must be stated within the body of the letter.

> Dear Hailey,
>
> *Assuming the writer of the letter knows Hailey or is in the same status as Hailey, a comma is appropriate here.*
>
> Love, Justin
>
> *"Love" is considered a closing. Other common closings are "Sincerely" and "Yours truly." A comma must follow the closing.*

A common error made by writers (as noted in Chapter 1) is when writers place a comma instead of a colon at the end of the salutation in a business letter. Here is how a salutation in a business letter should appear:

> To Whom It May Concern:
>
> *This is a common salutation for business letters when a person is writing to a company and does not know a specific contact person's name. Since there is no familiarity with the person being addressed, the appropriate salutation end mark is a colon.*

Rule 14: To Avoid Confusion

Sometimes, a comma is required because of the way your eyes tell your brain to read a sentence. Without the comma, the sentence cannot be comprehended easily. The comma is necessary for inflection or for clarity. This often happens when the same word is repeated consecutively in a sentence.

BTW

Many students think this is the rule of taking a breath or pausing, which, in fact, is **not a rule at all.** *That's right! There is no comma rule related to breathing or pausing. However, there is a rule associated with pausing when it comes to reading aloud. When one is reading aloud and comes to a comma, the reader often pauses for emphasis, inflection, or clarity.*

EXAMPLES

▶ The cat the boy had, had fleas.

If the comma were not in the sentence, the reader would automatically assume they misread this sentence, or they might misinterpret it as a typographical error. However, the word "had" in this sentence has two different functions. The first "had" means "owned." The second "had" means "acquired." Therefore, both "had" words make sense as long as the comma is between them so as to avoid confusion.

▶ Pick me, not him.

If this sentence did not have the comma, the reader's brain would automatically group "Pick me not" together and then read the word "him" separately. That would not make sense and would prompt the reader to begin reading the sentence again. This type of word grouping requires a comma between the words "me" and "him" for clarity.

Rule 15: To Set Apart Subordinate Clauses from the Sentence

The words listed below are called **subordinate conjunctions**. They are sometimes at the beginning of a sentence. When they are grouped together with other words to create a reasoning or explanation, that group of words is called a **subordinate clause**. Even though a subordinate clause contains a noun and a verb, it is not a complete sentence by itself. It is *dependent* upon the rest of the sentence to be a complete thought.

Common Subordinate Conjunctions

although	provided	when
as if	since	whenever
as long as	so that	wherever
because	though	while
if	unless	
in order that	whatever	

To consider whether or not a comma is required based on this rule, the subordinate conjunctions have to be the *first word* of the sentence.

Follow this test to see if you have placed the comma in the correct place:

- Identify the first word of the sentence as a subordinate conjunction. (**NOTE:** If these words appear elsewhere in the sentence, you *may* need to place a comma, but it will not be related to Rule 15.)

- Decide where you think the comma belongs in that sentence. Begin with the conjunction and follow the group of words along until the reasoning, condition, or explanation is complete.

- Move that entire group of words (from the conjunction to where you placed the comma) to the end of the sentence.

- See if the sentence makes sense in the inverted order. If it makes sense, then you placed the comma in the right place!

NOTE: This can be tricky! Sometimes, when a subordinate clause begins a sentence, you may see that there are *two identical words in succession* in the sentence. This doesn't mean it is automatically Rule 14 (To Avoid Confusion).

The way to know is to conduct the test we tried previously. Place the comma between the two words that are identical. Then, move the subordinate clause from the beginning of the sentence to the end of the sentence. If the sentence still makes sense, apply Rule 15. If it doesn't, apply Rule 14.

EXAMPLES

▶ Because the bad weather is affecting road conditions, after-school activities will be cancelled.

The word "Because" is on the list of subordinate conjunctions, and it appears as the first word of the sentence. If you read the sentence, the explanation for why activities are cancelled is "Because the bad weather is affecting road conditions." This means that "Because the bad weather is affecting road conditions" is a subordinate clause. It cannot be a sentence by itself, though it does contain a noun (weather) and a verb (is). To be sure the comma placement is correct, move the subordinate clause to the end of the sentence, and reread the sentence. Since "After-school activities will be cancelled because the bad weather is affecting road conditions" is a sentence, you know you have placed the comma in the appropriate spot (in the original sentence).

▶ Whenever there are several inches of snow, snow accumulates on cars.

Be careful! This looks so much like Rule 14 (To Avoid Confusion), but it is not. The difference is that the first word of this sentence is a subordinate conjunction. Since "Whenever" begins the sentence, find the condition or explanation. You should have found "Whenever there are several inches of snow." Even though there is a pronoun (there) and a verb (are), "Whenever there are several inches of snow" cannot be a sentence by itself. It is dependent upon the rest of the sentence in order to be a complete thought. Move that clause to the end of the sentence to see if it makes sense: "Snow accumulates on cars whenever there are several inches of snow." Since you can reverse the order of the subordinate clause and the remainder of the sentence, you know that the comma belongs between "snow" and "snow."

Remember when your teacher told you that the word "because" could never begin a sentence? As you can see, that is not entirely true. Your teacher told you that because many young students treat a subordinate clause beginning with the word "because" as an entire sentence. This would be a fragment without the help of an independent clause attached to it.

Phew! Did you have any idea there were so many rules for commas? It is time to do some more practice with exercises in isolation before attempting to compose the writing piece at the end of the chapter.

EXERCISE 2-3: Comma Rules 12–15

DIRECTIONS: *Using the rule bank below, complete the following tasks:*

- *Insert necessary commas in the sentences. (Not all sentences require a comma.)*

- *When an example contains a salutation, write either a comma or a colon (based on your knowledge of the use of these two punctuation marks in salutations).*

- *Write the number of the rule to the left of the question, or if the sentence does not require a comma, write **NC** (for No Comma).*

- **Never** *replace a period or any other punctuation mark with a comma.*

Comma Rules 12–15
Rule 12: To Set Apart Nonrestrictive Clauses from the Sentence
Rule 13: In Salutations and Closings
Rule 14: To Avoid Confusion
Rule 15: To Set Apart Subordinate Clauses from the Sentence

_____ 1. Dear Dr. Wilburt

    Please consider me for the summer internship. I look forward to meeting you in the near future.

                         Sincerely

                         Tobias Gordon

_____ 2. Remember not to place a comma before "because" when practicing Comma Rule 9.

_____ 3. When your tights have a run run to the mall to buy a new pair.

_____ 4. The spider that the bird ate ate two flies earlier that morning.

_____ 5. Dear Patrice

    I can't wait to have a sleepover once the school year ends!

                         Your friend

                         Mannat

_____ 6. As the roller coaster picked up speed the riders screamed loudly.

_____ 7. If you want to follow the speed limit limit the amount of pressure you place on your brakes.

_____ 8. My dearest Matthew thanked his friend sincerely.

EXERCISE 2-4: Writing with Commas

DIRECTIONS: In the space below, attempt to write a paragraph using **at least ten** *of the comma rules correctly. If you wish, you may use more than one comma rule within a sentence. Use parentheses after each sentence to write the number of the comma rule(s) you applied in that sentence.*

PROMPT: Write about an embarrassing moment in your life.

Comma Rules
Rule 1: Items in a Series
Rule 2: To Keep Numbers Clear
Rule 3: In Dates and Addresses
Rule 4: To Set Apart an Explanatory Phrase from a Direct Quotation
Rule 5: To Set Apart Interruptions
Rule 6: Introductory Words
Rule 7: When Directly Addressing a Person, Animal, or Group
Rule 8: To Set Apart Appositives from the Sentence
Rule 9: To Connect Independent Clauses
Rule 10: When Prepositional Phrases Begin a Sentence
Rule 11: To Separate Adjectives That Modify Equally
Rule 12: To Set Apart Nonrestrictive Clauses from the Sentence
Rule 13: After Salutations and Closings
Rule 14: To Avoid Confusion
Rule 15: To Set Apart Subordinate Clauses from the Sentence

An Embarrassing Moment in My Life

_____

_____

_____

_____

_____

_____

_____

_____

_____

_____

_____

_____

_____

_____

_____

_____

_____

_____

Flashcard App

Colons and Semicolons

By now, you must be very familiar with the most common forms of punctuation such as the period, comma, question mark, and exclamation point. However, colons and semicolons play important roles in our written language. In my experience, students often try to avoid these marks because they do not understand their usage clearly. Well, it is time to change that and broaden your punctuation horizons! This chapter will be divided between rules and exercises devoted first to the colon and then the semicolon. This should provide some clarity when making distinctions between the two punctuation marks.

The Colon

A **colon**, which looks like two dots in a vertical row (:), usually indicates that additional, related information will be provided. Often, that information looks like a list within a sentence. The purpose of a colon is to provide a signal to the reader. What follows a colon is usually something that the author wants to emphasize. However, a colon may also be used to separate numbers in certain situations.

Rule 1: Using a Colon to Introduce an Idea, Item, or List of Ideas/Items in Sentence Format

Have you ever seen a colon that appears before a *list of items*? This is one of the most common uses of a colon, but it is a little more complicated than you might think. This rule applies to a colon used before a list, as long as that list is continued on the same line of text as the sentence that precedes the colon. Here are the rules associated with this type of colon:

1. A colon *should not follow a verb (unless it is an infinitive) or a preposition.*

2. A *complete sentence* must *precede* the colon. (Most people don't know this one!)

3. There should be a *space* after the colon.

4. The *first word after the colon should not be capitalized* unless it is a proper noun or the word "I." Of course, there are *two exceptions*!

   ■ If the information following a colon requires more than one sentence, then the first word of all the sentences following the colon should be capitalized (to indicate that they all relate to that one colon).

   ■ If the information following a colon is a direct quotation, then the first word of the direct quotation may or may not be capitalized.

EXAMPLES

▶ When you go camping, you must bring these supplies: a sleeping bag, a lantern, a tent, a cooler, and a grill.

Read what comes before the colon. Since "When you go camping, you must bring these supplies" is a complete sentence, we are allowed to place a colon after that sentence if what follows it is a list of some sort.

▶ Here are some pieces of advice given to me by my grandfather: Work hard. Respect your elders. Listen before you speak.

Read what comes before the colon. Since "Here are some pieces of advice given to me by my grandfather" is a complete sentence, we are allowed to place a colon after that sentence as long as what follows it is a list of some sort. Read what comes after the colon. Since these are a series of complete sentences, it is necessary to capitalize the "W" in the word "Work" as well as the first letters of the sentences that follow this one.

There are several instances when colons are misused. Here are two common colon errors:

Incorrect: The recipe includes: sugar, flour, eggs, cinnamon, baking powder, butter, and baking soda.

Read what comes before the colon. Since "The recipe includes" is NOT a complete sentence, the colon is misused here. Remember that the word "includes" is a verb, and a colon should not be placed directly after a verb unless it is an infinitive. There should be NO punctuation mark after the word "includes."

Incorrect: During the summer, D.C. campers are being taken to: the Smithsonian, the White House, the Washington Monument, and the Pentagon.

Read what comes before the colon. Since "During the summer, D.C. campers are being taken to" is NOT a complete sentence, the colon is misused here. Remember that the word "to" is a preposition in this sentence, and a colon should not be placed directly after a preposition. There should be NO punctuation mark after the word "to."

Rule 2: Using a Colon in Vertical Lists

This rule looks very similar to the previous one, since items are listed after the colon. However, the way the items are placed on the page makes a difference. In Rule 1, listed items must continue on the same line of text. However, Rule 2 addresses the colons organized in a *vertical list*. A **vertical list** implies that the list of items following a colon appears on separate lines of the page (one line for each item listed).

Style guides (MLA, APA, Chicago Manual, etc.) have differing rules regarding colons with vertical lists. Many people wonder whether colons can be used even though the words that precede the colon are not a complete sentence. They also wonder about whether items in these lists should be capitalized or not. Furthermore, they are not certain about end punctuation for each line or for the final line of the list.

Here is the most common way to handle vertical lists that are *preceded by a complete sentence*:

1. Be sure the introductory sentence is *followed by a colon*.

2. *Capitalize the first word of each line* of the vertical list (even if it is not the beginning of a sentence, a proper noun, or the word "I").

3. *Do not place an end mark* after the vertical list unless the line of the list is a complete sentence.

EXAMPLE

▶ There are many attributes of a top student:

- Determination
- Creativity
- Dedication
- Motivation

Notice that every word in the vertical list is capitalized. Also, notice that there are no punctuation marks after each word in the list.

Here is the most common way to handle vertical lists that are *preceded by a fragment*:

1. If a vertical list is being utilized after a fragment, a colon *may* be used. This means that *even though* the words before the colon are not a complete sentence, if there is a vertical list that follows, that fragment can *still* have a colon following it. (Confusing, isn't it?)

2. Capitalize the first word of the vertical list (even if it is not the beginning of a sentence, a proper noun, or the word "I" and even if it is a continuation of one long sentence).

3. Commas are *not necessary* after each bulleted item.

4. To decide whether each line of your bulleted list requires a period, read each line. If they are a series of complete sentences, place periods after each of them. If they are fragments, no periods are necessary. However, some style guides state that a period is not necessary at all, since it is implied.

EXAMPLE

▶ To win the scavenger hunt, players must:

- Follow directions carefully.
- Solve difficult puzzles.
- Work quickly and efficiently.
- Use deduction skills.
- Work collaboratively with teammates.

Did you notice that the introductory phrase was a fragment? According to the rule of "vertical lists," a colon may still be placed after a fragment when it precedes a list of items on separate lines. Also, the first word of each of these lines is capitalized (which they would be anyway since they begin complete sentences). Finally, notice the periods at the end of each line in the list. This is because each line of the list contains a complete sentence.

▶ All hockey players must bring:

- Knee pads
- Helmet
- Stick
- Skates

Did you notice that the introductory phrase was a fragment? According to the rule of "vertical lists," a colon may still be placed after a fragment when it precedes a list of items on separate lines. Also, the first words of each of these lines are capitalized, even though they are not complete sentences. Finally, notice that there are no periods at the end of each line in the list. This is because these are not complete sentences.

Rule 3: Using a Colon for Emphasis After a Key Word That Precedes Something Important

Sometimes, colons are used to bring *emphasis* to something important. Think of a colon as a set of eyes looking at you, saying "Read this!" To grab your attention, there are times when a colon is *preceded by one important word* that is a directive. The most common ones are the words "Warning" and "Danger." These words, when used in other contexts within a sentence, are not followed by a colon. However, if specific information related to the warning or the danger follows that word directly, then a colon must be placed after that word. You may sometimes even see these words capitalized for further emphasis. Additionally, the word that follows the key word and the colon *must* be capitalized.

IRL Think about how many times you have watched ads or read product packages. It is part of our everyday life. Have you noticed the small print? Ironically, advertisers are required to include important information about their products, but they often do not want people to notice this information, especially if these products are detrimental to a person's health. Common allergens and side effects are two common pieces of information included on labels or in advertisements. If you look closely, you will usually find a colon following the words "Warning," "Danger," "Allergens," or "Side Effects."

Other popular catchwords before colons are "Directions," "Instructions," "Note," and "Example." You may have noticed some of these words in this book, and you most certainly have seen them on assignments and in textbooks.

EXAMPLES

▶ DANGER: Slippery when wet

This is meant to grab a person's attention. Notice that the colon follows the word "DANGER," which appears in all capital letters. Also, the words "Slippery when wet" are not a complete sentence, so they are not followed by a period. The first letter of "Slippery" is still capitalized even though it does not begin a full sentence.

▶ Warning: Enter at your own risk.

Even though the word "Warning" is not completely capitalized, it is still meant to grab the reader's attention. That is why it is followed by a colon. The "E" in "Enter" is capitalized as well. Since the sentence beginning with "enter" is a full sentence, a period belongs after "risk."

Those initial words are meant to catch your attention and get you to keep reading. That does not mean that you should use these words within a formal piece of writing. Chapter 8 is devoted to coming up with ways to capture readers' attention and keep them engaged.

Rule 4: Using a Colon with Direct Quotations

Most of the time, we use a comma between an explanatory phrase and a direct quotation. The **explanatory phrase** shows who is speaking. When it is at the beginning of the sentence, it is ordinarily followed by a comma before the quotation begins. (You learned this in Chapter 2.) However, there are instances when a colon should be placed before direct quotations (rather than a comma).

Use a colon when the explanatory phrase appears at the beginning of a sentence and is a complete sentence in and of itself.

EXAMPLE

▶ Ms. Garcia responded with disdain: "You must leave the classroom because your interruptions distract others."

Because "Ms. Garcia responded with disdain" is a complete-sentence explanatory phrase that appears at the beginning of a sentence, it should be followed by a colon, not a comma.

The following example shows when a comma should be used instead of a colon:

EXAMPLE

▶ Jonah said, "I am pledging a fraternity."

A comma should be used, since the explanatory phrase "Jonah said" is not a complete sentence.

Occasionally, you may see a colon used after an explanatory phrase that is not a complete sentence (but it is not the norm). This can *only be acceptable* if the *direct quotation that follows is a complete sentence.* Remember, this is *the exception* rather than the rule.

Sally stated, "I can't believe you went to lunch without me." OR Sally stated: "I can't believe you went to lunch without me."

Either form of the sentence is correct (comma or colon after the explanatory words), since the direct quotation is a complete sentence ("I can't believe you went to lunch without me."). However, it is more customary to use the comma.

You may *never* use a colon after an introductory phrase if the direct quotation is *not* a complete sentence, such as in the example below:

Lianne answered Ethan with disgust, "Not a chance!"

Even though the explanatory phrase is a complete sentence (Lianne answered Ethan with disgust), a comma must be used (not a colon) because the direct quotation is not a complete sentence ("Not a chance!").

You may *never* use a colon if the explanatory words in the sentence come *after* the direct quotation at the *end* of a sentence. The following example shows you an explanatory phrase at the end of sentence:

"Victor is a loyal boyfriend," Fabiola confided in her parents.

When the direct quotation is a statement (not a question or an exclamation) and it is followed by explanatory words (Fabiola confided in her parents), a comma must be placed before the end quotes. One may never use a colon after the dialogue if the explanatory words fall AFTER the dialogue even if the explanatory words form a complete sentence.

Rule 5: Using a Colon with Salutations in a Business Letter

When you learned the capitalization rule for salutations in Chapter 1, and you learned the comma rule for salutations (also called "greetings") in Chapter 2 (Rule 13), those rules focused primarily on salutations in friendly letters.

However, it is important to remember that if you are addressing someone in a company, an official person, someone *you don't know personally*, or a person whose name you *do not know specifically*, it is appropriate to use a colon rather than a comma after that salutation.

EXAMPLE

> Dear Dr. Brilliant:
>
> It was my pleasure to meet with you yesterday afternoon. I would love to have the opportunity to discuss more internship options for next summer.
>
> *The salutation "Dear Dr. Brilliant" is followed by a colon because the person to whom you are writing either is someone you do not know well personally or is a person in a position of authority.*

Rule 6: Using a Colon Within Titles

Sometimes, titles of books or courses include **subtitles**. This occurs when the second part of the title further explains the first part. Usually, when there is a subtitle that follows a title of a book or a course, a colon and a space separate them (*English Writing and Composition: The Basics*).

► Are you registering for French Language and Composition: An Introduction or French Language and Composition: An Intermediate Study?

The name of the first course "French Language and Composition" has a subtitle "An Introduction." Since "An Introduction" is a subtitle, a colon and a space need to follow "French Language and Composition." The same holds true for the second course listed. There are a colon and a space between "French Language and Composition" and "An Intermediate Study" since one is the title and what follows is the subtitle.

Notice that the first word after the colon is CAPITALIZED, even if it is one of the smaller words in the English language (An).

► *The Art of Crocheting: The Ins and Outs of Stitching* is one of the best books for people learning this craft.

Since the book title listed above has a main title (The Art of Crocheting) and a subtitle (The Ins and Outs of Stitching), they are separated with a colon and a space.

Notice that the first word after the colon is CAPITALIZED, even if it is one of the smaller words in the English language (The).

There are two exceptions to the subtitle rule: If the first part of a title ends in a *question mark* or *exclamation point*, a colon is *not* necessary. Here is an example of a title where a colon is unnecessary:

► Since you are constantly having car trouble, I bought you the book *Not This Time! Avoiding Flat Tires off the Beaten Path.*

Even though the book title Not This Time! Avoiding Flat Tires off the Beaten Path *contains a main title and a subtitle, a colon is not necessary between the two because the main title is followed by an exclamation point.*

Rule 7: Using a Colon in Time, Ratios and Odds, Biblical References, Volume/Page Numbers

Other uses of the colon are related to the *separation of numbers*. Most of the time, each set of these numbers represents something different. The colon provides *clarity* and increased *understanding* (without the use of words for an explanation). *None* of these examples require a space after the colon.

1. In Time

As you know, when you are telling time, it is customary to say the number of the hour followed by the number of minutes past the hour (12:15) The "12" represents the hour, and the "15" represents the number of minutes after twelve. When we are writing the time, we separate the hour from the minutes with a colon.

EXAMPLE

▶ Let's meet for dinner at 2:15, so we can be on time for the 3:00 movie.

When we are referring to a specific time of day, the hour is placed before the colon, and the number of minutes is placed after the colon (as in 2:15 and 3:00).

Have you noticed that some countries only count hours by 12 and then begin again, while other countries count hours up to 24 (also called military time) to indicate how many hours are in a day? Have you ever been confused by the time when you traveled to a different country or watched a foreign film? Countries that follow the 12-hour clock (also called meridian time) need to use a.m. and p.m. to specify the time of day. However, all countries count minutes up to 60.

Here is a list of countries that follow meridian time: Australia, Bangladesh, Canada, Colombia, Egypt, El Salvador, Honduras, India, Ireland, Jordan, Malaysia, Mexico, New Zealand, Nicaragua, Pakistan, Philippines, Saudi Arabia, and the United States.

All other countries follow military time (naming hours 13 through 24).

2. In Ratios and Odds

In the field of mathematics, the colon is used in two instances: ratios and odds. When a ratio is read aloud in math, the colon is replaced by the word "to." Instead of saying "There are ½ as many whales as sharks in the ocean," you can say, "The ratio of whales to sharks is 1:2."

The word "odds" can be confusing. This is because the word "odd" can be used for odd numbers (1, 3, 5, 7), but the word "odds" can have an alternate meaning. It can also refer to the probability that one thing will happen rather than another thing. Related to this, "odds" show the ratio between the amount that will be paid on a winning bet and the amount of the bet.

Learning how to calculate odds can be useful when playing games, and for some people, it makes the games more enjoyable.

EXAMPLES

▶ The ratio of acceptances to applications at the local university is 1:100.

This means that the university accepts 1 out of every 100 applicants.

▶ I placed a bet on Skippylongstocking at the Belmont Stakes, even though the odds were 20:1.

This means that if Skippylongstocking wins the race, $20 will be paid out for every $1 that is bet on the horse.

3. In Biblical Verses

The Bible is a text that is broken down into sections called "books." Within each book, there are chapters. Within each chapter, there are verse numbers. Since the Bible is such a big book, it is easier for people to find an excerpt if the chapter and verse are indicated. To note the chapter and verse in a book of the Bible, simply place a colon between the two.

EXAMPLE

▶ The song "Wherever You Go" is based on Ruth 1:17.

This means that the words to that particular song come from a Bible passage from the Book of Ruth, Chapter 1, Verse 17.

4. In Volumes and Series

Like Biblical verses, when using citations, a colon is used to separate the volume of a series from the page number(s) of that series.

EXAMPLE

▶ On the references page of his research paper, Keto cited *Encyclopedia Smarts* 6:88–89.

Keto took his information from the sixth volume of Encyclopedia Smarts, *pages 88 to 89.*

EXERCISE 3-1: Colon Rules

DIRECTIONS: *Read each sentence or set of sentences below.*

- *If the example requires a colon, place it in the correct location, and write the rule number on the space to the left of the question number.*

- *If the sentence requires no colon, write **NC** on the line provided.*

Colon Rules
Rule 1: Introduce an Idea, Item, or List of Ideas/Items in Sentence Format
Rule 2: Vertical Lists
Rule 3: After a Key Word That Precedes Something Important
Rule 4: Direct Quotations
Rule 5: Salutations in a Business Letter
Rule 6: Titles
Rule 7: Time, Ratios and Odds, Biblical References, Volume/Page Numbers

_____ 1. Here are the steps you should take when writing a paragraph
   - Read the question carefully.
   - Highlight key points in the essay question.
   - Write an outline or complete a graphic organizer.
   - Begin with a topic sentence.
   - Incorporate relevant details and excerpts (if applicable).
   - Write a closing sentence.

_____ 2. The sun will rise at 545 tomorrow morning.

_____ 3. WARNING Swim at your own risk!

_____ 4. "Don't forget to pay your cable bill," Steven's mother reminded.

_____ 5. Pastor Jim read the Golden Rule from Matthew 7 12.

_____ 6. *Are You There God? It's Me, Margaret* by Judy Blume is a classic for young adults.

_____ 7. Dear Governor Brooks

Thank you for considering me for the Distinguished Students of America internship. It would be my pleasure to serve as your intern this summer, as I am interested in pursuing a career in public service, and I am motivated to learn from one of our country's most respected leaders.

Sincerely,
Tabatha Marcus

_____ 8. Becoming a successful politician requires good public speaking skills, knowledge of the jurisdiction, corroboration with residents and fellow leaders, and the ability to remain composed under pressure.

_____ 9. When you want to express a ratio of 2 to 1, you may write it as 2/1 or 2 1.

_____ 10. At the assembly, Principal Stringer repeated his famous school rule "Be kind to each other."

The Semicolon

Semicolons are punctuation marks that replace a period. A semicolon looks like a period above a comma (;).

The most common use of the semicolon is to connect two sentences that are related directly to each other. A sentence that includes a semicolon is considered a *compound sentence*.

Rule 1: Using a Semicolon to Join Two Related Independent Clauses

Remember that the term **independent clause** means the same thing as **sentence**.

It is appropriate to use a semicolon instead of a period *only* if the semicolon is connecting two complete sentences that have a connection.

You might be wondering: When I use a semicolon between two related sentences, should I capitalize the first letter of the word that follows the semicolon?

No, the first word after the semicolon *should not* be capitalized unless it is a proper noun or the word "I."

There *should* be a space after the semicolon.

A semicolon must *never* replace a period at the very end of a sentence (because it is not connecting two things).

▶ Nettie has so many errands to run today; she will go to the bank, the post office, and the pharmacy before heading to work.

The semicolon is placed between two complete sentences: "Nettie has so many errands to run today" and "she will go to the bank, the post office, and the pharmacy before heading to work." These two sentences are directly associated with each other, since the second sentence explains

Nettie's errands. There is a space after the semicolon. The first word in the second sentence, "she," is not capitalized because it is not a proper noun or the word "I."

▶ Cocoa is the perfect name for your dog; he has such a lustrous brown coat!

The semicolon is placed between two complete sentences: "Cocoa is the perfect name for your dog" and "he has such a lustrous brown coat!" These two sentences are directly associated with each other, since the second sentence explains that the dog looks like the color of cocoa. There is a space after the semicolon. The first word in the second sentence, "he," is not capitalized because it is not a proper noun or the word "I."

Here is an example of a set of sentences that do not require a semicolon:

EXAMPLE

▶ Timmy traveled to Mauritania over the summer. The new school year begins on August 25th.

Although the reader might presume these sentences are related, there is no direct correlation between the two. We cannot presume that Timmy goes to school or that August 25th is the date his school begins. Even if Timmy did go to school, the sentences are not correlative enough for them to be considered "compound." That is why a period is utilized instead of a semicolon.

One common mistake is to use a semicolon with a **coordinating conjunction** (and, or, but, yet, as, so, since). A conjunction is *not necessary* to connect sentences when a semicolon is present. Here is an example of a sentence where a semicolon is not required, since a coordinating conjunction (along with the comma) already connects two related sentences:

▶ Sheldon likes to play video games, and he allots himself one hour a day to do so.

This is a compound sentence. However, this compound sentence is already connected with a comma and a conjunction (, and). Therefore, this sentence DOES NOT require a semicolon. The semicolon could replace the comma and the word "and," since these two sentences are related.

Rule 2: Using a Semicolon to Connect Two Independent Clauses Joined by Conjunctive Adverbs, Transitional Expressions, or Prepositional Phrases

This rule is like the first one. The difference is that some sentences are paired with others that begin with either a **conjunctive adverb**, **a transitional expression**, or a **prepositional phrase**. These words are *not* the same as *conjunctions* (and, or, but, yet, as, so, since, for).

Common Conjunctive Adverbs Used in Compound Sentences

accordingly	finally	moreover	regardless
additionally	furthermore	namely	similarly
anyway	however	naturally	still
also	incidentally	next .	subsequently
alternatively	indeed	nevertheless	then
besides	instead	notably	thereafter
consequently	ironically	notwithstanding	therefore
conversely	likewise	now	thus
certainly	meanwhile	otherwise	undoubtedly

Common Transitional Expressions Used in Compound Sentences

again	maybe	overall	though
all in all	if necessary	perhaps	to begin with
best of all	more or less	so far	to be sure
better yet	needless to say	so to speak	to say the least
equally important	no	strictly speaking	well
even though	not only	strange as it seems	whereupon

Common Prepositional Phrases Used in Compound Sentences

along with that	because of this	in other words	in this case
along with this	by the same token	in particular	of course
as a comparison	for example	in similar fashion	on the contrary
as a result	for instance	in the end	on the other hand
at last	for that reason	in the meantime	on top of that
at the same time	in addition	in the same way	to that end
because of that	in contrast	in that case	until now

If one of these **conjunctive adverbs**, **transitional expressions**, or **prepositional phrases** *begins the second sentence* of a pairing that is related (compound sentence), a semicolon should be placed at the end of the first sentence and before the conjunctive adverb, transitional expression, or prepositional phrase.

There *must* be a space after the semicolon.

If a prepositional phrase begins the second sentence of the series, remember to consider Comma Rule 10 (in Chapter 2) for that phrase or those phrases.

The conjunctive adverb, transitional expression, or prepositional phrase that follows the semicolon should *not* be capitalized.

▶ Anabella is allergic to cats; however, she is not allergic to dogs and even has one as a pet.

> *The semicolon is placed between two complete sentences: "Anabella is allergic to cats" and "however, she is not allergic to dogs and even has one as a pet." These two sentences are directly associated with each other, since the second sentence names the animal to which Anabella is not allergic. There is a space after the semicolon. The first word in the second sentence, "however," is a conjunctive adverb and is not capitalized.*

▶ Our plan is to drive straight through to Florida; if necessary, we will take some breaks along the way.

> *The semicolon is placed between two complete sentences: "Our plan is to drive straight through to Florida "and "if necessary, we will take some breaks along the way." These two sentences are directly associated with each other, since the second sentence names an alternative to driving straight to Florida. There is a space after the semicolon. The first word of the second sentence, "if," is not capitalized. "If necessary" is considered a common transitional phrase and should be followed by a comma.*

▶ Scott and Jack are so excited because they have tickets to the hottest concert; on top of that, their seats are ground level!

> *The semicolon is placed between two complete sentences: "Scott and Jack are so excited because they have tickets to the hottest concert" and "on top of that, their seats are ground level!" These two sentences are directly associated with each other, since the second sentence refers to the concert-ticket location. There is a space after the semicolon. The first word in the second sentence, "on," is not capitalized. Notice that "on top" and "of that" are two prepositional phrases in a row at the beginning of the sentence, so you need to place a comma after "that" based on Comma Rule 10, which states that if there are two prepositional phrases in a row at the beginning of a sentence, the comma should be placed after the last word of the final phrase.*

> *Remember that there is also a rule that two-word prepositional phrases that stand alone at the beginning of a sentence do not require a comma after the object of the preposition. Exceptions are the phrases "for example," "for instance," and "of course," which do require a comma despite having only two words in the phrases.*

A common mistake is to place only a comma between the two sentences. As you know, it is *incorrect* to use a comma to connect two sentences. Therefore, when connecting sentences that already have one of the conjunctive adverbs, transitional phrases, or prepositional phrases as a connector, remember to place a semicolon, not a comma, to establish the relationship between the two independent clauses.

Rule 3: Using a Semicolon to Avoid Confusion When Several Commas Are Present

There are other instances when a **semicolon** is used, though these instances are not as common. Sometimes, a semicolon is used to replace a comma but *only* in a situation when *commas are used in a listing situation* where several commas are already required. In this case, the *semicolon can help clarify or separate ideas*.

Warning: This does not mean that semicolons can replace commas all the time. Remember all the comma rules in Chapter 2? You cannot apply semicolons to *any* of those rules. Only under *very specific* circumstances can a semicolon replace a comma, as highlighted in the following examples.

▶ To become more proficient in Spanish, Liling vacationed in Punta Cana, Dominican Republic; Madrid, Spain; Buenos Aires, Argentina; and Cancun, Mexico over the past few summers.

> *If the semicolons were not in the sentence above, the reader might not understand the distinction between cities and countries due to the use of frequent commas. The semicolons replace commas after each country.*

▶ My English courses require so much reading: *Macbeth*, *Hamlet*, and *King Lear* in Shakespeare I; *The Scarlet Letter*, *Uncle Tom's Cabin*, and *The Red Badge of Courage* in Early American Literature; *Death of a Salesman*, *The Crucible*, and *Waiting for Godot* in Contemporary Drama.

> *In order to distinguish the required reading in each of the courses, commas are used to list the titles, and semicolons are used to separate the names of courses.*

Now that you have learned everything there is to know about colons and semicolons, it is time to test your knowledge.

The following exercises will present various challenges:

- Application of semicolon rules

- Distinguishing between colon and semicolon placement

- Incorporating colons and semicolons in your own writing

EXERCISE 3-2: Semicolon Rules

DIRECTIONS: Read each sentence or set of sentences below.

* *If the sentence requires a semicolon, place it in the correct location, and write the rule number on the space to the left of the question number.*
* *If the sentence requires no semicolon, write **NS** on the line provided.*
* *Do not replace any existing punctuation marks with a semicolon.*

Semicolon Rules
Rule 1: Join Two Related Independent Clauses
Rule 2A: Connect Two Independent Clauses Joined by Conjunctive Adverbs
Rule 2B: Connect Two Independent Clauses Joined by Transitional Expressions
Rule 2C: Connect Two Independent Clauses Joined by Prepositional Phrases
Rule 3: Avoid Confusion When Several Commas are Present

_____ 1. Jose is a very attentive listener when Malcolm needs a good friend likewise, Malcolm depends on Jose for advice.

_____ 2. Anne is a wonderful cook, yet she prefers to eat at restaurants.

_____ 3. Because she comes from a military family, Natasha has lived in several places including San Diego, California Cherry Point, North Carolina and Blount Island, Florida.

_____ 4. Reggie received a 99 on his last chemistry exam of course, three points of extra credit helped bring his score from an A to an A+.

_____ 5. In case of emergency, dial 911.

_____ 6. Jonathan plays soccer, football, and lacrosse, so he has hardly any time for socializing.

_____ 7. Blaze has had two injuries in the past year so far, he seems to have made a full recovery.

_____ 8. Patricia took the ACT three times she is hoping that her score will improve enough for her to be considered by her top-choice college.

_____ 9. Niran purchased the largest backpack available, but his books and laptop barely fit in it!

_____ 10. Coincidentally, two of the young ladies nominated for Prom Queen were wearing the same dress.

EXERCISE 3-3: Colon or Semicolon?

DIRECTIONS: Read each sentence carefully. Determine whether the sentence requires a colon, a semicolon, or nothing at all. Do not replace a punctuation mark that already appears in a sentence.

- **Insert either a colon, a semicolon, or no punctuation mark.**
- **On the line provided, write C if you inserted a colon.**
- **Write S if you inserted a semicolon.**
- **Write N if no punctuation mark needed to be added.**

_____ 1. Jeannie showed up for the audition without her sheet music thus, she was unable to try out for the musical.

_____ 2. Winter is a season that can be treacherous for the following reasons slippery roads, icy sidewalks, and frigid temperatures.

_____ 3. Dear Cathy,

I miss you so much! The summer has been so lonely without you. I can't want until you return, so we can go hiking on some new trails I discovered.

Your friend,
Louise

———— 4. Calvin ate four tacos at lunchtime, so he had no appetite for dinner.

———— 5. I asked the librarian to help me find *History of our Nation* 3 16–20 in the stacks.

———— 6. I heard that Sara recently contracted Covid-19 until last week, she had been able to avoid it.

———— 7. Remember to bring your bathing suit, towel, sunscreen, and sunglasses to the beach.

———— 8. Luciano's parents are opera singers naturally, he has some innate ability to carry a tune.

———— 9. Have you read *Take Deep Breaths An Insider's Guide to Managing Stress?*

———— 10. The child screamed at the puppy in awe "I want to take you home!"

EXERCISE 3-4: Writing with Colons and Semicolons

In the space below, attempt to write a two-page letter using **at least five** *of the colon and semicolon rules correctly. If you wish, you may use more than one colon or semicolon within a sentence. In parentheses after each sentence, write the number of the colon or semicolon rule(s) you applied in that sentence. Use a* **C** *before the number of the colon rule, and an* **S** *before the number of the semicolon rule* **(C6, S2).**

PROMPT: You and your French class went on a weeklong field trip to Quebec, Canada. As a culminating activity, your teacher asked you to write a letter (in English) to your school superintendent letting her know why this trip was so valuable.

Colon Rules

Rule 1: Introduce an Idea, Item, or List of Ideas/Items in Sentence Format
Rule 2: Vertical Lists
Rule 3: After a Key Word That Precedes Something Important
Rule 4: Direct Quotations
Rule 5: Salutations in a Business Letter
Rule 6: Titles
Rule 7: Time, Ratios and Odds, Biblical References, Volume/Page Numbers

Semicolon Rules

Rule 1: Join Two Related Independent Clauses
Rule 2A: Connect Two Independent Clauses Joined by Conjunctive Adverbs
Rule 2B: Connect Two Independent Clauses Joined by Transitional Expressions
Rule 2C: Connect Two Independent Clauses Joined by Prepositional Phrases
Rule 3: Avoid Confusion When Several Commas are Present

Letter to the School Superintendent

_____

_____

_____

_____

_____

_____

_____

_____

_____

_____

_____

_____

_____

_____

_____

_____

_____

_____

Flashcard App

Quotation Marks, Dialogue, and Formatting Titles

MUST KNOW

⚡ Quotation marks are used to represent the exact words of a person or character; we call this *dialogue* when the conversation occurs between two or more people.

⚡ Quotation marks are also placed around most direct excerpts (depending on their length).

⚡ Quotation marks are sometimes used for clarity, for deliberate separation, or even to signal to the reader a genre that is being referenced, in the case of a title.

Since you have been reading for many years, you have seen quotation marks in many contexts. Have you ever noticed that quotation marks come in sets of two? This is because the quotation marks (or quotes) need to precede what is being said and need to follow what is being said. You will never see an opening quotation mark (") without a closing quotation mark ("). Quotation marks looks like two apostrophes together. If you are typing a quotation mark, your computer will automatically change the shape of the quotation mark to distinguish between the one introducing something (") and the one ending something (").

Obviously, there is a lot to learn about quotation marks, so, as they used to say in the traveling circus acts of the early twentieth century, "Let's get this show on the road!"

Rule 1: Using Quotation Marks with Direct Quotations

When you hear the term **direct quotation**, it means that the exact words *spoken in conversation* are being cited. We distinguish the term direct quotation from excerpt. The term **direct excerpt**, which is sometimes just called **excerpt**, refers to the exact words that are taken from a film, broadcast, speech, piece of music, or piece of writing.

When citing the exact words of a person, an explanatory phrase is typically used at the beginning, in the middle, or at the end of the entire sentence (not included within the quotation marks). This phrase explains who did the speaking, and it sometimes explains how they said it:

"Don't make me come over there," *said Billy threateningly.*

It may also explain why they said what they said:

Disagreeing, Molly refuted, "We will never see eye to eye."

There are some *punctuation rules* to follow when using explanatory phrases. Some of these were reviewed in Chapters 2, 3, and 4, but to make things easier, here is a simple review.

If the *explanatory phrase* is *a fragment* and falls *at the beginning* of a sentence, it is followed by a *comma* that *precedes* the opening quotation mark.

EXAMPLE

> The tour guide exclaimed, "Please look to the left for a beautiful view of the Brooklyn Bridge."
>
> *Notice that when the explanatory phrase begins the sentence, the comma after the word "exclaimed" precedes the opening quotation mark.*

If the *explanatory phrase* is a *complete sentence* and falls *at the beginning* of a sentence, it is followed by a *colon*, which precedes the opening quotation mark.

EXAMPLE

> Nick buckled his seatbelt in anticipation: "This looks like the scariest rollercoaster I have ever seen!"
>
> *Because the direct quotation is preceded by a complete sentence, the explanatory phrase ends with a colon.*

If the *explanatory phrase* falls in the *middle of a sentence*, a comma is placed inside the closing quote. Then, the explanatory phrase ends in a comma before the next quotation mark begins the second direct quote.

▶ "Chapters 22 and 23," added Mr. Compass, "will be the basis of your geography quiz."

Since the explanatory phrase falls in the middle of the sentence, a comma is placed at the end of the first portion of the direct quotation and inside its closing quotation mark. An additional comma belongs after the explanatory phrase and before the next portion of the direct quotation.

If the *direct quotation* consists of *several sentences* in a row that are stated by the same speaker, *quotation marks* are only necessary *before the first sentence* and *after the last* in the series.

▶ The minister explained the respectful way to conduct oneself during a retreat: "Please be respectful of others. Many people will be praying quietly. Try to avoid excessive noise."

Because the direct quotation is preceded by a complete sentence, the explanatory phrase has a colon. It doesn't matter that the direct quotation has multiple sentences. Because the same minister stated all of these sentences in succession, only one set of quotation marks is necessary.

Punctuation becomes much more complicated if the sentence has a direct quotation followed by an explanatory phrase at the end of the sentence. These rules vary by country, so below, you will find the rules followed in the United States:

Commas and periods come *before* the final (second) quotation mark.

▶ "Find your mark before the music begins," instructed the director of the high school musical.

> *A comma is necessary after the director's instructions and before the closing quotation mark, since the explanatory phrase ends the sentence.*

▶ "Mix the liquids before adding the dry ingredients," Annette told her captivated podcast audience.

> *After Annette's direct quotation and before the closing explanatory phrase that ends the sentence, a comma must be placed after "ingredients" and before the closing quotation mark.*

Colons, semicolons, and dashes are placed *after* the final (second) *quotation mark.*

▶ "Remember to mix the liquids first"; we heard her say that a second time.

> *Since there are two complete sentences in this example, and one of them is a direct quotation and the other is not, but they are related to each other, the semicolon is placed after the direct quotation.*

Question marks and exclamation points are even trickier! If the question mark or exclamation point apply *only* to the quoted material, naturally, it belongs within the quotation marks. However, if the question mark or exclamation point applies to the *entire sentence*, it should be placed at the end of the sentence, regardless of the location of the direct quotation within the sentence.

▶ "Have you seen my stapler?" the librarian asked the students at the first table.

> *When the direct quotation is a question, the question mark belongs inside the closing quotation mark. Notice that the entire sentence is not a question; that is why the question mark only belongs inside the quotation mark.*

▶ "I cannot believe you have the audacity to enter my classroom late for a third time this week!" admonished Professor Alheure.

> *After Professor Alheure's sentence, an exclamation point is necessary before the closing quotation mark to indicate the emotion felt by the professor. Since the entire sentence was not stated with force, there should not be an exclamation point after "admonished Professor Alheure."*

▶ Wayne is incensed that you constantly say "Cool beans"!

> *An exclamation point is required at the end of the entire sentence, since the phrase in quotation marks is not necessarily stated with fierce emotion, but Wayne's reaction to it reflects irritation that warrants an exclamation point outside the closing quotation mark.*

There are *spacing rules* related to dialogue, specifically when *inserted within works of prose* (not poems or plays).

- When writing dialogue, press "enter" to begin begin a new paragraph every time the speaker changes.

- If indentation is used in that writing piece, don't forget to press "tab" to begin a new line of dialogue.

- When the dialogue ends, if the follow-up sentences are not related specifically to the last direct quote, press "enter" and "tab" to begin a new paragraph.

EXAMPLES

> "It's time to wake up, Darla," my mother said. "We are leaving for the airport in one hour."
>
> "Be right there, Mom!" I yelled with enthusiasm.
>
> We had been looking forward to this vacation for two years. Due to the pandemic, our annual trip to Disney World was postponed twice, so we were antsy to see Mickey and Minnie again.
>
> *Notice that each time there was a new speaker, a new paragraph was created. Once the dialogue ended, a new paragraph began.*

There are also *capitalization* rules related to direct quotations. You might have noticed that certain direct quotations begin with a capital letter whereas others do not. To know whether to place a capital letter at the beginning of a direct quotation or excerpt, the general rule of thumb is if the spoken words or excerpt being referenced is a complete sentence, it should begin with a capital letter. If it is not a complete sentence, it should begin with a lowercase letter unless, of course, it is a proper noun or the word "I."

When directly quoting a portion of a speaker's sentence, that portion should not begin with a capital letter. When typing a direct quotation that is interrupted by an explanatory phrase in the middle of the sentence, the second portion of the quotation should not be capitalized unless it is the word "I" or a proper noun.

EXAMPLES

> Mildred whined, "Why is my name so old-fashioned?"
>
> *Since the direct quotation is a complete sentence, the "W" in the word "Why" is capitalized.*
>
> "Because," her mother replied, "of the tradition in our family."
>
> *Since the portion of dialogue after the explanatory phrase, "of the tradition in our family" is not a complete sentence, the "o" in "of" is not capitalized.*

Of course, there is an exception, but since it applies to excerpts, it will be discussed in the subsection of this chapter that is related to excerpts.

One last note before we practice. Remember that the term **direct quotation** means *exact words*. This is not the same as an **indirect quote** or **paraphrase,** which describes when a statement is summarized rather than repeated exactly.

One way to distinguish between the two is to notice the word "that" before information about what someone said. In this sample sentence, someone is relaying what Felix said by using the word "that":

> Felix said *that* he needed a few weeks to recuperate after having surgery.

Still, a sentence can be paraphrased without the word "that." If the statement is not in quotation marks, the reader will know it is not a direct quote.

> Felix said he needed a few weeks to recuperate after having surgery.

Notice that the word "he" is used instead of the word "I." That is another way to tell that these were not Felix's exact words.

EXERCISE 4-1: Direct Quotations

DIRECTIONS: The following sentences contain dialogue.

- *For each example, insert quotation marks when necessary.*
- *If you add quotation marks to the sentence, write **Q** on the line provided.*
- *If quotation marks are not required in the sentence, write **NQ** to the left of the example.*

_____ 1. May I borrow a pen? asked Edward right before the quiz began.

_____ 2. The manager reminded the customers that they needed to stand in line and wait to be called before approaching the cashier.

_____ 3. The skills required for being a good server explained the restaurant owner include knowing the ingredients of the food, noticing the needs of the diners, and refilling water glasses constantly.

_____ 4. Ms. Steel conducted the orchestra class by raising her baton and explaining directions in a soft tone.

_____ 5. Cynthia reviewed the day's schedule with her twin daughters: When school ends, you will go to basketball practice and then attend Grandma's birthday dinner.

_____ 6. It isn't fair said Antonio to his Chinese teacher that you did not provide exam directions in English.

_____ 7. Ms. Zheng responded, You should know better than that, Antonio. One of the first things I taught you at the beginning of the year was that you needed to be able to decipher directions in Chinese.

_____ 8. Antonio relented: It was worth a try.

_____ 9. Bedtime is usually at 7:00 p.m., Cecilia explained to the babysitter, but because this is a special occasion, the babies should be put to bed by 8:30 at the latest.

_____ 10. Your brother's new sneakers are so cool! said Tyler to his friend, Nate.

Rule 2: Formatting Run-in and Block Quotations

So far, we have focused on on **direct quotations** (spoken). Now, we will shift gears to **direct excerpts**, also known simply as excerpts. An **excerpt** is a passage or extraction taken from a film, broadcast, speech, piece of music, or piece of writing. The rules for most excerpts are quite like the rules for direct quotations, but, of course, there are exceptions.

There are two types of direct excerpts: **run-in quotations** and **block quotations**.

Run-in Quotations

The term **run-in** represents the type of excerpts we are accustomed to utilizing most when we write essays or research papers. These excerpts from sources help us to develop a writing piece by proving our thesis and by supporting our statements.

Usually, when we are including excerpts within our writing, we provide one or two sentences directly from a source. Those sentences provide evidence to prove our point.

However, sometimes it is not necessary to excerpt an entire sentence. This is where the **ellipsis** comes in handy. It is important to understand the use of an ellipsis (. . .) within run-in quotations. Ordinarily, an ellipsis is used to indicate an unfinished thought or a lapse of time. It has a different purpose in the context of excerpts.

BTW

You are familiar with the term **run-on**. Even though it sounds similar, the term "run-on" has nothing to do with excerpts; it is related to the structure of a sentence.

If we are *excerpting only a portion* of a text that is *written in prose* (not a poem, song, or a play), an ellipsis may be used to indicate that a portion of the original sentence has not been included within the selected excerpt. An ellipsis may be used at the beginning of, in the middle of, or at the end of an excerpt. If the ellipsis is included at the end of the excerpt, an additional period is unnecessary.

▶ In the novel, the reader can assess the sincerity of Bixby's character through his treatment of others: ". . . listening with intent eyes . . . giving Stanley a reassuring hug as a sign of support during this difficult time."

The writer omitted the first portion of the excerpted sentence that appears in the novel because it was probably irrelevant in the discussion of characterization. A second ellipsis is used in the middle of the excerpt to eliminate other unnecessary words.

In Rule 1 of this chapter, there are notes regarding how to punctuate a direct quotation (spoken words) when the direct quotation comes at the end of a sentence. That rule states if a direct quotation is a complete sentence that would typically end in a period (not an exclamation point or a question mark) and it falls at the end of the entire sentence, only one period should be placed at the end of the entire sentence, and that period belongs inside the quotation mark.

▶ After a grueling twenty-hour race, the marathon runner said, "I am exhausted."

Notice that there is not an extra period after the final quotation mark of the sentence. Typically, the same rule applies when including an excerpt in a piece of writing.

There is an exception, however. In the case of **parenthetical citation**, *a period must follow the citation.* If your excerpt ends in a question mark or exclamation point, that mark belongs before the closing quotation mark, and there must also be a period after the closing parentheses of the citation. If there is any other type of punctuation mark at the end of the excerpt, you should eliminate it and simply place a period after the closing parentheses of the citation.

EXAMPLE

> The author exclaimed, "Drinking eight glasses of water per day is essential to good health!" (Ballen, 63).
>
> *Notice that the excerpt ends with an exclamation point. After the excerpt, there is a parenthetical citation (Ballen, 63). Since the excerpt ends in an exclamation point, that punctuation mark must remain, and a period is placed at the end of the parenthetical citation.*
>
> Many people live by the words of Plato:" Truth is the beginning of every good to the gods, and of every good to man" (Theos, 165).
>
> *Since the excerpt ends with a period in the text (not an exclamation point or a question mark), that end mark is eliminated, and a period appears after the citation.*

Block Quotations

There is another type of direct excerpt called a **block quotation**. The term **block quotation** or **block excerpt** refers to a longer extraction from a film, broadcast, speech, piece of music, or piece of writing. Many style guides differ in terms of how many lines of an excerpt comprise a block, but the common rule of thumb is anything *over five lines*.

When you have an excerpt that is exceptionally long, it needs to be *separated distinctly* from the rest of the writing in that paper, chapter, or book. This requires pressing the enter key twice, changing the margins to indent further, reducing the spacing from double-spaced to single-spaced, and/or changing the font to italic.

It is also important to know that when you set apart a long excerpt or a block, quotation marks are NOT used. You read that correctly! Since the block is a visual cue for the reader that a large excerpt is being included, quotation marks are unnecessary. Here is a sample paragraph from a research paper that includes a block quote:

> Square dancing derived from many traditional dances in Europe and became popular in the United States in the 1800s. Most square dances involve a caller (someone who tells the dancers which moves to use) and music (often a live band). Here are the lyrics to "Skip to my Lou," one of the most popular square-dance songs:
>
> > Flies in the buttermilk
> > Shoo fly, shoo
> > Flies in the buttermilk
> > Shoo fly, shoo
> > Flies in the buttermilk
> > Shoo fly, shoo
> > Skip to my Lou, my darlin'!
> >
> > Skip! Skip! Skip to my Lou!
> > Skip! Skip! Skip to my Lou!
> > Skip! Skip! Skip to my Lou!
> > Skip to my Lou, my darlin'!
> >
> > Lost my partner,
> > What'll I do?
> > Lost my partner,
> > What'll I do?
> > Lost my partner,
> > What'll I do?
> > Skip to my Lou, my darlin'!
>
> *Did you notice some ways the block excerpt looks different from the paragraph preceding it? The lines are indented, and there are no quotation marks around the excerpt (because this is a block quote).*

The example above happens to be a very common folk song, so there is no parenthetical citation. However, when excerpting a source that has an exact author and/or page number, place it on the same line as the last line of the excerpt after the final word or punctuation mark. *No period is required* after the closing parentheses (unlike in the case of run-in quotations).

Rule 3: Formatting a Play or TV/Film Script

Reading plays is often routine in a high school English class. Perhaps you read the role of a Shakespearean character in front of the classroom. You may have had to write a script for a language class and act it out. It is even possible that you acted in a video or in front of a live audience. If you have experienced any of the scenarios above, you have read **dialogue** in a different format. Did you notice anything different about dialogue when it appeared in the form of a play or script? By now, you might realize that plays do not use quotation marks to indicate a conversational exchange.

Why is this important? As you progress in your education, professors or employers may require you to develop videos, commercials, or live presentations to showcase your knowledge of a content area. They often require a typed copy of the script that accompanies that project. Therefore, it is important to recognize the features of scriptwriting and the different nuances between certain genres: stage plays, TV episodes, commercials, and screenplays.

The actual format of **scriptwriting** *varies based on the genre.* Since I direct plays and teach acting classes, I read various script formats for stage plays, TV scripts, and screenplays. As a rule, these three genres present dialogue in a similar way, yet their rules for spacing, capitalization, and punctuation differ.

What do all three have in common?

They *do not* use quotation marks to indicate that someone is speaking. This does not mean that quotation marks are *never* used in dialogue.

They can still be *used for emphasis* of a word or phrase.

EXAMPLE

▶ BETSY: Did she have to be "that" girl to him?

The word "that" is in quotation marks to help the actor/reader understand the meaning behind the inflection of that word.

Amid dialogue, quotation marks may also be placed around *titles*.

EXAMPLE

▶ MICHAEL: I haven't had a chance to read "The Gift of the Magi." Have you?

Michael is mentioning the name of a famous short story.

Writing Dialogue for Stage Plays

The most typical stage-play format for expressing dialogue is when a character's name is capitalized completely and followed by a colon. Speakers' names appear at the left-hand margin.

In a play written for the stage, you will also notice *parentheses*. The parentheses that follow an actor's name are called **character directions**. They tell an actor how to say a particular line. When actions or movements are necessary, actors are instructed in **stage directions.** In a script written for a stage play, stage directions appear on a separate line, form a complete sentence, and are centered and placed in parentheses.

EXAMPLE

▶ GOTHAM: (happily) I love the lights in the city. They shine so brightly!

(STAMEN shakes his head disapprovingly.)

STAMEN: (disgruntled) I prefer the grassy fields and the meadows of flowers.

Notice that the characters' names are capitalized completely and followed by a colon. When you are typing a play script, you must press "enter" once a character line is complete.

Also, the character directions (happily, disgruntled) appear after the speaker's name and before the spoken words. The stage directions appear on a separate line, centered and in parentheses.

Writing Dialogue for Television Shows and for Commercials

Television and commercial scripts are *like* stage-play scripts in that they both eliminate quotation marks, capitalize character names, and place character directions in parentheses (except that they appear *under* the character's name instead of *next to* the character's name).

They *differ* in a few ways. Television and commercial scripts center character names and do not include a colon. The spoken line is also centered. Stage directions are not centered and are not in parentheses.

Here is a sample snippet of a sitcom script:

EXAMPLE

▶ DAVID peers out the window looking very anxious, as LESLIE enters the room from behind him and tiptoes behind him.

LESLIE
(screaming)
Boo!

DAVID
(screaming louder)
Ahhhh! What did you do that for?

LESLIE
Do what?

DAVID
Scare me!

LESLIE
(teasingly)
It's fun!

DAVID
Ha! Ha! Very funny!

Notice how the stage directions begin at the left margin, are not centered, and are not in parentheses. The dialogue is completely centered including the character's name, the character directions in parentheses, and the character's lines. An extra space is used between character lines.

There is additional information necessary in TV and commercial scripts, since they involve *filming directions* as well.

The most popular ones are **FADE IN** (which is typed at the beginning of every new scene), **O.S.** (which stands for offstage and indicates that a character says a line from offstage), **V.O.** (which stands for voiceover and is often used in commercials when a narrator is explaining something while action is being shown), **CUT TO** (which means that one scene is quickly transitioning to another), **INT.** and **EXT.** (which appear at the beginning of a scene to indicate whether the scene is an interior or exterior scene), and **FADE OUT** (when a scene is finished).

For TV scripts, scenes are divided differently, since a **teaser** is a *very short opening scene* meant to lure a viewer into watching a show by providing a preview of the storyline for that episode yet the rest of these scenes vary in size based upon the *number of minutes between commercials* (if there are commercials on that network).

Similarly, commercials are written with a certain amount of *time in mind*. Some slots are 20 seconds, while others may be 60 seconds. This all factors into the amount of text that needs to be written and performed.

Here is an example of a scene intended to be a preview or teaser:

EXAMPLE

TEASER

FADE IN:

INT: COLLEGE ADMISSIONS OFFICE WAITING ROOM, 11:00 a.m.

A group of anxious teenagers sit quietly waiting to be called for an interview. A few overbearing parents are present as well.

> ADMISSIONS OFFICER (O.S.)
> Dylan Falls?

> MRS. FALLS
> Dylan, it's you! She called you!

DYLAN, wearing headphones and engrossed in a videogame, pays no attention to his mother.

> MRS. FALLS
> (louder)
> Dylan! She called you!

> DYLAN
> (flustered)
> Me? Oh snap!
> (to his mother)
> Okay, calm down.

As he jumps up, DYLAN gets tangled in his own feet and spills onto the floor. ADMISSIONS OFFICER has just entered the room to witness this.

ADMISSIONS OFFICER
(laughing aloud)
Did you say your name was Dylan Falls? I see what
you did there! Come into my office.

Notice how the scene begins with the word "TEASER," which indicates that this will be a very short scene meant to lure viewers into watching this episode. Then, the words "FADE IN" indicate that this is the beginning of the scene. The abbreviation "INT." prefaces the setting and time of the scene. Stage directions begin at the left margin, are not centered, and are not in parentheses. The dialogue is completely centered, including the character's name, the character directions in parentheses, and the character's lines. An extra space is used between character lines. The abbreviation "O.S." is used to show that the Admissions Officer is speaking from offstage.

Writing Screenplays for Films

Screenplays are scripts written for films. Screenplay scripts look almost identical to television scripts. One difference is they *do not* include teasers, fade-ins, or fade-outs. They *do not* include as many character or stage directions, since these decisions are often left up to the director and/or actor and may also be dependent upon where the movie is being shot. However, most screenwriters do include suggestions for *camera shots and angles*, though they may not be utilized in the final production of the film.

Now that you are a "star" in the dialogue department—have I taken it too far?—try to match the following terms with their definitions.

EXERCISE 4-2: Identifying Terms Related to Dialogue

DIRECTIONS: On the line provided to the left of each question number, write the letter of the definition which most closely matches the term or abbreviation related to dialogue.

_____ 1. run-in quotation

_____ 2. character directions

_____ 3. excerpt

_____ 4. fade in

_____ 5. dialogue

_____ 6. INT.

_____ 7. teaser

_____ 8. block quotation

_____ 9. O.S.

_____ 10. stage directions

a. conversation between two or more people

b. a line is being delivered offstage

c. tell the actor how to deliver a line

d. dialogue included within the text's normal format

e. short scene to tempt a viewer to keep watching

f. long excerpt set apart from the rest of a document

g. portion or passage taken from a text, song, etc.

h. show movement or action in a scene

i. indicates that the scene takes place indoors

j. marks the beginning of a scene

Rule 4: Using Nested Quotations

Have you ever seen a quotation within a quotation? This happens when a specific reference is made within an already existent line of dialogue. There is an actual name for a quote within a quote: **a nested quotation**.

In American English, when a quotation appears within a quotation, the original quotation takes quotation marks (" ") as it normally would. The nested quotation must be *surrounded by single quotation marks* (' '). On a keyboard, the *apostrophe* key is also used to type single quotation marks.

EXAMPLE

▶ Principal McElroy explained why I received detention: "When I asked Ms. Collins if you were late to class today, she said, 'Phil is always late to my class.'"

Principal Mc Elroy was explaining something to Phil. What he said to Phil was in quotation marks. However, within this explanation, Principal McElroy quoted Miss Collins. What Ms. Collins said to the principal is in single marks. Even though it might look strange to you, the single end-mark goes directly before the closing quotation mark in this sentence.

Rule 5: Using Quotation Marks for Clarity

Quotation marks are not only used in writing dialogue or in excerpting. They are also used in other contexts.

Sometimes, quotation marks are necessary *to separate information* from the rest of the sentence to *increase clarity*. In many of the example boxes in this book, if you look at the italicized explanations that I provided beneath examples, you will see that I used quotation marks to separate certain words (excerpted from the sample sentence) to highlight those words specifically.

EXAMPLE

▶ When using "I" in a sentence, always capitalize it.

If there were no quotes around the word "I," the sentence might be confusing to the reader. It may seem like there is a typographical error. The quotation marks around the word "I" help the reader to separate it from the rest of the sentence, increasing clarity in the sentence.

A common *mistake* made by writers is to place a word or words in quotation marks to emphasize something. Increasing clarity is *not* the same as emphasizing an idea.

Writers *should not* use quotation marks for the purpose of emphasis. In the past, features such as boldface print or italics were nonexistent. Before the use of a computer, the only way to emphasize a typed word was to underline it, to capitalize it fully, or to place it in quotation marks.

Nowadays, it is *not* grammatically correct to use quotation marks solely to emphasize a word. When a word is or words are in quotation marks (and not part of a direct quotation or excerpt), it is correct to assume that they are either for *separating certain words from the rest of the sentence for the purpose of clarity* or *to present information that is ironic or sarcastic.*

Rule 6: Using Quotation Marks to Depict Sarcasm or Irony

As you know, it is much easier to convey emotion or intent when speaking than when writing. People misinterpret texts and emails sent by others, and this can often lead to misunderstandings.

Believe it or not, there is a rule that allows quotation marks to surround words to suggest a *sarcastic* or *ironic tone*. These quotation marks are a visual cue to the reader that the writer is *purposely insincere* about the statement that is being made. Think of it this way. The word or words in quotation marks depict(s) how someone or something is *allegedly* supposed to be, but the reader can infer that the statement is not accurate. Writers, in a sense, distance themselves from that thought, often to show disapproval.

There is even a name for this specialized set of quotation marks: **scare quotes**.

EXAMPLES

Mallory, a "gifted and talented" senior, did not pass the basic comprehension exams in her core subjects.

The writer's intent is to show that Mallory may not be "gifted and talented" if she cannot pass basic exams in core subjects, though she might be labeled "gifted and talented" by her school or by her family members.

Bristol vowed to love his seventh wife "forever and ever."

By placing quotation marks around "forever and ever," the writer is poking fun at Bristol, since he obviously took the same vows six times prior to the seventh wedding day.

IRL As you know, **idioms** are expressions that are unique to a particular language and are, therefore, not translatable literally. There are a few idioms related to the word "quotes." I wonder how many of these you have heard before:

- "To get a quote" refers to a fixed price that is agreed upon and cannot be changed. The person providing the quote is the one who decides upon the price that must be offered for service.

- "Can I quote you on that?" This is used to suggest that the person who said something may not have been forthright **or** that someone wants to use that person's words as evidence for something.

- "Quote, unquote" This expression is used in spoken English and is often accompanied by hand gestures made in the shapes of quotation marks. Originally, this idiom was used to repeat someone's exact words. However, over time, it has evolved into something else. The person saying "quote, unquote" is often insinuating that the information they are relaying is surprising or even insincere. Of course, the context of the delivery is important, so the receiver of information can deduce the intent of the speaker.

Rule 7: Formatting Titles

As an English teacher, I correct my students constantly when it comes to the way they format titles. It almost seemed easier years ago when people used typewriters, not computers, and there were only two ways to format titles—quotation marks or underlining—but the truth is that many people were confused then as well. In Chapter 1, you learned how to capitalize titles of works. Now, it is time to learn how to format those titles in terms of punctuation.

What makes it more confusing is that, as time goes on, we have additional genres to include. With the rise in technology, we have more ways of communicating: social media, podcasts, blogs, vlogs, etc. When we refer to these platforms, there are correct ways to format them.

The way a title should be formatted depends upon if the title is being handwritten or typed digitally. Did you know that? Obviously, writing quotation marks and typing quotation marks are the same.

However, formatting certain genres requires *italics*. Since it is awkward to try to handwrite italics and distinguish that type of handwriting from the rest of the handwritten text, the rule remains that *works that are normally italicized when typed should be underlined when handwritten*. However, it *does not* work that way in reverse. In other words, if you are typing a title that should be italicized, you should *not* underline it when typing. Italics *replace* underlining in a typed document.

I also have students who italicize, underline, *and* place one title in quotation marks "just in case." See what I did there? I placed "just in case" in quotes to show that although my students think they are covering all bases by italicizing, underlining, and placing one title in quotation marks, they are just proving that they don't know how to format titles; they are *not* gaining credit by formatting a title in three different ways!

The easiest way to remember whether titles require quotation marks or italics is to follow this tip (which works most of the time):

Shorter works belong in quotation marks.

Longer works belong in italics (or underlined when being handwritten).

Since you might not be able to distinguish between short and long (it is sometimes confusing), I thought it would be helpful to provide that information to you in a chart listed by genre. It might even be a good idea for you to *take a photo* of this chart to keep as a quick reference, so you do not need to search for this chapter and page when you are writing. What would be most helpful, however, would be to *memorize* this chart, since you won't be able to use it as a reference while you are taking an exam (unless it is an open-book or open-device one, of course).

Also included in the chart are certain genres that should *not* have special treatment other than having title capitalization. Finally, style guides sometimes differ in terms of whether works should be italicized or not. Next to a few of the genres below, you will see the word *Chicago* or the abbreviation *MLA*. In those cases, that particular style guide requires special treatment, whereas the others do not require any.

How to Format Titles According to Genre

Quotation Marks	Italics	Capitalization Only
• short story	• full-length book	• section of scriptural works
• poem	• book-length poem (or epic poem)	• name of a prayer
• chapter title	• newspaper	• award
• article title	• magazine	• computer/digital application
• one-act play	• play that is longer than one act	• constitutional document
• TV commercial	• symphony	• software
• song title	• music/spoken album, soundtrack, or CD	• commercial product
• essay title	• editions, anthologies, or collections of works	• monument
• episode title (of a series)	• TV show	• famous building
• advertisement	• encyclopedia	• traditional game (board, pool, lawn, card, etc.) that has no punctuation marks within its name
• unpublished speech	• pamphlet title	
• short film	• full-length film	
• vlog entry	• name of vlog	
• blog entry	• name of blog	
• photograph	• journal	
• unpublished thesis	• published dissertation, speech, thesis, or manuscript	
• aria	• opera	
• lecture	• painting	
• board or card game that include a punctuation mark within the game ("Sorry!")	• computer/video game	
• comedy, live, or variety show (single event)	• musical theater production	
	• artwork (sculpture, statue, painting, drawing, mixed media, etc.)	
	• streaming service	
	• cartoon or comic strip	
	• online database (MLA but not Chicago)	
	• streaming service (MLA but not Chicago)	
	• website (MLA but not Chicago)	
	• name of ship, aircraft, spacecraft, train	
	• court case	
	• radio show	
	• art exhibition	
	• genus or species name	

EXERCISE 4-3: Formatting Titles

DIRECTIONS: *Each of the examples below contains a title. Determine whether the title should be placed in quotation marks, italicized, or left alone.*

- *If it should be placed in quotation marks, insert the quotation marks, and write **Q** on the line provided.*

- *If it should be italicized, underline the title, and write **I** on the space provided.*

- *If it requires no special treatment other than capitalization, write **CO** for capitalization only.*

_____ 1. Rodin's sculpture: The Thinker

_____ 2. Bruce Springsteen's song: Born in the U.S.A.

_____ 3. Movie soundtrack: Black Panther

_____ 4. Ship: Lusitania

_____ 5. Washington Monument

_____ 6. Play: Hamlet

_____ 7. Court case: Brown v. Board of Education

_____ 8. Inaugural poem: The Hill We Climb

_____ 9. The Lord's Prayer

_____ 10. Newspaper article: School Store Finally Opens

_____ 11. Video game: Minecraft

_____ 12. Nobel Prize

_____ 13. Board game: Guess Who?

_____ 14. Newspaper: The Washington Post

_____ 15. Broadway show: Hamilton

Rule 8: Depicting Thoughts in Writing

By now you know that **dialogue** is defined as a *conversation between characters*. We have spent a lot of time discussing the format of dialogue within stories, scripts, and papers.

Yet there is another type of dialogue that warrants consideration: **internal dialogue**, which can also be called **interior dialogue**. You might think this is a strange name for the inclusion of a character's thoughts, especially because there is only one character involved. Think about internal dialogue as if characters are having conversations with themselves.

Over the years, authors have handled internal dialogue differently. Some style guides believe that internal dialogue should be punctuated in the same way as direct quotations. This can be confusing for a reader. Others contend that authors should simply paraphrase, describing the author's thoughts without using exact words. Still, this seems to fall short of effective writer-to-reader communication.

In the recent past, the most common and, I believe, effective way to portray a character's thoughts is by utilizing *italics*. Using italics for internal dialogue seems to be most effective for several reasons: they cannot be confused with direct quotations; they provide exact words and thoughts of a character; and they are a clear visual cue to the reader that the character is thinking those words rather than saying them aloud.

Have you ever seen a book that contains both traditional dialogue and internal dialogue? The example below will show you how they can be used effectively.

> ▶ "Marc! Are you finished with your homework? Are you playing video games in there? Don't make me come up these stairs!" yelled Ms. Jensen in one long breath.
>
> *Ugh! Why doesn't she leave me alone? Can't she see that I am trying? I'd better get up and sit in my desk chair before she bursts in and starts screaming again.*

It all seemed like a jumble to Marc. He had been trying to focus on his schoolwork much more lately, but he just could not keep his eyes open. Maybe it was his hectic schedule. Maybe it was his lack of sleep. Maybe it was his recent breakup with Cameron. Whatever it was, he needed to figure it out—and quickly!

This is a typical example of a short story, a chapter from a book, or even a personal narrative. Many types of writing combine standard sentences, dialogue, and internal monologue. Do you see how the internal monologue stands out because of the italics? If the author placed Marc's internal dialogue in quotation marks instead, it would seem like he was answering his mother rather than thinking to himself. Especially in a third-person story, it is important for the reader to distinguish between internal dialogue (second paragraph above) and general narration (third paragraph above).

Well, my friends, our chapter is nearing its end, though I bet you "love it so much" (sarcasm). Well, maybe not. In any case, it's time to show what you know.

EXERCISE 4-4: Culminating Review of Quotation Marks and Formatting

DIRECTIONS: Read each sentence and decide whether it is punctuated and formatted correctly.

- *If it is punctuated and formatted correctly, write* **C** *on the line provided.*
- *If it is not punctuated and formatted correctly, write* **I** *on the line provided.*

_____ 1. Coach Morrow instructed the team, "Go to your locker; change into your uniform; gather all your equipment; board the bus within ten minutes."

_____ 2. Let's play "Old Maid" when you get home from school!

_____ 3. One of Shakespeare's most famous sonnets begins, "Shall I compare thee to a summer's day?" (Randolph, 130).

_____ 4. "You bought me a puppy!" Samantha shrieked with delight.

_____ 5. As my physical education class gathered around the track for our final assessment of the season, I was distraught. I was out of breath after running around the track once, and next, we were supposed to run a mile. I thought, "How am I ever going to pass this class if I can't run the mile?"

_____ 6. Ms. Li's class was so excited to take a field trip to see the Empire State Building and to take a tour of the famous ship, the Intrepid, while visiting New York City.

_____ 7. My sister's "fancy" outfit included a pair of ripped jeans and a dirty pair of Converse sneakers.

_____ 8. Always capitalize "I" whether it is at the beginning of a sentence or not.

_____ 9. Marvin explained to his group, "I think we should begin by highlighting important lines in "The Road Not Taken" before we write the analysis of the poem."

_____ 10. PIERRE: (thoughtfully) It seems to be raining. Would you like to share my umbrella?

MARIE: (enthusiastically) That would be great!

EXERCISE 4-5: Writing with Dialogue

DIRECTIONS: For this exercise, you will be writing about the same concept in two different formats. Follow the directions carefully to distinguish between the two tasks.

PROMPT: Think of a time when you persuaded someone to do something.

- _First, describe that event in the style of a **personal narrative**. Remember to include standard prose in addition to direct quotations. Review the punctuation and capitalization rules for direct quotations before beginning._
- _Then, write that same story in the format of a **stage play**. Follow the conventions of a stage play. Feel free to add the part of a narrator to fill in some of the details. Also, remember to include character directions and stage directions._
- _Finally, in a sentence or two, describe which of the two pieces you preferred writing and explain why._

Personal Narrative

_____

_____

_____

_____

_____

_____

_____

_____

_____

_____

_____

_____

_____

_____

_____

_____

_____

_____

_____

_____

_____

Stage Play

_____

_____

_____

_____

_____

_____

_____

_____

_____

_____

_____

_____

_____

_____

_____

_____

_____

_____

The One I Preferred Writing

_____

_____

_____

_____

_____

_____

_____

_____

_____

_____

_____

_____

_____

_____

_____

_____

_____

_____

Flashcard App

Apostrophes

MUST KNOW

 The most common use of the apostrophe is in the case of possession.

 Apostrophes are also used in contractions (when we shorten a word by eliminating letters and replace them with this punctuation mark) to establish a better flow.

 In other cases, apostrophes are used to replace letters but not for the same purpose as a contraction.

 The apostrophe can be used when forming plurals and when representing missing numbers.

Although an apostrophe looks the same in all situations, it serves many different functions in the English language. It may seem insignificant ('), but it bears great weight in our language. There is a lot to learn about the apostrophe, and since it is one of the most misused, misplaced punctuation marks, it is important to have a clear understanding of how and why it is included in words and in sentences.

Rule 1: Using Apostrophes for Single Possession

If you hear the word "possession," your first thought is most likely *ownership*. However, the word "possession" can also pertain to a *relationship* one person has with something, someone, or some place.

If you want to know where to place an apostrophe that belongs to a person, place, or thing, you need to take a careful look at the owner. Is it an *individual* person, place, animal, or thing in the sentence that is showing ownership or a relationship to something? If the owner is a *pronoun*, there is a separate rule for that.

Let's begin with the *ownership or relationship of a singular noun*. If you want to indicate the possessive case of a singular noun, *add an apostrophe and an "s"* to the end of the word (friend's skateboard).

EXAMPLES

▶ Cybil's sister looks exactly like her!

Cybil is a person's name. A person is one type of noun. Although Cybil doesn't "own" her sister, there is a relationship in this sentence. Since there is a relationship between Cybil and her sister, an apostrophe and an "s" need to be placed after the word "Cybil" and before the word "sister."

▶ Cory always finds his dog's toys buried in the backyard.

The singular noun does not have to be a proper noun. In the first example in this set, Cybil is a proper noun. However, the possession rule pertains to all nouns, not just proper nouns. Therefore, since "dog" is a noun and this sentence shows the dog's possession of the toys, an apostrophe and an "s" are necessary to indicate that possession. Otherwise, you need to write "the toys of the dog" or "the toys belonging to the dog," which would elongate the sentence unnecessarily.

Be careful, though. There are some nouns called **collective nouns**. These are challenging because they represent a group but are treated like singular words. The chart on the next page indicates the most popular collective nouns. If you *follow these words with the word "of,"* you will see that they represent a collection of something plural (a flock *of* geese, an army *of* soldiers) If you are deciding upon apostrophes for any of these nouns, treat them as **singular possessive nouns** (not plural possessive nouns).

NOTE: Sometimes, these words can be singular nouns when they are alone and don't show possession. What makes a noun "collective" is when it represents something that is plural (a book vs. a book *of* matches).

Popular Collective Nouns

PEOPLE	THINGS	ANIMALS
army	album	army
audience	basket	bed
band	anthology	brood
board	batch	caravan
body	block	colony
bunch	book	drove
cast	bouquet	flight
choir	bundle	flock
chorus	catalog	gaggle
class	clump	herd
company	collection	hive
congregation	fleet	host
crew	galaxy	litter
crowd	group	menagerie
ensemble	heap	murder
gang	pack	nest
group	packet	pack
horde	pair	plague
mob	pile	pod
panel	ream	pride
party	series	school
posse	set	swarm
regiment	sheaf	team
team	shower	tribe
tribe	stack	troop
troop/troupe	string	zoo

Not all collective nouns are listed in the chart above. If you are undecided about whether a noun should be treated as a collective noun, plug it into this sentence:

The _____ *of* _____ *is* very large.

If the noun fits correctly into this sentence, it is considered a **collective noun** and should be treated like a singular noun when it comes to apostrophes. If the noun does not fit into the sample sentence and requires the verb "are" instead of "is," it is considered a plural noun. Rule 2 in this chapter focuses on the use of apostrophes with plural nouns.

▶ The team's roster included twenty athletes.

This is an example that shows possession, not relationship. This is a tricky one. The word "team" makes you think of multiple people, so it seems like "team" is a plural noun. It is not a plural noun, however. The word "team" is a collective noun. It is singular but represents more than one person. The roster belongs to the team. Therefore, an apostrophe and an "s" need to follow the word "team."

So far, we have looked at people, animals, and certain things (used collectively) in terms of possession. If the possessor is an object (that is not a collective noun), room, building, place, or piece of furniture, it is *not customary* to add an apostrophe to show possession (the gymnasium floor, *not* the gymnasium's floor; the sofa cushions, *not* the sofa's cushions).

▶ Secure the backyard gate, so the turtle stays in the yard.

This sentence does not require an apostrophe, since "backyard" is a place, but it is not a collective noun.

Here are some examples of when a place's ownership requires an apostrophe:

▶ This laptop's defect is that it overheats too quickly.

Here is an example of the ownership of a thing, not a person or people. The defect belongs to the laptop; that is why there is an apostrophe and an "s" after the word "laptop."

▶ The town beach's waves have been so rough today!

This is an example of the ownership of a place, not a person or thing. The waves are located on that particular beach; that is why there is an apostrophe and an "s" after the word "beach."

Of course, the first rule applies only to common nouns. If the noun is a proper noun, an apostrophe is in order.

Some singular nouns end in an "s" or a "z." (mattress, jazz, Melina Sanchez), so you might be wondering how to show possession/relationship of such words. If a singular noun ends in an "s," simply place an apostrophe after it in order to indicate possession or relationship. If a singular noun ends in a "z" (whether or not it is a proper noun), add an apostrophe and an "s" to it to show possession/relationship.

Rule 2: Using Apostrophes for Plural Noun Possession

As you know, **plural** means *more than one*. When it comes to plural nouns, the apostrophe rule is a little more complicated.

After a *noun is made plural by adding an "s,"* should you simply add an apostrophe at the end of the word to indicate possession (the players' equipment), or should you add an apostrophe and another "s" (the players's equipment)? The answer is that it depends on the style guide you are following. Some require the additional "s," and some do not.

Certain style guides have even more specific rules about **plural possessives**: Some suggest adding an apostrophe and an extra "s" to possessive nouns that already end in "s" if they do not require a spelling change to be made plural (binoculars's). To show possession, some publications add an apostrophe and an "s" to common nouns ending in "s" but not to proper nouns ending in "s." (scissors's; Jones') Still, others just add an apostrophe to all plural possessive words ending in "s." (jeans'; Salinas')

In my opinion, the best way to approach a **plural possessive** is simply to *place the apostrophe without the extra "s."* The reasoning behind this is related to the way the word is *pronounced*. It is awkward-sounding to say, "The Williams's house is at the end of the street" because the word Williams's would then be pronounced "Williams*es*" (with an extra syllable at the end) when it is supposed to sound like the name always sounds "Williams." Therefore, I usually leave out the extra "s." Does that make sense?

Remember that *some nouns are irregular*, meaning that you cannot just add "s" to them to make them plural. If you want to show possession of a plural noun that is irregular, you need to change it to its correct form in the plural and then show possession (not gooses' but geese's; not shelfs' but shelves').

EXAMPLES

▶ The teachers' cafeteria is on the second floor of the building.

Since the cafeteria is shared by several teachers, the apostrophe belongs after the "s" in teachers (indicating that there is more than one teacher to whom the cafeteria belongs). It would also be correct to write the teachers's cafeteria, but doesn't it look strange? It even shows up as an error in most proofreading programs.

▶ The Davis' family adage is one that has been passed along for many generations: "Treat others the way you would have them treat you."

Since the last name of the family is Davis and it already ends in an "s," the best way to indicate possession is simply by adding an apostrophe to the end of the name. It would, in fact, also be correct to add an apostrophe plus "s" to the end of the name, but it would change the pronunciation when read aloud.

If a family name ends in a "y," simply add an "s" after the "y" to show that there is more than one person with that name. Many people confuse this and change the "y" to "i" and add "es." This is not correct when making a proper noun plural. (the O'Malleys, not the O'Mallies). Thus, when something belongs to the O'Malleys, the apostrophe should be placed after the s. It would not be placed after the "y" unless it was owned by or related to only *one* member of the O'Malley family. If a family name ends in a "z," and you are trying to convey plural possession by members of that family, place "es" and an apostrophe after the last name to make the proper noun plural and indicate possession.

EXAMPLE

> Maddy loves to sleep both at the Ruizes' local and summer homes, since Mr. Ruiz makes the tastiest pancakes in the morning, no matter where they are staying.
>
> *Since the last name "Ruiz" ends in a "z," the letters "es" and an apostrophe need to be added to the end of the name to indicate that the family that owns the homes has more than one member.*

You are probably wondering how you should approach **plural possessives** in your own writing. Here is my suggestion: If the teacher or professor requires you to follow a particular style guide, be sure to check the format of plural possessives in that guide and adhere to it. If you are writing a paper that does not need to follow a particular style guide, choose one of the rules noted above and remain consistent in the way you present plural possessives in your paper. Of course, if you are including a plural possessive as part of an excerpt, you must copy it exactly as it appears in the original document.

Some nouns have an "s" as their last letter to indicate that there is more than one of them. These words show *number* rather than *possession* or *relationship*. You should *never* place an apostrophe before an "s" in a word if you are not showing possession or a relationship (Los Angeles, *not* Los Angele's; baby carriages (plural), *not* baby carriage's (to indicate plural without possession); the Foo Fighters, *not* the Foo Fighter's).

Also, remember *never* to use an apostrophe to make a last name plural. ("The Moseys like to go to the movies," not "The Mosey's like to go to the movies.") Apostrophes are used to show possession or relationship, *not* number!

One more thing. The words to which we are adding apostrophes are *originally* nouns when they stand alone without an apostrophe. However, when we add an apostrophe to them, they function as adjectives in the sentence. (If I use the phrase "Yiwon's sweater," the word "Yiwon's" is the adjective that describes to whom the sweater belongs.)

EXERCISE 5-1: Punctuating Singular and Plural Possessive Nouns

DIRECTIONS: *Each phrase indicates possession by either a singular or plural possessive noun.*

- *Determine whether the noun in the phrase is singular or plural.*
- *Rewrite each expression by including the apostrophe in the correct place, according to the recommendations of this author.*

Remember that style guides vary when it comes to apostrophes, and you may have to adjust the apostrophe format based on the guide you are required to follow.

EXAMPLE: *the car of Melissa = Melissa's car*

1. snacks of the children = _____

2. shirts of the boys = _____

3. eggs of the quail = _____

4. frisbee of the dogs = _____

5. board of the Wounded Warriors = _____

6. medals of the athletes = _____

7. dishes of Grandmother Solis = _____

8. oven of the chefs = _____

9. office of the boss = _____

10. prison cells of Alcatraz = _____

Rule 3: Using Apostrophes for Personal Possessive Pronouns and Possessive Indefinite Pronouns

So far, we have covered apostrophe rules for singular and plural nouns. Although a pronoun takes the place of a noun, its apostrophe usage is not necessarily aligned with its singular or plural counterpart.

It is important to distinguish between two types of pronouns: **personal possessive pronouns** and **indefinite possessive pronouns**. This is because apostrophe rules differ between the two.

Personal Possessive Pronouns and Possessive Indefinite Pronouns

Personal Possessive Pronouns	Possessive Indefinite Pronouns
• hers	• another
• his	• anybody
• mine	• anyone
• *one* (when referring to a specific person) ours	• everybody
• theirs	• everyone
• yours	• nobody
	• no one
	• *one* (when not referring to a specific person)
	• somebody
	• someone

Let's start with the rule for **personal possessive pronouns**. Even though personal possessive pronouns show *ownership or relationship*, they *do not* need an apostrophe. The ownership/relationship is *already inherent* in these words, so an apostrophe would be redundant.

This is especially confusing for some people because the personal possessive pronouns *hers*, *theirs*, and *yours* have an "s" at the end of the word. Still, you should *never* add an apostrophe to these words *when they are indicating possession* or *relationship*.

It also *does not matter* if these pronouns are referring to one or more people or things. The number of items or people is irrelevant in determining apostrophe usage when considering personal possessive pronouns.

You may, therefore, be wondering why I even included these in this chapter, since they do not require apostrophes. The answer is threefold:

■ People often place apostrophes in or after these words, so I wanted you to be aware of that mistake.

■ There is an exception to the rule, and that exception is the word "one," which is why I italicized it in the chart. The word "one" can sometimes serve as a personal possessive pronoun and, as such, can require an apostrophe if it represents one specific person's *possession* of something or *relationship* to someone

Correct: Can you recognize that one's strategies for success?

In this case, "one" is referring to a specific person (indicated by the word "that"), so it is serving as a personal possessive pronoun.

You may also have noticed the word "one" in the right-hand column of the chart, since "one" can also serve as an indefinite possessive pronoun when it is *not* referring to a specific person or thing. The good news is that when it comes to apostrophe usage, if the word "one" is showing possession or ownership (whether it is serving a personal possessive pronoun or an indefinite possessive pronoun), it *always requires* an apostrophe and an "s" at the end of the word (one's). Here's the bad news: The word "one" can sometimes be plural (the *ones* who were accepted to Duke). In that example, "ones" is not showing possession or relationship and does not need an apostrophe.

The use of "one" as a **personal possessive pronoun** usually follows a sentence that specifies a person to whom "one" is referring.

The use of "one" as an **indefinite possessive pronoun** does not need to follow another sentence.

▶ Chad and Miranda are twins but do not have the same artistic ability. One's ability is in sketching, and the other can't draw at all.

You know that "one" in this sentence refers to either Chad or Miranda, not a random person.

▶ One's daily oral-hygiene habits should include flossing and rinsing.

The "one" in this sentence refers to any person in general.

■ Another common error is when people confuse the possessive adjective (also called a *determiner*) *its* with the contraction *it's*, and they also confuse the possessive adjective *whose* with the contraction *who's*. Although there is a separate section for contractions in this chapter, I would be remiss if I did not remind you that *its* shows possession/ relationship (the cat grabbed its toy) and does not mean "it is," just as *whose* shows possession/relationship (Whose pen is this?) and does not mean "who is."

Let's move on to **indefinite possessive pronouns**. These are pronouns that do not identify specifically who or what is being referenced. All indefinite possessive pronouns require an *apostrophe and an "s"* when they indicate *possession* or *relationship* (everyone's grades; another's perspective). Be careful, though. You still need to be certain as to *why* you are adding an apostrophe. Is it because you are indicating *ownership* or *relationship* (somebody's backpack), or is it because you are using that word as a *contraction* (somebody's blocking the hall)? Knowing *why* you add punctuation is just as important as placing it correctly within or after a word.

Before we finish the pronoun section, I want to let you know that even though certain words are considered **pronouns** when they stand apart from other words, they often function as adjectives (determiners) in a sentence when they precede a noun and explain to whom that noun belongs. These special adjectives (called *determiners*) also play a key role in compound possession, the next section of this chapter.

Here is an example of when a possessive pronoun functions as an adjective:

EXAMPLE

▶ Her new book is so heavy.

In this sentence, the word "her," which often functions as a pronoun, is serving as an adjective (determiner) in this sentence to indicate the owner of the book.

The word "one" is especially tricky; depending on its use in a sentence, it can serve as a pronoun (one's—indicating ownership), a noun (one who is tall), an adjective (when it is a number before a noun—one player), or even a verb (to one-up someone)!

Rule 4: Using Apostrophes for Compound Possession

So far, you have learned how to use apostrophes with an *isolated noun* and an *isolated pronoun*. What I mean by that is that there is only one noun/pronoun to which the apostrophe applies. There are many times, however, when *multiple* people or things have ownership. These **compound nouns** or **pronouns** do not necessarily have to be the subject of the sentence. They sometimes appear as *direct objects* or even *objects of a preposition*.

The key is to determine whether these owners have *joint ownership over the same item* or if they both have ownership, but over *different* items.

When you have a compound noun (two people who have *joint ownership over the same thing* or a *joint relationship with the same person*), the *final* noun in the series should show possession. This means that you *do not* need an apostrophe after each person's name, only after the *last* person's name in the series of names.

▶ We love to play cornhole in Dom and Marisa's yard.

This example implies that Dom and Marisa share the same yard.

▶ Tom and Mary Lou's pool has a lap lane.

Since Tom and Mary Lou both own the same pool, only one apostrophe is required after the last noun (Mary Lou).

Of course, if there happen to be multiple possessives in the same sentence but they are *not related* to each other or *not shared* by both parties, then the nouns take separate apostrophes.

▶ Pedro's turtle and Frankie's lizard play together.

Pedro and Frankie have different pets.

Even if the two nouns own the same type of item or have the same type of relationship, if the item/relationship is *not shared* by the two of them, each noun needs a *separate apostrophe*.

▶ Zander's and Max's surfboards need repair.

Zander and Max both own surfboards, but they don't share the same surfboard. That is why there are apostrophes after each of their names.

▶ Cici's mother and Bikram's mother are both Libras.

Cici and Bikram have different mothers even though their mothers both have the same astrological sign.

So far, so good. It is easy to indicate possession when it comes to nouns. Where it becomes more complicated is *when possessive nouns are mixed with possessive determiners* (also called possessive adjectives). These words (that look like pronouns and are sometimes labeled pronouns) show possession and modify a noun. Some **possessive determiners** include the words "my," "our," "its," "her," "their," "your," and "whose." Be careful, since many of these words look very similar to the possessive personal pronouns mentioned earlier in the chapter.

If there is shared possession in a sentence with a combination of a noun and a possessive determiner, the rule is that *the noun should take the apostrophe, despite the order* in which they appear.

EXAMPLES

▶ Peter's and my favorite food is pizza.

If you are mixing nouns and possessive determiners to show possession, both need to be in the possessive form. Since "my" already indicates possession, there is no need for an apostrophe after it.

▶ "Patrick's and your parallel parking need to improve before the road test," said the driving instructor to his students.

Patrick is a noun. The word "your" is a possessive determiner. When a noun and a possessive determiner show ownership, an apostrophe is only required after the noun (since the possessive determiner already shows ownership).

Note that there is no such word as "I's. The word "I" cannot show possession, though I have seen this mistake multiple times. You cannot have a sentence with "I" as the owner.

Incorrect: Peter and I's favorite food is pizza.

Remember, *we don't ever need to add an apostrophe to personal pronouns or possessive determiners*, as they already show possession and, therefore, do not require an apostrophe.

This is *not* the case, however, with **possessive indefinite pronouns**. Possessive indefinite pronouns function very much *like nouns*. Hence, we apply apostrophe rules to them very much like the rules for possessive compound nouns.

Let's begin with sentences that combine nouns with indefinite possessive pronouns. If a sentence indicates *shared* ownership over the *same* person or thing, only one apostrophe is necessary after the last noun/pronoun.

EXAMPLE

▶ Aydin and another's group project scored 100%.

This means that Aydin and someone else worked on that project together. However, if the noun and indefinite pronoun do not share ownership, they each take an apostrophe.

Here is an example of a sentence where two separate people have the same grade, but the grade is not based on a shared activity.

EXAMPLE

▶ Azaria's and someone's quarter grades are an A+.

This means that Azaria and someone else have an A+ for the quarter, but they did not work together to receive that score. A hint to help you decide is to look at the noun that is being owned (grades). Is it singular or plural? This is often helpful in determining if something is shared.

Finally, if two or more indefinite pronouns show ownership (without the presence of a noun), apply the same rules as the compound possessive noun rule. If they share ownership over the same item/person, only one apostrophe is needed.

EXAMPLE

▶ Everybody and anybody's behavior must be stellar.

It is implied that they share ownership of the behavior.

If they *do not* share ownership over the same item/person, then separate apostrophes are required.

EXAMPLES

▶ Someone's and another's philosophy on life may differ.

This sentence implies a contrast, so the philosophies are not shared; hence, there are separate apostrophes for each pronoun.

▶ Xavier's and somebody's cell phones were left on the bus.

Since Xavier and another person do not share the same cell phone, a separate apostrophe is used for the noun and for the indefinite possessive pronoun.

Apostrophes related to possession can be quite confusing. Let's see how well you retained the rules related to this subject matter.

EXERCISE 5-2: Correct or Incorrect Apostrophes to Indicate Possession

DIRECTIONS: *Read each of the following sentences. Determine whether the apostrophes are used correctly.*

- *If they are used correctly, write* **Correct** *on the line provided.*
- *If the apostrophes are incorrect, write* **Incorrect.**

_____ 1. The lobby's floor was slippery.

_____ 2. Cally's mother and Raquel's daughter travel together.

_____ 3. Emme and I's favorite ice cream flavor is strawberry.

_____ 4. Isaac's and Howard's aunt lives next door to their house.

_____ 5. Grandma Jo gave an heirloom to her son's wife.

_____ 6. The Empire State Building and the Pentagon's lobbies are huge!

_____ 7. Savannah and somebody's saddles were left behind in the stable.

_____ 8. Their teacher placed a prize in Hillary's and Jackie's backpacks.

_____ 9. The first-place medal was their's.

_____ 10. Quincy's and my vocal teacher won a Grammy Award.

Rule 5: Using Apostrophes to Represent Value, Distance, or Time

Like the rules we covered previously, **apostrophes** are sometimes used to represent a correlation between a noun and something else, but in the instances below, there is *no ownership* involved. These types of sentences relay information about *value*, *distance*, or *time*.

In the case of *value*, an apostrophe is used to denote the value/amount (but not time) spent on something. In such a sentence, the apostrophe must replace the word "of" and must fall between a noun and a number or value that directly follows that noun. (six days' laundry = six days *of* laundry = clothes that have been used over the course of six days and need to be laundered).

> She has already completed five chapters' classwork this quarter.
>
> *There are five chapters **of** classwork.*
>
> Seven stretches' legwork prepared Janie for the race.
>
> *The value of seven stretches **of** legwork helped Janie prepare for the race.*

Be careful, though. If you cannot substitute the word "of" for the apostrophe, you may have misplaced an apostrophe.

Incorrect: Five chapters' have been completed this quarter.

*Since "five chapters **of** have" makes no sense, an apostrophe cannot be placed after the word "chapters."*

Apostrophes also indicate an *amount of time* (but not the precise "o'clock" type of time).

In the case of *time*, the word "of" is a substitute for the apostrophe.

EXAMPLES

▶ It took three years' hard work to renovate the house.

*It took three years **of** hard work.*

▶ A day's pay was not enough for Celie to pay for her lunch and transportation.

*A day **of** pay was not enough for Celie. The apostrophe replaces the word "of" to indicate an amount of time.*

If you are uncertain as to whether you should use an apostrophe to indicate time spent, insert the word "of" after the word that indicates time spent.

Incorrect: It takes three years' to complete that project.

Since "three years of to" makes no sense, an apostrophe cannot be placed after the word "years."

Additionally, apostrophes may be used to indicate *distance* between items. In this case, the word "of" is *not always* a substitute for the apostrophe. However, in order to require an apostrophe, the word that indicates distance must modify a noun.

EXAMPLES

▶ Micah lived a stone's throw away from the farm.

The word "stone's" refers to the distance of the throw. He lived the distance of a stone (approximately 33 feet).

▶ A mile's walk in the countryside is all you need to feel refreshed.

Notice again that the word "of" does not have to replace the apostrophe in the context of distance. The word "mile's" refers to the distance of the walk.

If you are uncertain as to whether you should use an apostrophe to indicate distance, you will have to test it out on an individual basis to see if it makes sense.

Incorrect: Solomon lived six miles' from the ranch.

*Solomon did not live six miles **worth of** anything. The word "miles'" does not modify a noun.*

I bet you never realized the complications behind the apostrophe. Another issue is that we have come to use a straight mark (') that looks very similar to an apostrophe ('). This little, straight symbol (') represents items *other than possession or relationships.*

Rule 6: Using Apostrophes with Lowercase Plural Letters

This is not a rule that we see or apply often, but I wanted to let you know about it. Sometimes, we use a *lowercase letter to represent a word*. It does not happen often. When we do that and we want to make that lowercase letter plural, it is customary to *separate the lowercase letter from the "s"* at the end of the word.

EXAMPLE

Stephanie dotted her i's and crossed her t's before handing in her paper.

Understandably, the apostrophe is necessary between the "i" and the "s" because the reader can be confused and read this word mistakenly as the word "is." The apostrophes provide clarity for the reader.

Still, we apply this rule to lowercase letters *across the board*, not only when the lowercase letter and "s" form an actual word.

You may have noticed song titles or even companies that do not abide by these rules. In the case of a proper noun, even if it is grammatically incorrect, it needs to be spelled the way the author, creator, or corporation intended.

> Song: "Ex's and Oh's" by Elle King.
>
> *The word "Ex's" may be referring to an ex-loved one, in which case it is an abbreviation that begins with a capital letter. The word "Oh's" could be duplicating a sound rather than a letter. In either case, to make these plural would not require an apostrophe (could be "Exes" and "Ohs"), but we spell it the way the songwriter did.*
>
> Sports team: The Oakland A's
>
> *The actual name of the team is the Oakland Athletics. However, they have trademarked "A's" as an alternate name of their team. Even though it is not correct grammatically, we must write it or type it as it is trademarked.*
>
> Coffee and Donut Shop: Tim Hortons
>
> *This is an interesting one! The original name of this store was Tim Horton Donuts. Shortly thereafter, the name was shortened to Tim Horton's. Later, when it became popular in Quebec, Canada, instead of translating it to "Chez Tim Horton," the company dropped the apostrophe entirely, since apostrophes are not used to show possession in the French language. So, if we need to write the name of this business, we must spell it without the apostrophe (even though it is incorrect grammatically).*

When it comes to the apostrophe, there are some apostrophe rules in *British English* that *differ* from those in *American English*. Depending on where your book, essay, speech, etc. was published, you may notice these differences:

1. Sometimes, uppercase letters (besides the pronoun "I") are considered a noun when they are used to denote *someone's letter grade in school*. In that case, a lowercase "s" may be added to the word to represent the plural form of that letter grade, but *an apostrophe should not be inserted* between the letter grade and the "s."

▶ Kylie received Bs on all her tests.

Since there is no possession, the grade of B is just plural, so no apostrophe is necessary.

Remember, in American English, apostrophes should not be used to make capital letters plural when uppercase letters are substituted for words. Hence, there should not be an apostrophe in the "word" Bs.

2. Similarly, I have often seen people use apostrophes after an uppercase initialism when it is simply supposed to be plural. In American English, apostrophes should not be used to make initialisms plural when uppercase initialisms are substituted for words. In the following examples, the initialism A.P. stands for Assistant Principal.

▶ The A.P.s in every school building assume a great deal of responsibility, in order to alleviate some of the principals' work.

Apostrophes are not necessary to make an uppercase (A.P.) initialism plural.

3. Still, others often make a mistake in American English when they use an apostrophe to show plural numbers. In American English, we sometimes use numbers to represent words. If the word is written in numeral form (as it appears in the example), only an "s" is necessary.

EXAMPLE

▶ Walter answered this question on his math test: "How many 20s go into 100?"

"20s" only requires an "s" to make it plural.

The teacher could have written the word 20s as "twenties." If the word is written in numeral form (as it appears in the example), only an "s" is necessary to indicate that 20 is plural. There should not be an apostrophe in between the number and the "s."

4. There is one more error that I see often—*even in textbooks*! In American English, we do not place an apostrophe to represent the time period called a decade.

Incorrect: I love the fashion that emerged in the 1970's!

Be careful! Many proofreading programs won't even catch this one as a mistake, since it is used so frequently.

EXAMPLE

▶ I love the fashion that emerged in the 1970s!

Since the decade is plural to indicate all ten years of that time period, place an "s" after the year; an apostrophe is unnecessary.

Before moving on to the next rule, I need to stress something I have said before. For the most part, the information I provided for you regarding this rule is consistent with most American style guides. However, some style guides may vary with respect to this apostrophe rule, especially if they are not American. Additionally, some newspapers and magazines have adopted their own rules for apostrophes. If you are writing a research paper, be sure to refer to the guide recommended by your teacher or professor. Again, when citing an excerpt, be sure to copy the excerpt exactly as it appears, despite potential contradictions to the rules provided in this chapter.

Rule 7: Using Apostrophes in Contractions

As you know, **contractions** are *shortened forms of words or groups of words*. When a letter is omitted, an apostrophe is used to replace it. You may be wondering how apostrophes for contractions were derived. It is believed that apostrophe usage began in the 1500s by poets, who wanted to adjust the meter of a line of poetry by reducing its amount of syllables. By eliminating vowels and replacing them with apostrophes, poets had the freedom to adjust the number of "feet" in a metric line of poetry, thereby conveying their intended rhythm more effectively.

There is an apostrophe that we use almost daily, but you might not even realize what it represents.

HINT: It answers the question, "What time is it?"

Have you ever thought about the word *o'clock*? It is a contraction we never really think about. Did you know that *o'clock* stands for "of the clock?" It is one of the few contractions where the apostrophe takes the place of multiple words.

Most contractions replace letters found in certain **helping verbs** (will, shall), **linking verbs** (am), or **adverbs** (not).

Most Common Contractions

Contraction	Word(s) it Replaces
I'm	I am
I've	I have
I'll	I will
I'd	I would or I had
it'll	it will
you'll	you will
you're	you are
you've	you have
you'd	you would or you had
we're	we are
we've	we have
we'd	we would or we had
he's/she's	he is/she is
he'd/she'd	he/she would or he/she had
he'll/she'll	He will/she will
they'd	they would or they had
they're	they are
they've	they have
they'll	they will
who's	who is
who'll	who will
who've	who have
what's	what is
what'll	what will

(continued)

Most Common Contractions, *continued*

Contraction	Word(s) it Replaces
what're	what are
what've	what have
where's	where is
why's	why is
shouldn't	should not
should've	should have*
couldn't	could not
could've	could have*
wouldn't	would not
would've	would have*
didn't	did not
can't	cannot**
don't	do not
shan't	shall not
aren't	are not
mightn't	might not
doesn't	does not
hadn't	had not
haven't	have not
isn't	is not
mustn't	must not
wasn't	was not
weren't	were not
oughtn't	ought not

Contraction	Word(s) it Replaces
that's	that is
there's	there is
who's***	who is
it's***	it has or it is
won't****	will not
let's	let us
'tis*****	it is
'twas*****	it was

* "Should have" is the correct meaning of should've. "Could have" is the correct meaning of could've. "Would have" is the correct meaning of would've. However, in my many years of teaching, I have noticed that students write "should of," "could of," and "would of." Perhaps it is because of the pronunciation of the contractions. In any case, the word that follows should, could, and would must be "have," not "of."

** "Cannot" is the only single word in English that can be transposed into a contraction (can't). Never separate the words "can" and "not"; they are one word and must be written without a space in between. All other English contractions represent two or more words.

*** I know I mentioned this earlier in the chapter, but I thought I should mention it here as well. The words *it's* and *who's* are tricky because these words are commonly confused with their homophones: *its* and *whose*. Remember, **possessive adjectives** (its and whose) *do not* need an apostrophe. On the contrary, the word *it's* stands for "it is," and the word *who's* means "who is," so these both require an apostrophe to replace the letter that is missing (i). Hopefully, you will test these when you write them to be sure you have used the correct form.

**** Obviously, the word *won't* has an "o" in it, but it represents the words *will not*. In case you were wondering why, I thought I would tell you. Years ago, the verb *will* was actually spelled *woll*, but it evolved into *will* over time. Strangely, the spelling of the contraction (won't) remains the same to this day.

***** There are two contractions on the chart that differ from the others: " 'tis" and " 'twas." This is because rather than eliminating a letter from the second word, they *eliminate a letter from the first word*. The "i" in "it" (which is the first word of the two-word sets: "*it* is" and "*it* was") is being eliminated in both instances.

If you live in the United States, you know that in certain parts of our country, there is an expression that is used to address people: *y'all*. It is a contraction for "you all," and it is used when more than one person is being addressed. It is not exactly considered "proper English," but I thought it was worth noting, since it appears in many works of literature.

Another informal word that is sometimes used in the United States is "ain't." It originally replaced "am not," but today, it loosely replaces "am not," "are not," "is not," "has not," and "have not." It is considered informal and should not be used in formal writing. The only instance when it might be acceptable is in a fictional piece of writing when the author is attempting to depict a particular time period or region's language for effect. Naturally, if you excerpt a piece of writing that includes "ain't," you must copy it exactly as it appears in the text.

Now that I have explained the contraction rule in depth, I have some news: *Contractions are frowned upon in formal written English*—especially on college application essays, on college entrance exam essays, in research papers, and in business correspondence. Whenever I assist rising seniors in their college application journey, I remind them to avoid contractions and, instead, to spell words completely.

Rule 8: Using Apostrophes in Omissions

There are occasions when *an apostrophe is used to replace a letter* but the word in which it appears *does not form a contraction*. Remember when I told you about the derivation of contractions by poets long ago? There are other instances when letters from words were dropped to change the sound or flow of words. These words, however, are not considered contractions, since they do not combine multiple words with an apostrophe. The apostrophe simply *replaces a letter or letters within a single word*. These words are called **omissions**.

Many of these words are obsolete and are no longer used in modern English. However, you will certainly come across them in your reading, and

you may have to include them in excerpts in your papers. When doing so, you will copy them exactly as the author intended.

Here are the most popular **omissions**:

o' = of

o'er = over

ne'r = never

e'en = even

'fraid = afraid

s'pose = suppose

'til = until

'twixt = betwixt (which we now call "between")

'tween = between

 IRL | Here's a quick aside about a new word added to our language recently. The word **'tween** has been a contraction for many years, and it represents the word "between."

However, in our society, we have a new word that is spelled **tween** without the apostrophe. This word means a youngster whose age falls between small childhood and teenage years—namely, ages eight to twelve.

There is a subset of omissions that is attributed to the United States as well. In certain parts of our country, words ending in "ing" are shortened to end in "in" plus an apostrophe to represent the dialect of that region.

Nothin' and *somethin'* are the most common examples of regional omissions in the US.

As I explained earlier, another type of omission is used in numbers, specifically *years*. When we refer to particular years or time periods, we sometimes replace the century number with an apostrophe (Class of '22; icons of the '80s).

Again, in formal writing, it is *frowned upon* to utilize such shortcuts. The entire year should be typed.

> ▶ My Irish grandfather always greeted me by saying "Top o' the mornin'!"
>
> *There are two omissions in this quote. The first one, "o'," stands for "of." The second one, "mornin'," represents the word "morning."*
>
> ▶ They were members of the Class of '07.
>
> *Of course, the reader or listener needs to know the context behind this statement, since the graduates could have been graduates of 1807, 1907, 2007, etc.*

Now that we are finished discussing apostrophes, I want to remind you that the misuse of apostrophes is one of the most common grammatical errors. *Do not* add a random apostrophe to a word *just in case* it belongs there. Use these notes as a reference, practice using apostrophes, and try to commit the rules to memory.

When Is an Apostrophe *Not* an Apostrophe?

1. Many people confuse the distance rule mentioned earlier in the chapter with the indication of someone's height in feet and inches (in the US, of course). Typically, when we write someone's height, we use a straight single mark called a single prime (which looks like an apostrophe but is not curly) to represent feet.

    We use a double set of those straight marks called a double prime to represent inches.

    Ava is 5'6" means that Ava is five feet, six inches tall.

These marks are not called apostrophes or quotation marks, since they are shaped differently and have different purposes than for English grammar. Prime and double prime symbols can be found in the "Symbols" menu in software such as Word, but for regular use, straight quotation marks can be substituted for them.

Do you know how to make these symbols straight rather than curly? In Word, you press the apostrophe button (or quotation marks) and then press the rounded "undo" symbol in the toolbar. Voila! The apostrophe/quotation marks are no longer curly!

Now, do not say I never taught you anything. ☺

2. If you recall, when you were learning about direct quotations in a previous chapter, you learned about a quote within a quote. This is when something specific is referenced within existing dialogue. Even though the typical curly apostrophe symbol *is* used to surround a quote within a quote, that symbol *does not* function as an apostrophe. In this use, it is called a *single quotation mark*. There are opening and closing single quotation marks that face opposite directions, just like regular double quotation marks. (Software such as Word will format these automatically, so they face the correct direction.)

EXERCISE 5-3: Culminating Apostrophe Review

DIRECTIONS: *Read each sentence carefully.*

- *Place apostrophes in appropriate places in each sentence.*
- *If the sentence also requires an **S** or **ES**, add that/those as well.*
- *If you added at least one apostrophe, write the rule number on the line provided.*
- *If the sentence requires no apostrophe, write **NA** on the line provided.*

Apostrophe Rules
Rule 1: Using Apostrophes for Single Possession
Rule 2: Using Apostrophes for Plural Noun Possession
Rule 3: Using Apostrophes for Possessive Personal Pronouns and Possessive Indefinite Pronouns
Rule 4: Using Apostrophes for Compound Possession
Rule 5: Using Apostrophes to Represent Value, Distance, or Time
Rule 6: Using Apostrophes with Lowercase Plural Letters
Rule 7: Using Apostrophes in Contractions
Rule 8: Using Apostrophes in Omissions

_____ 1. In two decades time, technology usage has quadrupled.

_____ 2. Ruth Bader Ginsburg was appointed a Supreme Court justice in the 90s.

_____ 3. The Class of 2020 was unable to have a graduation ceremony due to the global pandemic.

_____ 4. "Lo, How a Rose E er Blooming" is a popular holiday hymn.

_____ 5. Roberto and her birthday is the same, since they are twins.

_____ 6. Since his arm is broken, someone needs to carry Chess bookbag to his next class.

_____ 7. The Gomez youngest son, Darren, is featured on a reality TV show.

_____ 8. "Cant you see that I am busy?" asked Sra. Placida when Milo interrupted her repeatedly.

_____ 9. Because Herminia received all Cs on her tests, she did not qualify for the honor society.

_____ 10. After Mr. Scribner checked the penmanship quizzes, he noticed that most students had difficulty writing qs and as in cursive.

EXERCISE 5-4: Writing with Apostrophes

DIRECTIONS: You will be incorporating several apostrophe rules while completing the following writing task.

PROMPT: Over the summer, your parent organized a family reunion. You did not know many members of your extended family, and you were apathetic about the event, which was held at your home.

Describe the event, ensuring to include your meetings with individual relatives, the activities in which you participated, and the conversations you had in order to get to know family members better. Try to incorporate words that reflect the correct usage of a variety of apostrophe rules.

_____

_____

_____

_____

_____

Flashcard
App

 # Hyphens and Dashes

MUST KNOW

- Hyphens, en dashes, and em dashes are punctuation marks that are often confused with each other.

- Hyphens (-) are punctuation marks that help us make and understand connections between words.

- The purpose of an en dash is to indicate date or number ranges. The en dash (–) looks like a shorter version of an em dash.

- An em dash is used to emphasize, interrupt, or explain something further. It also can be used to convey a tangential thought within the context of a sentence. The em dash is a longer line (—) than the en dash.

D o you know the difference between a hyphen (-) and a dash (–)? Did you know there were two types of dashes (– and —) and that they serve different functions? Most people simply type the hyphen key (-) to represent all three symbols, but they are not supposed to be the same line length. Besides, the meaning behind their usage varies. Many texts classify hyphens under the umbrella of dashes, but because the functions of hyphens and dashes differ, we will be analyzing them separately in this chapter. It is time to learn how these punctuation marks can help us become better readers and writers.

In my experience, people often use **en dashes** (a type of dash that looks like this –), sometimes use **hyphens** (that look like this -), and hardly ever use **em dashes** (that look like this —). I am pretty sure most students use these from memory rather than from understanding.

Since we will begin with hyphens, the function of a **hyphen** is to make connections (for example, "snow-covered hills"). Throughout the chapter, we will discuss the types of connections they make.

Hyphens

As you may know, a **hyphen** (-) is a line that is often used to join two or more words together. To type a hyphen, simply type the key that has the underscore on top and the hyphen beneath it. You do not have to press a special function key to type a hyphen.

Why is a hyphen necessary to connect words? If the hyphen that is supposed to be placed between two words or parts of words is not present, the reader may misunderstand the meaning of the sentence. Hyphens help readers develop *clarity of understanding*. Therefore, it is essential that you understand when to hyphenate words to portray them as adjectives.

Rule 1: Using Hyphens to Form Compound Adjectives

As you know, **compound** means more than one. A **compound adjective** *does not* mean that there are multiple adjectives in a sentence. Compound, in this case, means *connected*. The hyphen is the connector between words that, when connected, *function as one adjective* in a sentence and describe a noun that follows the adjective.

So, how do you know when to use the hyphen to connect words to form a **compound adjective**? Even though a hyphenated set of words describes a noun, placing the word "and" between the adjectives *would not* make sense. Separating the words and trying to place them before the noun individually may only work for the *last word* in the compound adjective or may not make any sense at all.

One final note: Hyphens *never require a space* before or after them.

EXAMPLES

▶ Going on safari was a never-to-be-forgotten experience.

  In this sentence, "never-to-be-forgotten" serves as a compound adjective to describe the noun "experience." If you try to place "and" between these words, it does not work to connect them ("never and to and be and forgotten and" does not make sense). If you try to use these words separately as adjectives, that does not work. As a matter of fact, the word "forgotten" by itself would change the meaning of the sentence.

▶ The sun-kissed fruit was a bright shade of orange.

  In this sentence, "sun" and "kissed" are serving as a descriptor of the fruit. They need to be connected by a hyphen, since separating them would cause the reader confusion. There is an actual fruit called a "sunfruit," but that is not what is being expressed in this sentence. Also, the fruit was not "kissed" literally. "Sun-kissed" is a figurative expression meaning that the fruit received a lot of sunshine to help it ripen. This is why the two words need to be hyphenated to form one adjective.

Rule 2: Using Hyphens in Numbers and Units of Measure

We use hyphens so commonly when *spelling out two-word numbers* that we may not even think twice about it (for example, thirty-six). The hyphen rule related to numbers that are written as words is that a hyphen is required for two-word numbers *from twenty-one through ninety-nine*. However, we *do not* use hyphens for hundreds, thousands, millions, or billions, unless a two-word number is part of that number (one million six hundred forty-two).

The same rule applies when numbers that are spelled as words serve as **compound adjectives** (twenty-six million dollars).

EXAMPLE

▶ The thirty-four students in the last row of the auditorium could not hear the guest speaker.

The number "thirty-four" is a number that falls between twenty-one and ninety-nine, and, in this sentence, it is spelled out rather than written as a numeral. Therefore, it must be hyphenated.

Hyphens are also used *when fractions are written as words* when serving as compound adjectives (one-quarter cup of flour). However, if the fraction is being used as a noun, it becomes a little more complicated. Some style guides say that a hyphen is not required if the fraction is a noun (Skylar ate two thirds of the cake), while others require the hyphenation (Skylar ate two-thirds of the cake). I am accustomed to seeing the hyphen in all contexts of word fractions (spelled out), so I usually hyphenate the words, regardless of the part of speech.

EXAMPLE

▶ The gardener added one-quarter pound of fertilizer to the soil.

The fraction "one-quarter" is serving as a measurement of the noun "pound," and the fraction is spelled out in words. That is why it must be hyphenated.

As you know, there are other types of measurements besides fractions. One rule that can be confusing is if the measurement has a *combination of numeral and word*. You must read the sentence to know whether a hyphen is required.

If the numeral and word combination form a *compound adjective before a noun*, then a hyphen is required. (25-pound puppy). However, if the numeral and measurement *do not* form an adjective, a hyphen is not required (20 ounces of milk).

EXAMPLE

▶ The three-legged stool wobbled every time someone sat on it.

This sentence has a compound adjective that is composed of two adjectives where one adjective is a number and the other is not ("three" and "legged"). However, these two adjectives cannot function apart from each other in this sentence (without the hyphen). You cannot place the word "and" between them, right? (The three and legged stool? That makes no sense.) You also cannot use "three" as a separate adjective to describe "stool," since "three" indicates something plural and "stool" is singular ("three stool" doesn't make sense). So, the way to describe the stool as having three legs is to hyphenate "three" and "legged." Of course, you can say "the stool that had three legs," but that changes the structure of the sentence.

In addition, if the numeral and measurement end the sentence, a hyphen is not necessary (Nate led the other runners by 15 feet) unless, of course, the number is between twenty-one and ninety-nine and is spelled out (Ned led the other runners by sixty-two feet).

There is an exception to hyphenated words in measurements. If the measurement appears as an abbreviation, the number preceding it is always written as a numeral rather than a word (17 ft. instead of seventeen ft.).

EXAMPLE

▶ It was a 30-ft. jump from the cliff into the sea.

The reason why "30" is typed as a numeral is because the word "foot" is abbreviated. Still, there needs to be a hyphen between "30" and "ft." because this measurement is describing the distance of the jump.

The same is true when a two-word number precedes a symbol like the degrees sign (76°) or if is part of an exponential number (36^1).

We are also accustomed to seeing hyphens between numbers like *serial numbers* (RT5-6B612-489Z), *bank accounts* (91200-5066734), *credit card numbers* (2201-5694-0908-2265), and *telephone numbers* (143-964-0877). These hyphens are used to separate digits for a purpose.

EXAMPLE

▶ Every time I try to dial Santa Claus at 451-262-3062, it goes directly to voice mail!

This phone number has hyphens to separate the area code from the exchange and from the four-digit specific number.

Did you know that originally, when telephone numbers were linked to home phones (before mobile phones), the first two sets of numbers were geographical indicators? The first three numbers represented a specific city or region (area code). The second set of numbers represented the first two letters of a neighborhood's name plus an additional digit, and the last four numbers were a unique combination assigned to a particular person's household.

I can still remember my grandmother's home phone number in the Bronx from many years ago: 212-**O**Linville 2-0249.

The area code (212) indicated that the phone number was in New York City. **O**Linville was the neighborhood in the Bronx where my grandmother lived. How did I dial the letter "**O**" and the letter "**L**?" To know which numbers represented the **O** and the **L**, I needed to look at the telephone dial and substitute numbers for letters—in this case 6 represents **O**, and 5 represents **L**. The last four digits of the telephone number were assigned randomly. Of course, after a short time, neighborhoods became more populated, and a larger sequence of numbers was necessary for differentiation, so the names of neighborhoods (second set of numbers) were left by the wayside.

If you still have a home telephone, it might be fun to discover whether your second set of numbers corresponds with the first two letters of the name of your neighborhood.

Although most area codes are still linked to geographical locations, some are specific to mobile phones.

Other area codes were created to represent toll-free (800) or corporate (866) phone numbers.

Of course, you may also see the area code surrounded by parentheses (212), in which case you would not need a hyphen between the area code and the exchange.

Country codes have also been added to the beginning of phone numbers. In the US, our country code is 1 or 01. That is why we often dial the number 1 before the rest of a telephone number.

One of the most popular ways people use hyphens with numbers is when they *indicate someone or something's age*, but much confusion surrounds this usage.

What if the words "two" and "year" and "old" are all serving as an adjective to describe something? Should you hyphenate them all together? Should there be a comma between the age and the word "old?"

Here is the rule: If there is a noun directly after the number, the year, and the word "old," *all three words* need to be hyphenated.

EXAMPLES

▶ The forty-year-old panda was a favorite at the San Diego Zoo.

The word "panda" is the noun that comes after "forty-year-old," so all three of those words become a compound adjective that need to be linked together with hyphens.

▶ Whenever Alicia is around her one-year-old niece, she puts on a baby voice and crawls around the floor with her.

The words "one" and "year" and "old" are serving as a compound adjective to describe the age of Alicia's niece. That is why they are linked together by hyphens.

However, sometimes, age is used as a noun. Most people do not think of the word "old" as a noun, but it can be one, when it refers to an age and is grouped with numbers. Therefore, it is correct to type out a person's age in a certain way.

EXAMPLE

▶ A two-year-old has so much energy.

The words "two" and "year" and "old" function as one noun in this sentence. They are not describing anything. They are the receiver of the action "to have." Therefore, they function as the subject of the sentence as a noun. All three words should be hyphenated here also.

However, if the word is "years" and not "year," all bets are off (except if the number is between twenty-one and ninety-nine—you know the drill). Here is an example with the word "years" in the sentence:

> ▶ That book is 100 years old.
>
> *No hyphen is necessary in this sentence, since it contains the word "years" rather than "year."*

Rule 3: Using Hyphens with Prefixes and Suffixes

As you probably know, a **prefix** is a partial word that is placed before a root word to modify or embellish its meaning. Most words that contain a prefix do not require a hyphen, though some do.

Here is a list of the prefixes that must be hyphenated before the main word:

Prefixes That Require a Hyphen

Prefix	Meaning	Example
ex	former	ex-Marine
self	personal	self-starter
all	totally	all-consuming
cross	across	cross-section
quasi	seemingly	quasi-friendly
ultra*	super	ultra-exotic

*I have noticed a recent change in words including the prefix "ultra," as certain words have recently appeared without the hyphen, such as "ultraconservative." In order to be sure of correct hyphen usage when it comes to specific words beginning with "ultra," consult an online dictionary.

▶ Spike Lee is a self-proclaimed basketball fanatic.

The prefix "self" always requires a hyphen before the root word with which it is associated.

There is another instance when prefixes are required, but the rule applies to the noun that follows it rather than the prefix itself. If you are *adding a prefix to a proper noun,* a *hyphen must be utilized* (un-American as opposed to unpatriotic).

▶ Brandt was named All-American Athlete at the awards ceremony.

Since the prefix "All" precedes a proper noun (American), it requires a hyphen.

Another reason why a hyphen should be used before the main word is if the *same vowel* is used consecutively between the prefix and the main word. This is *to avoid confusion.* (ant**i-i**ndustrious, **re-e**ligible).

Of course, there is an exception! If the double vowel is an "o," and the letter "o" makes a *different sound* in the prefix than it does in the main word, then a hyphen is not necessary (cooperative). However, a hyphen *should* be used in a word such as co-owner, since "co" and "owner" both make the long "o" sound.

Similarly, a hyphen should be used after a prefix to avoid confusion when the prefix plus the noun *look very much like a word with a different meaning*: re-sign (sign again) as opposed to resign (to quit).

As you know, **suffixes** are partial words added to the end of a main word. Most suffixes do not require a hyphen when they are added to words. However, there are some rules related to hyphens and suffixes, and they are much more *specific* and much *trickier* than the prefix rules.

There are only *three suffixes* that *always require a hyphen* between the main word and the suffix.

Suffixes That Require a Hyphen

Suffix	Meaning	Example
elect	one who has been elected but has not yet assumed the position	treasurer-elect
type	the way lettering should appear in text	bold-type letters
designate	one who is assigned a job	ambassador-designate

Those are easy enough to remember. However, there are a few hyphen rules that *depend on circumstances of the spelling* of the words or even the number of syllables in a word!

One of the tricky ones is the word "like" when it is used as a suffix. Use the hyphen before "like" when

- The root word is a **proper noun**: That website has a Google-like quality.

- The root word is *three or more syllables*: The coffee shop has a library-like décor.

- *The word that precedes the word "like" has two "l" letters consecutively* at the end of the word: a bell-like sound.

EXAMPLE

Ms. Gullitti conducts her AP class as a Socratic seminar, which is a university-like setting.

Since the word "university" has more than three syllables, a hyphen must be used to connect it with the suffix "like."

Isn't this complicated? Well, here are a few more, and then, I promise, we will be done with suffixes and hyphens.

The suffix "*fold*" needs a hyphen if the number that precedes it is greater than ten (eleven-fold) OR if an exact unit that includes a *decimal is used* (1.5-fold). Numbers ten or lower do not require a hyphen before "fold" (twofold). Of course, there is an exception! If you are combining single-digit number words in the same sentence with "fold" as their suffix, the first one requires a hyphen but does not have "fold" (three- and fourfold harvests).

Despite all these suffix rules, remember that if any of these suffixes are used to form a compound adjective that appears before a noun, the hyphen will be required.

Rule 4: Using Hyphens for Word Breaks

Have you ever handwritten an essay and found yourself trying to squeeze a long word at the end of a line? Perhaps you were typing a long word at the end of a line only to find that the software program you were using moved the entire word to the following line, leaving a gaping space at the end of the previous line. Of course, typing on a computer is easier because you can adjust the margins to make that word fit. That doesn't mean it will look good or be aligned with the rest of your lines of typing.

What am I getting at, you ask? There is a hyphen rule that involves separating a word between two lines of either written or typed text. The hyphen goes at the end of the first line, and the word is continued on the next line. These types of separations are called **word breaks**.

You may think you can separate the word wherever it is convenient as long as you use a hyphen. Come on, now! This is English we are talking about. You may be surprised at how many rules apply to writing/typing word breaks correctly.

When I was little, we used a paper dictionary (a book) to look up word breaks in a particular word. All we would do is look at the phonetic breakdown, and wherever a bullet point appeared in the word, that was a signal that we could use a hyphen to break up the word from one line of text to the next. You can still use that trick if you search the word in an online dictionary.

However, I thought I would give you a few tips about when it is appropriate to use a hyphen to indicate a word break and when it is not.

Here are the correct ways to use line breaks:

- Be sure least *two letters at the beginning of the word* appear on the first line before the hyphen is used. There also need to be at least *three letters of the word on the following line.* Therefore, no word with fewer than five letters may be divided.

- Divide words between syllables, *as long as separating the syllables does not change the meaning of the word.*

- Divide *compound words between the two words* that are connected.

- Divide *hyphenated words where the hyphen already appears.*

- Divide words *after the prefix or before the suffix* of words.

Here are some additional reasons you **may not** use hyphens for word breaks:

- If the word is only *one syllable*

- If the word is a *proper noun*

- If you *cannot place more than two letters on the first line* before the hyphen (even if the word has multiple syllables)

- If you are *on the last line of a page*

- If you are typing a *heading* or a *headline*

- If it causes the *pronunciation of the word to change* (child-ren would not work)

- If it creates *confusion* (is-lander would not work)

- If you must *split up a URL* (especially if it is a hyperlink). However, if it is essential to do so, simply press enter after one of the "slashes" in the URL, and *do not* add the hyphen.

> When Mr. Pace told me I would be working with Katie on a co-operative learning project, I knew I would be carrying most of the weight.
>
> *The word "cooperative" falls at the end of the first line. It was separated after the prefix "co," which is a natural place for the word to be broken.*

> To get to Santa Monica, drive yourself, take a Lyft, or take a cross-town bus from Hollywood.
>
> *The word "crosstown" is a compound word. The hyphen splits the word in between "cross" and "town," which is acceptable.*

NOTE: You may have seen hyphens instead of bullets in a list of items. You may also have seen hyphens between headings and subheadings (Exercise 1-1). These are not considered rules of the hyphen. They are merely visual cues of something additional that is mentioned.

EXERCISE 6-1: Practicing Hyphen Usage

DIRECTIONS: Decide whether any of the words in the following sentences require a hyphen.

- **If the sentence requires at least one hyphen, insert it/them accordingly.**
- **If the sentence does not require a hyphen, write NH on the line provided.**

_____ 1. Twenty two students from my school were named National Merit Semifinalists!

_____ 2. I stopped dating Paul due to his ultrastrange belief that aliens from Mars live in our neighborhood.

_____ 3. For my Sweet Sixteen invitation, I would like calligraphy type lettering.

_____ 4. I considered having a coauthor for this book but decided that might be too difficult.

_____ 5. After calling off their engagement twice, Elizabeth and Richard decided to get reengaged last month.

_____ 6. To save money, Josephine self designed her wedding gown and asked her sister to sew it.

_____ 7. Have you noticed that most planets have a balllike shape to them?

_____ 8. Copy down the following phone number: 7185460239.

_____ 9. "Join me for a once in a lifetime safari," said the tour guide at Animal Kingdom.

_____ 10. Dr. Denton gave me a threefold treatment plan to rehabilitate my sprained ankle.

It has been fun learning the many rules associated with hyphens, but it is time to move on to dashes, which—in my opinion—are underappreciated. (See what I did there?)

Dashes

Dashes are different from hyphens in both *appearance* and *function*. When you are reading, you may notice that the *lengths of certain horizontal lines* used to connect or separate words is different. You may also notice that sometimes, these *lines have spaces* separating them from words or numbers, and sometimes, they do not. It takes a keen eye to notice these subtle differences and an even more keen mind to understand the functional distinction between all three.

Dashes fall under two categories: **en dash** and **em dash**. I know they sound like the letters "n" and "m," but they are spelled "en" and "em" when described. An **en dash** is approximately the length of a lowercase "n," and an **em dash** is approximately the size of a lowercase "m," so it is a little longer horizontally.

When you are handwriting a document, it is simple to distinguish between a *hyphen*, an *en dash*, and an *em dash*—just make them shorter or longer when you draw them.

However, when you are using a computer (which most of you do), it is a different story.

The hyphen is the easiest, since it already appears on your keyboard (-). It is the key with the underscore above it. This is not the same key as the minus sign.

However, depending on which software you are using, you will need to press a different series of keys to create either an *en dash* or an *em dash*. Here is how you make them in three popular programs: Microsoft Word, Google Docs, and Mac.

Microsoft Word:

- To make an *en dash*, click where you want to insert the en dash and press Control + the minus-sign key on the numeric keypad simultaneously (–). It will not work if you press the hyphen key. It must be the minus-sign key.

- To make an *em dash*, click where you want to insert the em dash and press Control + Alt + minus-sign key on the numeric keypad simultaneously (—). It will not work if you press the hyphen key. It must be the minus-sign key.

Google Docs:

- To make an *en dash*, be sure the number-lock button is lit before beginning. Then, hold the Alt key and type 0150.

- To make an *em dash*, be sure the number-lock button is lit before beginning. Then, hold down the Alt key and type 0151.

Mac

- To make an *en dash*, press the option key and the hyphen key.

- To make an *em dash*, press shift + option key + hyphen key.

Note: On some Mac keyboards, the option key is called "alt."

Besides having a different function from hyphens, *en and em dashes have different functions from each other.*

Before we begin our study of dashes, I thought you should know that most style guides do not require additional space between em dashes and other words. However, if you are in doubt, check with your school to see which style guide is followed. En dashes *never* have spaces around them.

Let's begin with the easier one: *the en dash.*

Rule 5: Using En Dashes for Time and Number Ranges

The **en dash** is closest in usage to the hyphen but in different contexts. Often, an **en dash** is used in mathematical and scientific writing. It can be confused with the hyphen because the hyphen is also used with numbers in certain situations.

Here's how to know the difference. The purpose of an **en dash** is to indicate *date or number ranges*. An easy way to test whether you should be typing a hyphen or a dash between numbers is by substituting the word "to" for the horizontal line. If that makes no sense, you probably have a hyphen on your hands. If it does, you are dealing with an en dash.

By the way, an **en dash** *does not* have to be part of a sentence. Time frames and year ranges often appear outside of the conventional sentence.

EXAMPLES

▶ 3:00–6:00 is the typical range of hours for our dress rehearsal, so we can do a full run-through.

> *Did you notice that I purposely included both an en dash and a hyphen in this sentence? I wanted you to see the difference in the length and in the function of these punctuation marks. Since there is a range between 3:00 and 6:00 and we can replace that symbol with the word "to," we must use an en dash. Since there is no range of time between "run" and "through" and we cannot place the word "to" between those two words, that grouping requires a hyphen.*

▶ Abraham Lincoln's life (1809–1865) was cut short at a pivotal time in our country's reconstruction.

> *The range of years in which Abraham Lincoln lived is indicated by the en dash between 1809 and 1865. I can replace the en dash with the word "to," and it makes sense.*

Now that you know the long and short of en dashes, it's time to learn more about the least-known mark in this chapter: the em dash.

Rule 6: Using Em Dashes for Interruptions

An **em dash** is a bit more complicated. It varies in function and sometimes acts similarly to one or more of the following punctuation marks: commas, colons, quotation marks, and parentheses. However, em dashes are considered *more emphatic* than these punctuation marks.

What is important is the purpose of the em dash. Usually, an **em dash** is used to *emphasize, to interrupt, to explain something further,* or to *convey a tangential thought* within the context of a sentence.

Remember that the em dash is the *longest* of the horizontal punctuation marks. Think of the width of the letter "m," and you will remember that it is the longest (—).

First, we will explore how *em dashes set off interruptions*. If you remember the comma chapter (Chapter 2), there was a comma rule about interruptions (Rule 5). It stated that commas should surround an interruption. But there is a difference between the commas that surround an interruption and the em dashes that surround one. To apply the comma rule, the interruption cannot add any detail or information to the sentence. Words and phrases such as "of course," "therefore," and "in fact" are examples of interruptions that can be surrounded by commas.

When it comes to the *em dash*, however, *the interruption does provide information*, even if the information is an "aside" or an afterthought. It is also *surrounded* by em dashes, just as commas surround non-informative interruptions.

▶ Silvia looked stunning in her hot-pink dress and her six-inch—a bit too high for my taste—heels.

Did you notice that I also included hyphens in this sentence, so you could distinguish between hyphens and em dashes? The phrase "a bit too high for my taste" adds the speaker's opinion but is not directly about the appearance of Silvia. That is why it is an example of an interruption (including an opinion) surrounded by em dashes.

▶ I firmly believe—I mean, barely believe—that you are the best candidate for the position.

The way this interruption disclaims the initial statement is important. A certain tone is set with this interruption, and the em dashes enable the reader to notice it glaringly.

Rule 7: Using Em Dashes to Signify Digression of Thought

This rule is like the previous one. However, the digression does not provide information that is relevant to the main sentence.

This technique is used often in the creation of fictional pieces such as plays and poetry. When a character is distracted, the *em dash separates the digression from the original thought process.*

▶ Please clear your desks for the—wait, that sounds like hail hitting the window—for the quiz, everyone.

The phrase surrounded by the em dash is irrelevant to the main sentence. The speaker was distracted by the weather, mid-sentence.

Rule 8: Using Em Dashes for Emphasis

Like the previous rule, *em dashes* set information apart from the rest of the sentence. However, *in the case of emphasis*, there *do not have to be two em dashes*, as the emphasis does not always fall in the center of the sentence. Many times, when the em dash is used for emphasis, it can replace a colon.

EXAMPLES

▶ My boyfriend took me to see Dave Grohl—the best front man ever!

It is obvious that the speaker is a fan of Dave Grohl's music, especially when, at the end of the sentence, they call him the best.

▶ Tami swam ten laps in under five minutes—that is an amazing school record—and she wasn't even trying hard!

The fact that it is a school record makes it important to set apart from the rest of the sentence with the use of em dashes.

Rule 9: Using Em Dashes to Explain Something Further or Illustrate Something

This is the *most common use of the em dash* that I have seen. When a writer wants to *explain something further* in a way that is noticeable, the *em dash* is often used to replace parentheses (which some readers ignore) and the colon.

EXAMPLES

▶ Susan baked a variety of pies—pecan, pumpkin, and apple—for the Thanksgiving gathering.

The types of pies offer more specific information and are more obvious to the reader due to the em dashes.

▶ Voyagers on the Titanic expected a thrilling adventure—but not one so thrilling that it would lead to their imminent death.

The em dash in this sentence illustrates the type of adventure the voyagers experienced as something different than the one they had anticipated originally.

Rule 10: Using Em Dashes to Summarize or Condense Information

We are accustomed to seeing a list of items following an introductory phrase or sentence and a colon. Well, sometimes, the em dash switches this order. Some *sentences begin with a list* of items *followed by an em dash* and an *explanation or summary* of those items. Other times, the *summary may appear mid-sentence.*

EXAMPLES

▶ Winter, spring, summer, fall—the Northeast is famous for experiencing all four seasons in the course of a year.

If the sentence were flipped, the writer would most likely use a colon to preface the seasons, though an em dash would not be incorrect.

▶ Algebra, Geometry, Trigonometry—the essential math courses—are required in many high schools across the country.

The phrase "the essential math courses" is a summary of the type of courses that are required.

Rule 11: Using Em Dashes to Set Off Appositives That Contain Commas

In Chapter 2, you learned that an **appositive** is a word or group of words that further describe(s) a noun or pronoun that precedes it (them). You learned that if an appositive falls in the middle of the sentence, it is surrounded by commas (Rule 8). If an appositive ends a sentence, one comma precedes the appositive, and the sentence ends with the period.

You are probably wondering how an em dash plays into this rule. Well, the *em dash* is basically used to *replace the appositive's commas* if there are *so many commas in the sentence* that their purpose becomes confusing. If the first comma in the appositive causes confusion for the reader due to the other commas that are nearby, we *substitute an em dash for the comma.*

By the way, I have also seen *em dashes* used to *separate nonrestrictive clauses* from the rest of the sentence. Comma confusion is not usually an issue, so writers might simply use the em dash as a *visual cue* more than anything else. For this reason, I am not lumping together the appositive with the nonrestrictive clause.

EXAMPLE

▶ Three teachers—Ryan, Henry, and I—attended a live theater production of *The Taming of the Shrew.*

If a comma were placed after the word "teachers," the reader would not know if six people attended this trip or if three people attended the trip. The comma would group the three teachers together with the other people, totaling six. Therefore, the comma that begins the appositive can be easily confused with a comma in a series. That is why the em dash is necessary in a sentence like this one.

Rule 12: Using Em Dashes for Quote Attribution

Have you ever begun an essay or a paper with a famous quotation that was set apart from the rest of your writing? Perhaps you have walked around your school building and have seen some famous quotations posted in the hall, the library, or even in your classrooms.

When that quote appears by itself, *beneath it, you will often find the speaker's or author's name.* A traditional byline with the word "by" before the person's name (by Ernest Hemingway) is not used in this instance. Instead, the author's name is preceded by an em dash.

EXAMPLE ▶

"Ask not what your country can do for you—ask what you can do for your country."

—John F. Kennedy

Notice the em dash before John F. Kennedy's name. That is an indicator that the person wrote or said that exact sentence (in this case, he said it, since it was excerpted from a speech).

Coincidentally, did you see the em dash in the middle of the quotation? That one is there for a totally different reason. Besides, whenever anything is an exact excerpt, the words and punctuation must be copied exactly as they appear. I had nothing to do with that first em dash. ☺

EXERCISE 6-2: En Dash or Em Dash?

*DIRECTIONS: Read the following sentences. Decide whether an **en dash** or an **em dash** is appropriate for that sentence. After drawing it in the correct place(s), write either **en dash** or **em dash** on the line provided.*

_____ 1. "Give me liberty or give me death."

Patrick Henry

_____ 2. 1920 1933 was the range of years when Prohibition was enforced in the United States.

_____ 3. The three coaches Andrew, Martin, and Ian attended the swim meet to gather information for their teams.

_____ 4. Reading, writing, listening, speaking all are essential elements of an English Language Arts Curriculum.

_____ 5. 1200 1500 calories per day is the goal for maintaining a healthy lifestyle.

EXERCISE 6-3: Culminating Review of Hyphens, En Dashes, and Em Dashes

DIRECTIONS: Read the following sentences. They each have hyphens, en dashes, and/or em dashes. On the line to the left of each example, write the hyphen or dash rule number that is being applied in that sentence.

Rule Bank
Rule 1: Using Hyphens to Form Compound Adjectives
Rule 2: Using Hyphens in Numbers and Units of Measure
Rule 3: Using Hyphens with Prefixes and Suffixes
Rule 4: Using Hyphens for Word Breaks
Rule 5: Using En Dashes for Time and Number Ranges
Rule 6: Using Em Dashes for Interruptions
Rule 7: Using Em Dashes to Signify Digression of Thought
Rule 8: Using Em Dashes for Emphasis
Rule 9: Using Em Dashes to Further Explain or Illustrate
Rule 10: Using Em Dashes to Summarize or Condense Information
Rule 11: Using Em Dashes to Set Off Appositives That Contain Commas
Rule 12: Using Em Dashes for Quote Attribution

_____ 1. I'm running so late—where is my left shoe?—that I may miss the bus!

_____ 2. "Now is the time to make real the promises of democracy."

—Martin Luther King Jr.

_____ 3. Charles Lindbergh went from living a once-happy existence to a life of solitude and desolation.

_____ 4. Can you believe the Vietnam War lasted for two decades: 1955–1975?

_____ 5. Cover letter, résumé, interview, background check, references—there are so many steps in securing a job nowadays.

_____ 6. The Tate is my least favorite museum in London, since I do not favor ultra-modern art.

_____ 7. I cannot believe Chiara had the nerve to go to the party without me—especially since I was the one invited, and she was only attending as my guest!

_____ 8. I learned many new words over the summer including circum-spect and infamy.

_____ 9. You might think it is overcautious and excessive of me, but I decided to apply to twenty-two colleges.

_____ 10. In *The Wizard of Oz*, the principal actors—Dorothy, Scarecrow, Tin Man, and Lion—were so talented.

EXERCISE 6-4: Writing with Hyphens and Dashes

DIRECTIONS: Often, when you apply for a job, you must provide a cover letter and a résumé. This writing task will involve your cover letter in which you will use hyphens and dashes correctly.

PROMPT: Today, you will write a cover letter. Pretend you are applying for a position as a tour guide for incoming freshmen at your high school. Within the letter, include **at least five correct uses of the hyphen, en dash, and/or em dash**. Address the letter to your principal.

Cover Letter

Dear Principal _____:

_____

_____

_____

_____

_____

_____

_____

_____

_____

_____

_____

_____

_____

_____

_____

Flashcard
App

Usage

MUST KNOW

 There are several types of errors that do not fall under the category of capitalization and punctuation.

Agreement is important in sentence structure. Knowledge of alignment in subject/verb agreement, number, and parallelism will help you ensure that your sentences are clear and correct. Pronouns play a big part in the topic of agreement.

 Knowing common errors in spelling, abbreviations, and word choice will help you to write clearly and correctly.

 Recognizing and correcting informal language will help you become a more sophisticated writer.

In the past, how have your English teachers notified you that you made grammatical errors in a writing piece? Did they write out the specific error on the paper, use codes and/or symbols to indicate an error, place comments in the margin of the document, or, perhaps, make note of errors on a grading rubric? Most learners say that it has been a combination of those listed above, depending on the teacher, the grade level, and the course.

The exercises in this chapter will differ from those in the previous ones. This is because instead of covering several rules related to the same topic, a variety of topics will be explained in this chapter. Even the writing task differs from those in previous chapters. Certainly, it will test your ability to recognize and correct common errors in usage.

Topic 1: Subject/Verb Agreement

Let us begin with a review of the meaning of the words **subject** and **verb**. When someone mentions the subject of a sentence, they are *not* referring to the typical meaning of the word *subject*, which is *topic*.

Instead, the word **subject** refers to *the part of the sentence about which something is being said*. Many books will define **subject** as the person, place, thing, or idea that is performing an action. That definition is *not incorrect*, but it is *incomplete*. This is because we have some verbs in English that are not actions; they are states of being. Therefore, an action is not being performed. That does not mean those sentences without action verbs lack a subject.

When you are checking subject/verb agreement, it is customary to rely on the **simple subject**, the *noun or pronoun without additional words*. Be aware that there can be more than one noun or pronoun serving as the subject. They would still be considered the *simple subject* if they are both experiencing the state of being or action of the *same verb* in a sentence.

A **complete subject** refers to the *noun or pronoun plus some additional words* that offer information (usually articles and/or adjectives).

Verbs can be described in a similar way, with regard to simple or more complicated forms. You also may have heard the word "verb" referred to as the **predicate**. If the verb in the sentence is only one word, is called a **simple predicate**.

If the verb requires a **helping** or **auxiliary verb** (is going, was climbing), we call it a verb phrase.

When a **verb phrase** contains additional words such as adverbs and prepositional phrases (was climbing carefully), we call that combination of words a **complete predicate**. The **complete predicate** says something about the subject, and it is composed of the *verb and all the accompanying words* that help describe the action or the state of being.

Now that you have the basic background of the meaning of subject and predicate, it is time to analyze a common error made by English learners. Sometimes, the subject of the sentence does *not agree* with the verb form. The word **agree** means that the verb does not correspond with the **number** of subjects. This is a common error made by people who are in the process of learning English, but I have seen my native-speaking students make errors in subject/verb agreement from time to time.

Let's begin with the simplest type of sentence—the action-verb sentence. If the verb is a **regular** action verb, the number of subjects needs to match up in number with the verb.

For now, to keep it simple, we will focus on verbs in the present tense. In English when a simple subject is singular, the action verb usually ends in an "s" when it is in the present tense. In some cases, we add "*es*" to present-tense verbs.

EXAMPLES

▶ The doorman waves his hand to hail taxis.

The word "doorman" is the subject. The doorman is doing the action. The word "waves" is the simple predicate. "Waves" is the action the doorman is doing. Since the doorman is one person, the action verb ends in an "s" (waves), since the verb is in present tense.

▶ Your skirt matches your shirt perfectly.

The word "skirt" is the subject. The skirt is, technically, doing the action. The word "matches" is the simple predicate. "Matches" is the action the skirt is doing. Since the skirt is one item, the action verb ends in "es" (matches).

This is not so bad, right? Buckle up! It gets more complicated.

In English we have several verbs that are *irregular*. This means that when the tense changes to past tense, they do not have typical endings added to them such as "ed." The spelling of the root verb changes based on the tense of the verb.

EXAMPLE

▶ The bird flew over the lake.

The subject is "bird." The original form of the verb (or infinitive) is "to fly." However, we do not use the word "flied." The verb changes when the tense changes. "To fly" is an irregular verb. However, even though the verb is irregular, it is still an action verb. "To fly" is an action. You can see things fly because they move. That makes "fly" an action verb.

So far, so good. Well, we also have verbs called **linking verbs**. These are verbs that show *state of being*. They do not perform an action.

Let's start with the basics. The verb *to be* is the most common linking verb. If you have studied Spanish, French, or Italian, you may remember your teacher setting up the conjugation of a verb in a chart like this:

To be

I am	We are
You are	You are
He is She is It is	They are

Does that look familiar? That is the conjugation of the verb "to be." It is the most common verb in English, and it is called a **linking verb**, not an action verb. **Linking verbs** *show states of being, but they do not describe actions.* Of course, the verb "to be" is also an **irregular verb** since the spelling of its forms totally change depending on the subject (I *am*; You *are*; It *is*) and the tense. We don't just add an "s" to the verb to make it match the subject (ams; ares; ises).

All forms of the verb *to be* are considered linking verbs, including *was*, *were*, *being*, and *been*.

However, there are some linking verbs that are *not* a form of the verb *to be*. These verbs are confusing because they sometimes serve as linking verbs and sometimes serve as action verbs. It depends on their use in a sentence.

Most of those verbs are the ones that *involve the senses.* The following chart includes sentence examples, so you can look at the function of the verb when it is a linking verb as opposed to when it is an action verb. In the *linking verb* column, you will notice that the subject *cannot actually perform the implied action of the verb.*

You might be wondering why it is important to know whether those verbs are serving as linking or action verbs, since their endings seem to be the same in either case. This will become important when we discuss **predicate adjectives** a little later in the chapter.

Linking/Action Verbs

Verb	Example of when it is a linking verb	Example of when it is an action verb
look	That pizza looks delicious.	Look at me skate down the block, Mom!
smell	This locker room smells horrendous!	My grandmother loves to smell the roses whenever she passes the bush.
touch	Your kind sentiments touched my heart.	The toddler places everything he touches into his mouth.
sound	That sounds like a great idea!	The bell sounded at exactly 11:00.
taste	The cupcake tastes so sweet.	The chef tasted his bechamel sauce before serving it.
feel	Are you feeling tired or achy?	Simon felt all of the fabrics before deciding upon the comforter for his bed.
appear	It appears sunny outside today!	The magician appeared from behind the curtain.
turn	The food turned bad after being left out all day.	"Turn around three times before landing your split," instructed the choreographer.
remain	The truth remains to be seen.	The children remained on the ride until the worker removed their seatbelts and told them to exit.
prove	Your brother has proven to be a trustworthy friend to me.	On mathematics exams, it is important to prove your answer by showing your work.
grow	The dean was growing tired of reprimanding the same three students daily.	Daisies grow wild along the highway.
became	Josef became increasingly impatient as the drizzle turned into a downpour.	The caterpillar finally became a butterfly!
act	"Try not to act immature in front of your new teacher," advised Perpetua's mother.	Lauren can't wait to act in the upcoming talent show.

EXERCISE 7-1: Linking Verb or Action Verb?

DIRECTIONS: *Determine whether the verb in the sentence is functioning as a linking verb or an action verb. Write the word* **linking** *or* **action** *on the line provided.*

_____   1. The science teacher sounded the fire alarm.

_____   2. Jason looks so tired today.

_____   3. Turn toward the front of the room.

_____   4. Let me feel your cashmere sweater!

_____   5. The kitten grew into a cat so quickly.

_____   6. This gum tastes like watermelon.

_____   7. Look at my new locker decorations!

_____   8. A rainbow appeared in the sky after the storm.

_____   9. Heather feels upset about her Spanish grade this quarter.

_____   10. The lawyer proved that the defendant was not guilty by using evidence.

In Chapter 5 (Apostrophes), I provided a list of **collective nouns** for you. Remember that collective nouns *represent a group but are still considered singular in number.* This means that the *verbs that appear with collective nouns will end in "s" or "es"* because that indicates that a verb corresponds with a singular noun in the present tense.

> ▶ The basketball team acquires new uniforms every year.
>
> *Even though the word "team" represents a group of people, it is considered a collective noun. This means the verb that follows it must end in "s" or "es" when it is in the present tense. We would never say "The team acquire new uniforms."*

The most difficult scenario in subject/verb agreement involves a particular type of pronoun called an **indefinite pronoun**. When an indefinite pronoun serves as the subject of the sentence, many people become confused as to whether the verb should correspond with something singular or plural. The answer? It depends!

Certain **indefinite pronouns** are *always considered singular;* certain ones *are always considered plural.* But—you guessed it—for *certain indefinite pronouns, it depends* on other words in the sentence.

You will have to commit these indefinite pronouns to memory, noting which ones are *always singular, which ones are always plural, and which ones vary.*

Indefinite Pronouns

Singular	Plural	It Varies
• another	• both	• all
• anybody	• few	• any
• anyone	• many	• more
• each	• others	• most
• either	• several	• none
• everybody		• some
• everyone		
• everything		
• much		
• neither		
• nobody		
• no one		
• nothing		
• one		
• somebody		
• someone		
• something		

So, the first column seems easy enough. When one of those pronouns is the subject of the sentence, we treat the verb as if it were connecting to something singular.

EXAMPLE

▶ Neither speaks properly.

In this sentence, "Neither" is an indefinite pronoun, and it serves as the subject of the sentence. "Neither" is considered a singular pronoun, which means the action verb that follows it must have an "s" or "es" when it is in the present tense. Do you see how the present tense of the verb ends in "s" just like a regular verb would? The correct verb to follow "neither" is "speaks," since it is a verb in the present tense that ends with an "s."

Things become more complicated when there are words placed in between the pronoun (subject) and the verb (predicate).

EXAMPLE

▶ Neither of the boys speaks properly.

The phrase "of the boys" describes those to whom "neither" is referring. However, "boys" is not the subject of the sentence. "Neither" is the subject of the sentence, and since it is singular, the verb that goes with it must end in an "s" when it is in the present tense.

Look at the second column of plural indefinite pronouns in the chart on the previous page. These are fairly simple, since we treat these pronouns as if they are plural subjects, and the verbs will match just like they normally would.

EXAMPLE

▶ Many arrive at the amusement park early.

When the subject of the sentence is plural (many), the present tense of the verb does not have an ending (arrive).

So far so good. Even when we place a phrase between *Many* and *arrive*, the verb stays in the plural form.

EXAMPLE

▶ Many of the employees arrive at the amusement park early.

"Many" is still the subject of the sentence (not "employees"). The verb "arrive" matches up with "Many" (not with "employees").

As you can see, determining subject/verb agreement with indefinite pronouns can be a little tricky. Here is a hint I often offer to students: *Substitute a person's name for the singular indefinite pronoun.* That will make it easier to determine the ending of the verb.

EXAMPLES

▶ Nobody wants to go bowling.

▶ Susie wants to go bowling.

> *Of course, placing "Susie" in the sentence changes the meaning of the sentence, but we are simply replacing the pronoun with a name temporarily, so we can test out the verb's ending to make sure it makes sense.*

Similarly, *if the subject is a plural indefinite pronoun, substitute two names for the pronoun.* This will make it much easier to determine the ending of the verb.

▶ Several apply for the clerical position at the law office each year.

▶ Myra, Chloe, and Denise apply for the clerical position at the law office each year.

> *We know the sentences are not the same in meaning. We only substitute names temporarily to test the ending of the verb.*

Now it's time for the tough ones—the "it depends" **indefinite pronouns** found in the third column of the chart.

There are *two ways* to tell whether these pronouns are singular or plural in a sentence.

The first way to determine whether a singular indefinite pronoun (from the third column of the chart) is functioning as a singular or plural pronoun is to *look at the noun in the prepositional phrase that falls in between the subject and the verb.*

EXAMPLES

▶ All the milk spills on the table when the first graders have snack time.

Since "all" can sometimes be a singular subject and sometimes be a plural subject, you need to look at the prepositional phrase that comes between the subject (all) and the verb (spills). Since the object of the preposition (noun) is "milk" and the word "milk" is singular, you need to place an "s" on the verb "spills."

▶ All the rugby players gather around their injured teammates for support.

Since "all" can sometimes be a singular subject and sometimes be a plural subject, you need to look at the prepositional phrase that comes between the subject (all) and the verb (gather). Since the object of the preposition (noun) is "players" and the word "players" is plural, you do not place an ending on the present-tense form of the verb "gather."

This is the exact opposite of what I instructed you to do with the indefinite pronouns that are *always singular*. Remember this sentence?

Neither of the boys speaks properly.

The prepositional phrase that falls between the subject and the verb *only matters* if the singular indefinite pronoun is one listed in the *third column* of the chart. Otherwise, ignore those objects of the preposition. They are inconsequential in determining the ending of a verb when the subject of the sentence is an indefinite pronoun that is *always* singular or always plural.

Be careful! To avoid that type of confusion, you really need to commit these indefinite pronouns to memory according to their categories.

Sometimes, you will not be fortunate enough to have one of those prepositional phrases between an "it depends" indefinite pronoun and the verb. You may be wondering how you can tell which verb ending you should use in that situation.

The answer is to use **context clues**. Read the sentence prior to the one with the "it depends" indefinite pronoun as well as the sentence following it to try to determine if the "it depends" indefinite pronoun is referring to one or more people, places, things, or ideas.

EXERCISE 7-2: Subject/Verb Agreement with Indefinite Pronouns

DIRECTIONS: *Using your knowledge of indefinite pronouns, underline the present-tense verb that matches correctly with the indefinite pronoun (subject) of each sentence.*

1. More of the adults (own, owns) credit cards.

2. Both of the clubs (meet, meets) on Wednesday.

3. Somebody in the crowd (smell, smells) horrible.

4. Everything in the dorms (need, needs) to be cleared out by May 10th.

5. All of my hard work (pay, pays) off in the long run.

6. Many of the seals (swim, swims) close to the shore.

7. None of my homework assignments (is, are) difficult to complete.

8. Each of my science labs (is, are) challenging.

9. Some of the residue (remain, remains) on the desk.

10. All of the balls (roll, rolls) off the table when it is tilted.

Topic 2: Predicate Adjectives vs. Adverbs

Earlier in this chapter, I mentioned that it would be important to know the difference between a linking verb and an action verb. The type of words that follow these verbs will be dependent upon the *type* of verb in the sentence. In other words, action verbs are not followed immediately by adjectives; linking verbs are hardly ever followed by adverbs.

Let me show you what I mean.

In this sentence, choose the word that should follow the verb:

> I feel (bad, badly).

I am not going to tell you the answer yet. Keep reading to figure it out.

Here is the rule: If the verb in the sentence is a **linking verb**, it is *followed either by an adjective* (called a **predicate adjective**) or a *noun* (called a **predicate noun** or **predicate nominative**). It is *not* followed by an **adverb** (usually a word that ends in "ly").

Conversely, if the verb is an **action verb**, it does not need to be followed by anything at all. Still, if there are words that follow an action verb immediately, they will either be **nouns** (called a **direct object**, **indirect object**, or **object of the preposition**) or **adverbs** (most often a word that ends in "ly").

Why is this important for us to know? Well, one of the most common errors made is when people use a linking verb with an adverb following it immediately. They may think it sounds formal or fancy, but it is incorrect.

Are you ready for the answer to the sample question I gave you earlier? Here it is:

> I feel bad.

Do you understand why the word after "feel" needs to be an adjective? "Feel" is a linking verb in this sentence. Linking verbs cannot be followed by adverbs (badly). They must be followed by either nouns or adjectives. That is why "bad" needs to follow "feel."

This becomes especially tricky with the verbs that are sometimes linking verbs and sometimes action verbs. You need to analyze the way the verb is functioning in the sentence to be sure the words that follow the verb are the proper parts of speech, especially when it comes to adjectives and adverbs.

Read these two sentences. Which sentence is correct?

I feel good.

I feel well.

The answer is . . . both!

Knowing what you learned just a moment ago, you would say **I feel good** is correct, since **feel** is a linking verb in this sentence and **good** is the predicate adjective. Good for you! You are correct!

However, in today's world, there is a time when **I feel well** is acceptable.

As you know, the word **well** is often used as an adverb meaning **healthy.**

We do accept the sentence **I feel well** (even though **well** is an adverb) in one situation! If someone used to be sick and has now recovered, it is acceptable to say **I feel well** in that context. There has to be some type of implied recovery from sickness in order for it to be valid.

I think it is time for a little practice. Let's see how well you remember linking verbs and action verbs from earlier in the chapter. You will need this knowledge to determine the proper word to follow the verbs in the following exercises.

EXERCISE 7-3: Predicate Adjective or Adverb?

DIRECTIONS: *The following sentences contain either a* **linking verb** *or an* **action verb**. *After reading the sentence, decide whether the word that follows the verb should be an* **adjective** *or an* **adverb**. *Underline the correct answer.*

1. Angeline sat (quiet, quietly) in the back of the auditorium.

2. My dog, Muffin, appears (happy, happily) when she wags her tail.

3. Will the protagonist in *To Kill a Mockingbird* prove (loyal, loyally) to her initial beliefs?

4. Grandma was sick last week, but this week, she is feeling (good, well).

5. Robin remains (dutiful, dutifully) by Batman's side when they are fighting the villains.

Topic 3: Agreement Between Subjects, Linking Verbs, and Predicate Nouns

As you know, some sentences have **linking verbs**, and the nouns that following linking verbs are called **predicate nouns**. You learned all about the importance of subject/verb agreement, but I would be remiss if I did not tell you that subjects and verbs can agree with each other in number, but there still may be agreement issues with other parts of the sentence.

When teachers correct your work, they might comment on this type of error as a *s/pl* or a **singular/plural** error.

In the previous section, we learned that the *number* of people, places, things, or ideas in the subject impacts the form of the verb that matches it (singular or plural).

In certain sentences with linking verbs that are followed by nouns, we need to take it a step further to match the number in the subject with other words beyond the verb. This is not an issue in all sentences, but it is relevant to sentences that provide an explanation of the subject.

Here is an example of a sentence that has an error due to a difference in number:

EXAMPLE

> The best reason for living in New York is the Broadway shows and the variety of museums.
>
> *If you look at the subject (reason) and the verb (is), those match up well, since they are both singular. However, if you look further in the sentence, you will notice that instead of one reason being named, two reasons are named (shows and museums). To correct this sentence, the subject needs to be "reasons" (plural), and the verb needs to be "are" (plural) so that the entire sentence has an aligning number (plural).*

The following example provides a sentence that demonstrates singular agreement:

EXAMPLE

▶ The best assignment in last year's English class was the Shakespeare project.

The sentence begins with "the best assignment," which suggests that one item will be named after the verb. Since "the Shakespeare project" is one item, the sentence has correct, singular agreement.

Here is another example of a common error I see:

EXAMPLE

▶ If I could make three wishes, they would be to be a billionaire. I would also wish for a healthy family and for a happy life.

The first sentence begins by stating that three wishes will be listed, but only one wish is stated in that sentence. This is unacceptable. All three wishes need to be included in that first sentence for the sentence to be correct.

Here is an alternate way to fix this error:

EXAMPLE

▶ If I could make three wishes, one would be to be a billionaire.

This clarifies that only one wish will be stated in that first sentence. The reader can infer that the other two wishes will be forthcoming in the sentences that follow the first one.

Topic 4: Parallel Structure in Sentences

I know you are familiar with the word *parallel* as it relates to mathematics. You know that two parallel lines run next to each other without crossing. Did you know that **parallelism** is also a term used in writing?

We already spent a good amount of time discussing the agreement between subjects and verbs. **Parallel structure** corresponds to situations where common *words, phrases, or clauses need to match, predominantly in number or tense.* Think of it as keeping your writing aligned or symmetrical. If your sentences show consistent parallel structure, your writing will have greater clarity and seem more sophisticated.

Many students write sentences where the verbs are not in the same tense. If there are multiple verbs in the sentence, *follow the tense of the first verb in the sentence to determine the tense of the verbs that follow.*

Here is an example of a sentence where the verbs are not in the same tense:

> **EXAMPLE**
>
> ▶ One thing I do well is drawing.
>
> *Since the first verb in the sentence is "do," all the other verbs in the sentence need to be in the present tense. The word "drawing" in this sentence is a gerund (verb that functions as a noun). However, it still needs to maintain the same structure as the original verb (do), so "drawing" should be "draw." Otherwise, it is considered faulty parallelism.*

One of the most common issues with parallel structure is related to **coordinating conjunctions: and, or, but, yet, as, for, so, since,** and **because.**

If words, phrases, or clauses are connected by one of these words, we need to concern ourselves not only with commas (except for *because*) but also with ensuring that the words that precede and follow these conjunctions are in the same form.

Here is an example of a sentence where the subject and verb agree, but the word/phrases that follow them *do not*:

> My favorite hobbies are gardening and to take long walks.
>
> *Since the word "and" is used to connect two items that are being listed, these two items need to be in the same form. Since the first hobby is "gardening" (which ends in "-ing" and is a gerund), the second hobby needs to be "taking" long walks not "to take" long walks. "Gardening" and "taking" need to be in the same form (-ing).*

That was one type of **faulty parallelism**. Of course, the sentence can also be changed to this:

My favorite hobbies are to garden and to take long walks.

Besides coordinating conjunctions, another set of words that need to be followed by parallel words, phrases, and clauses are *correlative conjunctions*:

not only . . . but

both . . . and

either . . . or

neither . . . nor

Sentences with **correlative conjunctions** have a *set* of conjunctions in the sentence that present a *comparison, contrast,* or *relationship* between two people, things, items, actions, or ideas.

Here is an example of a sentence that *does not* have correct correlative structure:

EXAMPLE

> Herbie not only loves to walk but swimming.
>
> *Do you see the problem? Herbie loves "to walk." Once that infinitive has been established (to walk), when another activity is introduced after the second correlative conjunction (but), it must also be in the infinitive form (to swim). It cannot be a different form of the word "swim." Otherwise, it is considered faulty parallelism.*

There are other sets of words that require parallel structure. They do not fall under the category of conjunctions, but when they are grouped together, they function in a similar way. These are called **comparative expressions**. Some examples (to name only a few) include

> **more than**

> **less than**

> **as much as**

Once the first word, phrase, or clause in the comparison is established, the word, phrase, or clause *after the comparative expression* must match it in form.

Here is an example of a comparative-expression sentence that *does not* have parallel structure.

▶ Sandra likes to talk on the phone more than she likes texting.

This might be a tough one for you. Does it look right to you? Many students make the mistake shown above. Since "to talk" is the form that is established prior to the comparative expression, what follows must be "to text" (not "texting"). Otherwise, there is faulty parallelism.

Another error that is made often is when items in a series are not parallel. You might remember the *Items in a Series* rule and the *Adjectives that Modify Equally* rule from Chapter 2 (The Comma). When a sentence contains a list of some sort, besides being concerned about commas, one needs to be concerned about keeping the form of the words or phrases the same.

Here is an example of a sentence that *does not* have parallel structure:

EXAMPLE

▶ Walter is smart, athletic, and cooking.

This might look pretty good to you. The commas are in the right place. It seems like a list. Well, we have a problem here. The sentence begins with adjectives (smart and athletic). Therefore, that third item needs to be an adjective as well. The word "cooking" is not an adjective in this sentence. This is considered faulty parallelism. Parallelism concerns items within the same sentence.

Other words that require parallel structure are certain words in a *bulleted list*. We covered lists in Chapter 3 (Colons and Semicolons). If the bulleted list begins with *verbs*, the *verbs need to be in the same tense*.

Here is an example of a list that *does not* show parallel structure:

EXAMPLE

▶ There are many requirements necessary to become an Eagle Scout:

- Be active in the troop
- Show dedication to the oath and laws
- Providing references from family, work, church, and/or other groups
- Earn 21 merit badges
- Serve at least six months in a leadership position.

Can you spot the error? All the verbs are in the present tense except for one (providing), which should be "provide." This is considered faulty parallelism.

IRL There is one instance when bulleted lists **can differ** in tense. This is in the case of a résumé.

On your résumé, in the Employment Experience section, you often begin by naming your most recent job. Many people are still employed in that position when they are applying for a new or different job. When delineating skills you utilize in your present job, it is appropriate to list them in present tense (since you are still working in that capacity).

However, you will also include previous employment experience on your résumé (if you have any that is relevant to the position to which you are applying). When you list the skills performed in previous jobs or positions, you should list them in past tense.

Overall, remember to look for parallelism between coordinating conjunctions, correlative conjunctions, and comparative expressions. Plus, ensure that items in a series and in bulleted lists are aligned in form. Naturally, verbs within the same sentence should also be in the same tense. If you can remember to check for parallel structure in your sentences, your writing will improve tremendously!

Topic 5: Pronouns and Antecedents

As you know, a **pronoun** is a word that *takes the place of one or more nouns*. It stands for one or more than one person, place, thing, or idea.

The **antecedent** of that pronoun is the *noun to which the pronoun is referring*.

In some sentences, that noun appears in the sentence. In other sentences, the antecedent is not stated. **Personal pronouns** such as "he," "she," "it," and "they" may also refer to antecedents.

> Billy admitted that he did not know what he was talking about.

> *The pronoun in the sentence is "he." "Billy" is the noun to which "he" is referring. Therefore, "Billy" is the antecedent.*

There are some sentences that have **personal pronouns** *without* **antecedents**. A good way to determine whether there is an antecedent is to know that an antecedent must come *before* the personal pronoun.

Here is an example of a sentence that contains a pronoun but does not contain an antecedent:

EXAMPLE

> They were able to break out of the Escape Room in forty minutes.

> *"They" is the pronoun in the sentence. However, we don't know the name(s) of the people to whom "they" is referring. Therefore, there is no antecedent in this sentence.*

For many years, **pronouns** were specific to gender. Possessive Determiners such as "his" and "her" were designated for people who were assigned male and female at birth. Nowadays, people often notify others of their pronouns and determiners. You may have seen emails that end with a person's name followed by she/her, he/his, they/their, they/he, or they/she, to name a few. Also, it has become customary to use "their" to refer to a person if you do not know their determiner.

I must admit that it took me some time to adjust to this. In my mind, "their "referred to people plural in number. To use "their" to refer to one person seemed like faulty parallelism, since the number of people in the sentence did not align (Shelley gave me their sweater, since I was cold.). However, it is important to respect people's sense of identity. Yes, I am a stickler when it comes to grammar, and yes, I correct mistakes all the time. This is different. This rule is an assumption that people have made for years.

Therefore, unless I know for certain that a person identifies as "he," "she," or "their," I accept "their" as the pronoun that refers to that person, both in speaking and in writing.

There will be purists who disagree. They will argue that grammar is not flexible—that singular is singular and plural is plural. I understand their point, but I must remind everyone that languages change all the time. We add new words, omit outdated words, and even change punctuation rules. Those changes *do not ever* offend people personally.

For the sake of teaching the rule, it is necessary for me to show you how to use pronouns/determiners and antecedents in the singular and plural form. In the examples below, I provide four different types of sentences with antecedents. Presume that I know, for a fact, that the person in the first sample sentence identifies as female and the person in the second sample sentence identifies as male. Sentence three shows you a plural determiner based on multiple antecedents. In sentence four, I am uncertain about the antecedent's determiner.

If you are completing exercises in pronoun or determiner/antecedent agreement for an English assignment, double-check with your teacher or professor to know how to proceed.

▶ Malala Yousafzai was so grateful for all the support from her fans.

 "Her" is the determiner that refers to Malala Yousafzai (the antecedent).

▶ Muhammad Ali is still remembered for his unusual boxing style.

 "His" is the determiner that refers to Muhammad Ali (the antecedent).

▶ Willow and Blake ordered their school supplies online rather than waiting in line at the store.

 "Their" is the determiner that refers to Willow and Blake (the antecedents).

> Casey chose to write a rap poem for their English project.
>
> *Since I do not know Casey's determiner, I defaulted to "their." Casey is the antecedent.*

Let us move on to a different type of pronoun. Some pronouns that connect nouns or noun phrases to clauses are called **relative pronouns**. The most common ones are *who*, *that*, and *which*.

Often, these pronouns appear at the beginning of a group of words called a relative clause. **Relative clauses** are dependent clauses (not complete sentences) that introduce further information about a noun or phrase (also called the **antecedent**) that precedes it.

A relative clause is considered a **defining relative clause** (also called a **restrictive clause** or **essential clause**) if it *contains words that are essential in the meaning of the sentence*. Defining relative clauses can begin with the relative pronouns "who" or "that." Defining relative clauses do not require commas to separate them from the rest of the sentence.

On the other hand, sometimes, relative clauses provide additional details about a preceding noun or noun phrase (antecedent), but the information in the relative clause is not essential to the meaning of the sentence. In that case, we call that clause (which begins with a relative pronoun) a **nondefining**, **nonessential**, or **nonrestrictive clause** (which we covered in Chapter 2, The Comma). The information in this type of clause can be removed without affecting the meaning of the sentence. Nonrestrictive clauses can begin with the words "who" or "which." These clauses require the use of commas to separate them from the rest of the sentence.

Many people wonder when to use "who," "that," or "which" at the beginning of a relative clause.

The relative pronoun "who" is the easiest because it only refers to people. However, whether or not you should surround the clause with commas will depend upon whether the clause that begins with "who" is restrictive or nonrestrictive. If the word "who" begins a clause that is essential in the meaning of the sentence, it does not require commas. If the clause that begins with "who" can be removed from the sentence without compromising its meaning, it requires commas.

EXAMPLES

▶ The artist who painted this picture won an award.

This is an example of the relative pronoun "who" beginning a clause that is essential to the sentence's meaning. We need to know that this particular artist is the one who won the award. Note that commas are not used because the relative clause is defining or essential.

▶ Rembrandt, who was from the Netherlands, was world-famous for his paintings.

This is an example of when the pronoun "who" begins a clause that is not essential to the sentence's meaning. The fact that Rembrandt was from the Netherlands does not add information about his fame or his paintings. Therefore, "who" is considered a relative pronoun that begins a nondefining or nonrestrictive clause, so that clause must begin with a comma. Ordinarily, the clause would end with a comma as well, but since the clause appears at the end of a sentence, no final comma is necessary.

Recently, I have also seen the word "who" in reference to particular animals such as pets with specific names or famous animals at the zoo even though they are not considered people. The jury is out on this.

Whether to use the relative pronoun "that" or "which" is more complicated because it depends on whether the relative pronoun begins a restrictive clause or a nonrestrictive clause. Use "that" at the beginning of a restrictive clause, and use "which" at the beginning of a nonrestrictive clause.

▶ Don't wear the blue sweater that has a hole in it.

The reason why the relative pronoun "that" is necessary in this sentence is because it suggests that there are multiple blue sweaters, and the directions are to avoid the one with the hole in it (out of all the blue sweaters). If "that has a hole in it" were not in the sentence, there would be a lack of clarity as to which blue sweater should be avoided. Since "that has a hole in it" is considered a defining relative clause, no commas are necessary.

▶ The striped blouse, which is my favorite, has pearl buttons.

The reason why the relative pronoun "which" is necessary in this sentence is because the clause "which is my favorite" is not an essential part of the sentence. It does not add information that is essential in the sentence's meaning, since this information has nothing to do with the way the blouse is designed. Therefore, it is considered a nondefining or nonrestrictive clause, and as such, the relative clause "which is my favorite" must be surrounded by commas.

Reminder: If "who," "that" or "which" is the first word of the sentence, it is not functioning as a relative pronoun. This is because a relative pronoun refers to a noun or phrase that precedes it.

Topic 6: Additional Abbreviations

As you know, an **abbreviation** is the *shortened form of an original word or words.* Though many abbreviation rules were covered in Chapter 1 (Capitalization), there are others that do not require capitalization.

In the age of texting, abbreviations have become second nature for all of us. The problem is that students are carrying over their informal texting abbreviations to the world of formal writing, and it is not going well for them. There are only certain abbreviations allowed in formal writing. The rest need to be replaced with actual words. Here are a few of the most common abbreviation issues faced by young writers.

- **The "&" symbol**

  There are several symbols used to replace the word "and." These are *not acceptable* in formal writing pieces *except if they are part of a title, brand, or company* (Ben & Jerry's).

- **Numbers below eleven**

  Did you know that you are supposed to *spell out numbers below eleven*? Most people do not know this rule. This rule applies in the context of writing. Exceptions are when stating dates, telling time, and referring to money. Of course, you don't need to spell out numbers while doing math problems! Solving math equations is not considered formal writing, even when you are explaining how you came to your answer.

  There is one more thing to know about this rule. *When a number is the first word of a sentence, even if the number is above ten, it should be spelled out*, except in the case of time of day (12:00) or year (1945).

■ Abbreviations for versus

The abbreviations "v." or "vs." are often used to represent opposing sides. In the past, they were not acceptable to use *except in law reports or cases* (*Plessy v. Ferguson*). Recently "v." has become the more acceptable abbreviation for "versus."

■ Latin terms

Even though we do not speak Latin, many of our words and expressions derive from Latin.

 IRL You may know about Latin abbreviations used to denote time periods: BCE and CE.

There has been a recent movement to shift from BC (before Christ) and AD (anno Domini, "in the year of the Lord") to BCE (before Common Era) and CE (Common Era). Obviously, this is due to the religious implications of BC and AD.

There are still several *Latin abbreviations* that are acceptable to use in English.

They are not all punctuated in the same way, so take note of that. Here are the most popular ones used in English:

Common Latin Abbreviations

Latin abbreviation	What it stands for	What it means	When it is used
i.e.	id est	that is	to explain something further
etc.	et cetera	and so forth	when you list some examples but not all of them*
et al.	et alia	and everyone else	when you do not want to mention an entire list of people*
ibid.	ibidim	in the same place	With regard to footnotes, you may use "ibid." to indicate that you are making reference to the exact same source as the previous footnote (so you do not need to type out the entire footnote again).
sic	sic erat scriptum	thus, it is written	When there is a grammatical or typographical error in a direct quotation or excerpt, use [sic] after the error to indicate that you are aware of the mistake, but you are copying it in the exact same manner as it was written or spoken.
a.m.**	ante meridiem	before noon	This indicates a time of day that is before noon. Notice that this is a lowercase abbreviation.
p.m.**	post meridiem	after noon	This indicates a time of day that is after noon. Notice that this is a lowercase abbreviation.

*Remember that you must list at least two people prior to using etc. or et al.

**Remember that many countries function on a twenty-four-hour clock and do not use a.m. or p.m. at all, since they are not necessary.

■ Acronyms and initialisms

We covered these in Chapter 1 (Capitalization). However, I wanted to add that if you are using an acronym or initialism in a formal piece of writing, you need to *spell out the entire name the first time you mention it* and *place the acronym in parentheses immediately afterward*. Thereafter, you may use the acronym without spelling it out.

There are two more important points to note in the study of **abbreviations**. One involves *punctuation*, and the other involves *articles that precede abbreviations*.

We have discussed whether certain abbreviations require periods, but we did not discuss what happens when an abbreviation that requires a period comes at the end of a sentence. Here is the rule: If an abbreviation that requires a period ends a sentence, *only one period is required at the end of the sentence.* It is not necessary to add an additional period to end the sentence.

> **BTW**
>
> *Have you ever heard of R.A.S.? It stands for Redundant Acronym Syndrome, a tongue-in-cheek expression that pokes fun at abbreviation expressions that mistakenly repeat a word that already exists in the abbreviation itself such as ATM machine or PIN number.*

The second point that needs to be addressed is the use of "a" and "an" before certain abbreviations, especially acronyms and initialisms. To determine which to use, *listen to the sound of the first letter of the abbreviation.* (Notice that I did not tell you to look at the first letter of the abbreviation. That is because consonants sometimes make vowel sounds and vice versa.) If the abbreviation begins with a consonant sound, use the word "a" before it:

EXAMPLE

> It is my goal to meet a US president within the next five years.
>
> *Yes, I know it is confusing. You were always taught to place "an" before a vowel word, right? Wrong. You only place "an" before a word that begins with a vowel sound. The "U" in United sounds like a "y" similar to the initial sound made in the word "you." Since the "y" in "you" makes a consonant sound, the word "a" must come before "US."*

Here is an example of when to use "an" before an initialism:

EXAMPLE

> ▶ An ADA recommendation is to brush one's teeth twice daily.
>
> *Since the initialism "ADA" begins with the "a" sound, it must be preceded by the article "an."*

Since we have covered so much additional information related to abbreviations (that was not covered in the capitalization chapter), it is important for you to try a quick review.

EXERCISE 7-4: Abbreviations

DIRECTIONS: In the following sentences, you will see an abbreviation. Decide whether the abbreviation is capitalized/punctuated correctly and if it is appropriate to use that abbreviation in the sentence.

- *If the abbreviation is correct, write **Correct** on the space provided.*
- *If the abbreviation is incorrect, write **Incorrect** on the space provided.*

_____ 1. Chloe needs to go to the bank, etc. after work today.

_____ 2. Do you prefer M&M's or Skittles?

_____ 3. "How do you like them [Sic] apples?" is a famous quote from *Good Will Hunting*.

_____ 4. Benjamin Franklin, Thomas Jefferson, James Wilson, et al. were famous men who authored and signed both the Declaration of Independence and the Constitution.

_____ 5. Twelve players advanced to the next round.

_____ 6. *Roe v. Wade* was one of the most controversial Supreme Court cases.

Topic 7: Double Negatives

There are words in the English language that imply something is opposite, against, or negative in some respect. The most popular words used to negate an idea are **no**, **not**, **none**, **never**, **no one**, **nothing**, and **hardly.** Remember that sometimes, *"not"* can be represented as *"n't,"* in the case of a contraction.

There is a rule in English that states that one *may not use two negatives in the same sentence.* The use of two negatives in a sentence when only one is needed is called a **double negative**.

Many English teachers might say that when two negatives are used, it creates a positive. (Think of math.) However, that is not always the case. Two negatives simply make a sentence *unclear* and, thus, should be avoided.

> Correct: Billy hardly did anything.
> Incorrect: Billy hardly did nothing.

> Correct: I haven't been to Ireland.
> Incorrect: I haven't never been to Ireland.

> Correct: I can hardly wait for my SAT results.
> Incorrect: I can't hardly wait for my SAT results.

NOTE: Yes, I know there is a famous movie *Can't Hardly Wait*. When a double negative appears in quotation marks/italics or if the double negative is a part of a proper noun (like the name of a business or a film), we do not correct it.

EXAMPLES

▶ Holden Caulfield doesn't have any filter.

> *One negative is sufficient to express the idea in this sentence. The word "any" should not be replaced with a negative word such as "no."*

▶ We don't have anything left to give the trick-or-treaters.

> *One negative is sufficient to express the idea in this sentence. The word "anything" should not be replaced with the word "nothing."*

Topic 8: Who and Whom

Children and adults alike struggle with the usage of the words *who* and *whom*. In fact, most people are inclined to use *who* in all contexts due to their uncertainty. Of course, this is an error that is easy to fix.

The word "who" should be used when it *replaces the subject of a sentence* (the noun/pronoun that receives the action or state of being of the verb). Another instance when "who" would be appropriate is when *it refers to a noun/pronoun that follows a linking verb.*

EXAMPLES

▶ Aidan is flying here from Dublin.

Who is flying here from Dublin?

Aidan is the subject of the sentence, so the pronoun "who" must be used instead of "whom."

▶ She was the recipient of the gold medal.

Who was the recipient of the medal?

Sometimes the subject of the sentence can be a pronoun (not a noun). If the subject of the sentence is a pronoun, the word "who" should still be used when posing the question. Therefore, the answer to the word "who" is "She," and "She" is the subject of the sentence.

You might be wondering when to use "whom." The word "whom" refers either to a noun that comes after an action verb or the object of the preposition (when it is preceded by the word "to," "from," or "by").

▶ I believe Jenna because she is trustworthy.

Whom do I believe?

The answer to the question is "Jenna." The name "Jenna" comes after the action verb "believe." It is called a direct object. When you are asking a question about the direct object, and the direct object is a person, you must use the word "whom."

▶ You should address the check to the Assistant Treasurer.

To whom should I address the check?

The subject of the sentence is "You," but the question is not asking about the subject of the sentence. The question is asking about the noun after the preposition, which is also called the object of the preposition (Assistant Treasurer). Since the answer is found in a prepositional phrase (to the Assistant Treasurer), the preposition "to" must precede the word "whom."

▶ Dom inherited his green eyes from his mother.

From whom did Dom inherit his green eyes?

The subject of the sentence is "Dom," but the question is not asking about the subject of the sentence. The question is asking about the noun after the preposition, which is also called the object of the preposition (mother). Since the answer is found in a prepositional phrase (from his mother), the preposition "from" must precede the word "whom."

NOTE: Have you heard the term **dangling modifier**? It is a common error.

Some people make a mistake and pose the question this way:

> ▶ Whom did Dom inherit his green eyes from?
>
> *The preposition "from" should not end the sentence. It should precede "whom" in this sentence. When people mistakenly place the preposition at the end of the sentence instead of placing it before the "who" or "whom," we call it a dangling modifier because there is not a word following it that it can modify or explain. It is just dangling by itself at the end of the sentence.*

Here are tips to help you determine whether to use *who* or *whom*.

- If you can substitute *"he," "she,"* or *"they"* for the word, then use *"who."*

- If you can substitute *"him," "her," "it,"* or *"them"* for the word, then use *"whom."*

Topic 9: Homophones

Homophones (also known as homonyms) are *words that sound the same but are spelled differently and have different meanings.*

Here is a chart with the most common homophones, their spellings, and their meanings. I have also taken the liberty of including in this chart words that do not have the exact same pronunciation but sound so similar that they are confused.

Homophone Chart

Homonym	Part of speech	Meaning
to	preposition	toward
to	verb	part of the infinitive (to + verb)
too	adverb	very; much
two	adjective or noun	the number after one (double)
there	adverb, pronoun, noun, adjective, interjection	a location or state of being
their	pronoun	belonging to someone or to people
they're	pronoun + verb	contraction for *they are*
it's	pronoun + verb	contraction for *it is*
its	pronoun	belonging to something
principal	noun	person who leads a school or corporation
principle	adjective	most important; primary
principle	noun	value; moral
compliment	verb	to say something nice about
compliment	noun	nice words that have been said about something or someone
complement	noun	something that goes well with or completes something else
complement	verb	to complete
effect	noun	a result or consequence of an action
effect	verb	to cause a change; to bring about
affect	verb	to produce a response to something; to influence

Homonym	Part of speech	Meaning
affect	noun	facial expression, gesture, or reaction that reflects an emotion
whether	conjunction	links doubt or choice between two alternatives
weather	noun	the state of the atmosphere
weather	verb	to wear away the appearance of; to come safely through something
aloud	adverb	audibly; meant to be heard
allowed	verb	past tense of giving/having permission to do something
capital	noun	important city or town; wealth in the form or money or assets
capital	adjective	related to a legal charge or offense; large in size (as in a capital letter)
capitol	noun	building in which a legislative body convenes
loose	adjective	larger than necessary
lose	verb	unable to find the whereabouts

Topic 10: Verbs That Are Confusing

Many verbs are similar in meaning and are, thus, confused. However, their meanings are not interchangeable. Thus, you must be able to decipher the differences between them. Here are some sets of commonly confused verbs:

Can and May

The verb "can" means having the ability to do something.

EXAMPLE

▶ Josh can run a mile in six minutes.

Josh has the ability to run the mile.

The verb "may" has multiple meanings. It can mean having permission to do something, but it can also mean "might."

EXAMPLE

▶ May I leave class early today?

The speaker is asking permission to leave class early.

Lay and *Lie*

The verb "to lay" means to place something down carefully. It must be followed by an object. The past tense of "lay" is "laid." The present participle is "laying."

EXAMPLE

▶ The kindergarten teacher lays the mats on the floor before naptime.

The mats are the objects that are being placed.

The verb "to lie," besides meaning not telling the truth, can mean to put oneself in a flat position. The past tense is *lay* (not "laid"). The present participle is "lying."

EXAMPLE

▶ Denise loves to lie in the sun.

There is no object after Denise, just a prepositional phrase (in the sun), so you know that the verb in this sentence cannot be "to lay," since that verb would require an object after it and before the prepositional phrase.

Hung and Hanged

The past tense of the verb "to hang" can be confusing. Basically, you will always use "hung" as the past tense of "to hang" unless you are referring to a person who is sentenced to die by hanging.

EXAMPLES

▶ Enson hung the picture on the wall.

The picture is an item Enson was hanging.

▶ The serial killer was going to be hanged at sunset.

This killer is going to be executed with a noose.

Topic 11: Words Often Confused with Each Other

Just like commonly confused verbs, there are some words that have such similar meanings that people tend to use them interchangeably. It is important to recognize the difference.

Fewer and Less

These are often confused because the antonym for both words is "more." It is usually easy to distinguish whether to use "fewer" or "less" by looking at what is being measured. If it is something that can be counted, use "fewer." If it is something that cannot be counted, use "less."

EXAMPLES

▶ Brody has fewer freckles than his sister.

Freckles can be counted, but who would bother to do that?

> ▶ Pamela has less patience than her mother.
>
> *Patience cannot be counted.*

Naturally, there is an exception to this rule. If what is being measured is a collective noun (presented in singular form), then "less" should be used, even if the item can be counted.

> ▶ Erica has less money than her brother.
>
> *Even though money can be counted, it is a collective noun that does not end in "s." Therefore, we use "less" instead of "fewer."*

Many and Much

Speaking of counting things, the rules for "many" and "much" are very similar to the rules for "fewer" and "less." In the same manner, one must look at the item that is being described. If it is something that can be counted (and is plural), the word "many" should be used. If it refers to something that can't be counted (whether or not it is plural), the word "much" should be used.

> ▶ Mohammed has many posters on his wall.
>
> *Posters can be counted; therefore, the word "many" refers to them.*
>
> ▶ Mr. Compiti assigns so much homework.
>
> *Homework is not a plural word. It does not have an "s" at the end. Therefore, the word "much" needs to precede it.*

Although and *Though*

The words *although* and *though* are mistakenly used interchangeably, but they do not have the same function in sentences.

Although is a word that begins a *dependent clause*. A *dependent clause* is a group of words that cannot function as a sentence in and of itself.

Though is a word that may be used as part of a dependent clause or in an *independent clause (sentence)*. This means that the group of words that begins with *though* can usually function as a sentence by itself if the word "though" is serving as a substitute for the word "however." A sentence that begins with *though* usually follows another sentence and provides an explanation or a contrast to the preceding sentence.

EXAMPLES

▶ Although I was very tired when I arrived home from play rehearsal, I still did my homework.

The clause that begins with "Although" and ends with "rehearsal" is connected to a complete sentence.

▶ I planned to complete two school projects when I came home from school. Though, I was very tired when I arrived home from play rehearsal.

The sentence beginning with "though" works as an independent clause only because of the sentence preceding it. It is a substitute for the word "however" that suggests a shift from something conveyed in the preceding sentence.

Incorrect: Although I was very tired when I arrived home from play rehearsal.

This is a fragment because there is no sentence connected to the dependent clause.

After and Afterward

Like *although* and *though*, the word *after* is often used incorrectly when the word that should be used is *afterward*. Often, this error is made at the beginning of a sentence.

> ▶ Afterward, we went for ice cream.
>
> *The word "afterward" establishes time in the proper manner. It is used correctly in this sentence to indicate that the ice cream trip followed a previous activity.*

Incorrect: After, we went for ice cream.

The word "after" in this sentence is being used as a preposition. As you know, a prepositional phrase begins with a preposition and ends with a noun. If the sentence said, "After the movie, we went for ice cream," that would be fine. However, simply placing "after" with a comma is incorrect.

Regardless or Irregardless?

Do you know which is correct?

The answer: Regardless

Here's why: The suffix "less" already suggests negation. There is no need for the prefix "-ir" (which also suggests the opposite of or negation of). Therefore, "irregardless" is redundant and unclear. "Regardless" is the correct form of the word.

Topic 12: Common Spelling Errors

People write entire books about the spelling rules of the English language. Even if you follow all the rules, there will still be so many exceptions to them! I decided to provide a list of the most-commonly misspelled words in the English language, hoping you will commit these to memory for occasions when you have to handwrite something and do not have the luxury of a grammar-correction program to catch the mistakes.

- acceptable
- accommodate
- acquaintance
- acquire
- acquit
- a lot (instead of allot, which has a different meaning)
- arctic
- argument
- broccoli
- buoyant
- bureaucracy
- business
- calendar
- camouflage
- Caribbean

- cemetery
- college
- colleague
- column
- congratulate
- connoisseur
- conscientious
- conscious
- conscience
- consensus
- controversy
- deceive
- definite
- desperate
- disappoint
- embarrass

- entrepreneur
- exhilarated
- fluorescent
- foreign
- fulfill
- gauge
- grammar
- guarantee
- hierarchy
- hors d'oeuvres
- hygiene
- indict
- inoculate
- jewelry
- judgment
- led

- liaison
- license
- liquefy
- maintenance
- medieval
- memento
- millennium
- miniature
- mischievous
- misspell
- necessary
- neighbor
- noticeable
- omission
- occurrence
- parallel
- parliament
- pastime
- precede
- privilege
- pronunciation
- publicly
- queue
- receive
- recommend
- relevant
- renaissance
- repetition
- rhythm
- separate
- sergeant
- successful
- supersede
- surprise
- tomorrow
- twelfth
- tyranny
- underrate
- unnecessary
- vacuum
- weird
- whoa
- willful
- withhold

Topic 13: Informal language

There are several instances when spoken language allows us to say certain words or use certain expressions that are considered informal or slang in written form. I have included the most popular in this section.

Got and *Gotten*

I can thank my seventh-grade ELA teacher, Miss Doyle, for breaking me out of this habit. She explained that the words *got* and *gotten* are not translatable into other languages, so they should not be utilized in formal written English. The words *get* and *getting* are allowed, however. What has happened is we have come to use *got* to replace so many different words that it becomes ineffective and vague.

Here is an exercise that can help you break the habit of using the word "got" by substituting it with a word that matches your intended meaning more closely.

EXERCISE 7-5: Have You GOT a Better Word?

DIRECTIONS: *Try to replace the word* **got** *in these sentences.*

- *On the line to the left of the number, replace the word* **got** *with a better word (or better words).*

- *Remain in the same tense.*

- *Do not repeat an answer!*

- *You may remove or add words to make the sentence flow better (without changing the meaning).*

- *On the line provided, please list any other substitutions for "got" that work well in the context of this sentence.*

_____ 1. I got an A on my test.

(other possible answers: _____)

_____ 2. Joe got out of the car.

(other possible answers: _____)

_____ 3. Suzanne got there early.

(other possible answers: _____)

_____ 4. Jill got fired today!

(other possible answers: _____)

_____ 5. Jack got tired of waiting.

(other possible answers: _____)

_____ 6. You got so tall!

(other possible answers: _____)

Another bone of contention for me is when students refer to their parents in an informal way, especially when writing. I know that correct capitalization of family members was discussed in Chapter 1 (Capitalization), but the issue addressed here goes far beyond a capitalization error.

It is very common to hear people say, "*My mom* picked me up from school." Is that what you say?

The rule is simple. Refer to your relatives as mother, father, grandmother, grandfather, etc. when preceding those terms with the word "my." Also, you should not refer to parents or grandparents by nicknames unless those nicknames are part of dialogue or unless you are using that nickname as part of a proper noun.

EXAMPLE

▶ Grandpa Jones is coming over for Thanksgiving.

Since the name "Jones" comes directly after Grandpa, that makes "Grandpa Jones" his title, so the capitalization of "Grandpa" is correct.

Incorrect: My nanny gives the best hugs.

In this sentence, "nanny" is an informal way of saying "grandmother." The word "my" is a visual cue that the word following "my" should not be a nickname for a grandmother.

As you know, people speak differently in various regions of our country and of every country. This becomes problematic when people transfer their speaking habits into their formal writing. In fact, many people have begun to spell certain words and phrases the way they are pronounced regionally. We cannot let the way we pronounce things influence us in the way words are spelled.

Here are the most common examples I have heard and seen:

- ■ *Should of* **and** *could of*
  I know I mentioned this in the contraction section (Chapter 5), but I want to make sure it sticks. We may pronounce the word *have* similar to *of* when we are speaking English, but that doesn't mean it is okay to write this way. There is no such expression as "should of" or "could of." The correct expressions are "could have" and "should have."

- ■ *Gonna* **and** *kinda*
  There is an informal word you may have heard: "gonna." We may say this word when we are rushing or are in casual conversation with friends, but the formal expression is "going to." Another one I read often is "kinda." The correct form is "kind of."

One more thing: Writing is different than speaking. While speaking, we have become accustomed to using **pause words/phrases** such as "like," "you know," and "um." That does not mean it is okay to include these words in formal writing. If you are writing dialogue or a fictional piece and you add those for effect, that would be more acceptable than in an essay or paper.

Topic 14: Awkward Sentence Structure

Word placement is an important part of language and sentence structure. When phrases within a sentence are misplaced, *they create confusion and reduce clarity.*

Here is an example of **awkward word placement**:

Incorrect: Howie delivered an oral presentation on porcupines in sixth grade.

First, that must have hurt! How did Howie stand on porcupines while presenting? Next, those porcupines must be intelligent. They are in sixth grade already?

Of course, I am joking to make a point. Be mindful of where you choose to place words and phrases; the entire meaning of the sentence can change or become unclear. Also, you may need to replace words to provide more clarity for the reader.

> In sixth grade, Howie delivered an oral presentation about porcupines.
>
> *Notice how I moved "in sixth grade" to the front of the sentence to increase clarity. I also replaced the word "on" with "about" to help avoid confusion.*

Topic 15: Other Common Errors

There are other common errors that do not fall under any of the preceding categories, but they are still worth mentioning, since they are fairly common.

"However" Misused as a Coordinating Conjunction

In Chapter 2 (Commas), we learned about run-ons and how to prevent them. We learned about the **coordinating conjunctions**: and, or, but, yet, as, so, since, for, and because.

There is a common error made by students. They use the word "however" as a coordinating conjunction when it is not one. In other words, they try to connect two complete sentences by placing a comma before the word "however." This is not allowed. The word "however" may begin a sentence, may be used after a semicolon, or may be inserted elsewhere in a sentence as an interruption or a closing word. It may not connect two sentences with a comma.

Incorrect: I studied so much for the test, however, I did not receive a high score.

Since the word "however" cannot connect two sentences with only a comma, a comma splice was created in the example above.

▶ I studied so much for the test. However, I did not receive a high score.

"However" is the first word of a follow-up sentence. This is correct.
A semicolon could have been used between the words "test" and "however."
If the semicolon were used, the word "however" would not be capitalized.

Could Care Less or Couldn't Care Less?

I have heard this expression both ways. Do you know which is correct?

The answer: couldn't care less

Here's why: If you could care less, it means you actually could care a little less than you do right now.

However, if you "couldn't care less," you could not go any lower than the limited amount you care right now. That is the lowest.

As this chapter draws to a close, I hope you realize that these are a sampling of common issues in the English language. Furthermore, it is one thing to be able to recognize these areas of confusion in isolation (such as in exercises), but it is another to retain these rules when doing our own writing. That will be the challenge for you. In the meantime, attempt the writing practice that follows to see how much information you have grasped from this chapter.

EXERCISE 7-6: Writing Practice—Correcting Common Errors

DIRECTIONS: *The writing practice for this unit is going to be a bit different. Since this chapter included many types of usage rules and issues, it is important for you to be able to recognize common errors and learn how to correct them. Therefore, I am providing for you, in the space below, a writing prompt that contains all types of errors.*

Your job is to rewrite the writing sample, eliminating the common errors. Feel free to remove words, replace words, add punctuation, and remove punctuation. Try not to change the meaning, though. It is not as easy as it sounds. Good luck!

Writing Prompt with Errors

Irregardless of what others think, I decided to take a gap year between my senior year of high school and freshman year of college. Although this seems like a bad idea to most. Whom is it that has to pay for college tuition, you ask? None other then, um, myself. You might think I did not consider asking my parents before making this decision, especially after they already hanged my graduation picture on the wall and paid for Parents' Weekend at two prospective colleges, however, that is simply not true.

When I explained my reasoning to my parents, they had less concerns then I thought they would. After all, they were the ones that planted the traveling bug in me: taking me to countries from Mexico to Spain, from Norway too Japan. "Enjoy your life while your young," and "You only live once" were mantras in my family home. It only makes perfect sense that I can't "lie my hat down in won place" for too long.

So, I got a part-time job teaching English online who will help me play my expenses, and I am looking forward to traveling across Europe. My favorite country in Europe is Italy & France, so it will be interesting to see where I land firstly. There will be much opportunities to take selfies and videos in order gain viewers on social media. I know that's gonna be fun! After all, I'm the one that all my friends ask for advice when it comes to posting. What may go wrongly?

My parents said as long as I call them once a week, seperate my money into savings and spending money, and don't run off with a whine connessewer, they are fine with the decision. I don't want to become a full-fledged adult and think back on my late teens as a time I should of done more with my life. Now is the time, rite?

Once I return from my jaunt in Europe, I will apply to colleges and follow the "traditional" path. After, I plan to pursue a career in education, so teaching online will be great life experience to include in my application essay. Hopefully, colleges will like me better than much other applicants. Who else will they get an application like this from? This is the reasons why I am taking a gap year. I hope I persuaded you that it's a good idea.

Writing Prompt Without Errors

_____

_____

_____

_____

_____

_____

_____

_____

_____

8 Sentence Structure and Variety

MUST KNOW

 If you can tell whether you have a fragment, a complete sentence, or a run-on sentence, you will be on the road to becoming a more sophisticated writer.

 Writers who vary their sentence structure engage readers and raise their interest level.

 Another way to raise reader interest is to diversify your word choice by considering synonyms, incorporating sensory imagery, and including figurative language.

 Mastering the fundamentals of sentence writing is the first step in perfecting paragraphing style and essay writing.

The foundation of the English language is the **sentence**. Sentences can be as short as one word (a verb with the word *you* as the understood subject), or they may take up lines upon lines of text. All the grammar and usage rules we have covered will help you become a better and more sophisticated writer if your sentences are correct, clear, and comprehensive.

Topic 1: Fragments

It always fascinates me that many students can identify **fragments** in isolated exercises, but they have trouble identifying fragments in their own writing. It is as if they proofread their own writing with so much familiarity that they overlook the functionality of sentence structure.

Of course, it doesn't help matters that people text fragments all day long. I wonder if they start to believe that the texts they are sending are actual sentences. Furthermore, students are accustomed to reading fiction, where fragments are often included.

However, when you are writing an essay or a paper, not only are fragments frowned upon, but they are often penalized. This is because they lack clarity and sometimes confuse the reader.

Without getting into elementary-level instruction, I want to be sure you know the fundamentals of a sentence and can identify and correct fragments. Though some of the following material was covered in Chapter 7, it is presented here to identify and correct fragments rather than to check for agreement and parallelism.

So, what makes a **sentence** a sentence? It is complicated. In elementary school, they tell you that a sentence is composed of a noun and a verb, but that is not always the case.

First, we need to consider the **verbs**. The *type* of verb in a sentence impacts so much!

If the verb is an **action verb**, it is almost always preceded by a noun or a pronoun that carries out that action. We call that noun/pronoun the **subject** of the sentence. However, in the case of a command (Walk!), a sentence can be one word (when the subject is called an "understood you"). This means that the sentence is actually "*You walk!*" but that seems to change the meaning. Hence, the word "*Walk!*" by itself clarifies and enhances the tone of the command.

If the verb is a **linking verb** (remember covering these in Chapter 7?), there must be a *subject, a verb, and a word that follows the linking verb* (either an adjective or a noun). I have seen and heard this rule broken constantly in spoken English.

> ▶ The teacher asks the class who is prepared for the test. Three students yell, "I am!"
>
> *Is "I am!" a sentence? Everyone understands that the students are saying that they are prepared for the exam. Just because we understand it does not mean that "I am" is a complete and correct sentence. Since "am" is a linking verb, it needs to be preceded by a noun or pronoun. (The word "I" is a pronoun, so the subject is fine.) The linking verb is supposed to be followed by a noun or adjective. In this example, it is not followed by anything. Technically, the correct way to say the sentence is like this: "I am prepared."*

We are much more accepting of these types of errors in spoken English, but written English is a different story.

Suppose your friend texted you and told you about a situation when they were asked to apologize but felt they had done no wrong.

You may have seen someone write this:

> Not sorry.
>
> *We may hear this expression often, but that does not mean it is a sentence. There is no subject in this sentence. Even if you tried to say that the subject is an "understood you" (which it is not), "You not sorry" is not a sentence. For this to be a complete sentence, a subject and helping verb need to be added: "I am not sorry" would work.*

What complicates things more is that most sentences in our language have more than two or three words in them. There are articles, adjectives, adverbs, conjunctions, prepositional phrases, etc. This makes it more difficult to proofread for fragments. Sometimes, all those words may make you *believe* you have written a sentence.

Here is my advice. Look for the verb. Find the subject that is completing that action or state of being. If you have trouble finding those two, you may have a fragment on your hands.

Here are some examples to review what I have discussed.

> Hurry!
>
> *This is an example of a one-word sentence. The implied subject is "you" even though it is not present. One-word sentences must have an action verb that provides a command.*

> Marcus drives.
>
> *Again, this is a simple sentence, but it has two words. In this sentence, "drives" is the action verb. The noun that conveys the action is "Marcus," so "Marcus" is the subject of the sentence. Since this sentence includes an action verb, it does not require any words after it.*

▶ Elroy is enthusiastic.

There is a linking verb ("is") in this sentence. A linking verb needs to be preceded by a subject that is either a noun or pronoun. "Elroy" is a noun. The linking verb must also be followed by a noun or adjective. "Enthusiastic" is an adjective.

Again, fiction writing is an entirely different ball game. It is not uncommon to see fragments in novels, poetry, or plays. When it comes to formal essay writing or research, however, fragments are unacceptable.

BTW

Sometimes, verbs and their subjects can be inverted when verbs consist of a helping verb and main verb. This means the subject and verbs are not always in consecutive order. This usually happens when a helping verb is used in forming a question. Even though they are not in the traditional order of subject and then verb, they are considered a complete sentence.

- *Are you going to the party with me?*

In this sentence, "Are" serves as a helping verb to the action verb "going." The subject "you" falls between the two verbs ("Are" and "going").

EXERCISE 8-1: Fragment or Sentence?

DIRECTIONS: Read each example.

- *If the example is a fragment, write **F** on the line provided.*
- *If the example is a sentence, write **S** on the line provided.*

_____ 1. To the game!

_____ 2. Maxine walked away.

_____ 3. Don't run!

_____ 4. Exhausted by it all.

_____ 5. I have been.

_____ 6. Ron sings.

_____ 7. Round the bases!

_____ 8. Do I annoy you?

_____ 9. Very, very scared.

_____ 10. Stop!

Topic 2: Run-Ons

The topic of **run-on sentences** was mentioned briefly in Chapter 2 (The Comma), but it is necessary to delve more deeply into this topic, as it is a prevalent error that is not often detected by grammar-correction software.

As you know, many people continue to write run-on sentences. This is considered a significant error on standardized tests. Therefore, you need to be able to recognize and correct run-on sentences, both on grammar sections of exams and in your own writing.

When I ask my students how they identify a run-on, they usually tell me they look for "a really long sentence." Most English learners do not really understand that *run-ons have nothing to do with the number of words involved*. The reason why something is called a **run-on** is because *multiple sentences have been treated as if they are a single sentence*. These sentences can be short or long.

Furthermore, there are different types of run-on sentences, so the way they can be corrected may differ.

The first type illustrated below should be more obvious for you to recognize.

> Jeanette is the smartest student in the class she always receives perfect scores on her tests.

Can you spot the error? This example above has two sentences in it, but they are being treated as if they are one sentence. There are three ways to correct this run-on. See if you can figure out how to correct this run-on using **three different methods**. On the lines below, describe three different ways you can correct the "Jeanette" sentence.

1. _____

2. _____

3. _____

How did you do? Were you able to figure out how to fix them?

1. Most students can tell me that a **period** can be placed after the word "class" and before the word "she." They also let me know that the "s" in "she" should be capitalized. Is that the answer that was easiest for you?

2. Others recognize that a **semicolon** is appropriate between these two sentences. Remember that a semicolon can replace a period if the *consecutive sentences are related to each other.* The semicolon should be placed after the word "class" and before the word "she." However, as you may remember, the sentence after the semicolon does not begin with a capital letter unless the first word should be capitalized ordinarily (as in the cases of the word "I" or as the first letter of a proper noun).

3. This is the tricky part. Some students tell me to place a comma between "class" and "she." Since when does a comma by itself connect two sentences? In Chapter 2, we learned that the error of using a comma by itself to connect two sentences is called a **comma splice**. Others tell me to add a conjunction such as "and." This is not entirely correct either. A conjunction alone usually cannot connect two sentences. So, have you figured out the answer?

    If you are trying to connect two sentences by using a **coordinating conjunction**, you **must place a comma before that conjunction**. Otherwise, it is still considered a run-on!

    Of course, it would not be English without *an exception*. Remember, the word "*because*" is considered the *only* coordinating conjunction that can connect two sentences *by itself*. It should *never* be preceded by a comma if it is functioning as a connector between two sentences.

I still think that most of you would have noticed the error in that "Jeanette" run-on, and you would have known how to correct it. It is the second type of run-on that stumps my students. Take a look at this example:

Hector plays soccer so well but he stinks at basketball.

Do you see it?

Reread the explanation next to number 3 above. If you use a **coordinating conjunction** (*connecting word*) *to connect two complete sentences* (also called *independent clauses*), you *must place a comma before that conjunction*, or you risk writing a run-on. Of course, you also may drop the conjunction and add either a period or a semicolon.

Once again, here are the most common conjunctions that must be committed to memory if you ever hope to master the identification and correction of run-ons in your own writing:

and, or, but, yet, as, so, since, for

REMINDER: Do not forget that **because** can also be a conjunction that connects two sentences, but it *never* requires a comma before it when it is connecting sentences.

What is tricky about this rule is that some students place commas before every conjunction they see, just in case. This is unacceptable.

Avoiding this type of run-on takes practice. After a while, you will be able to "eyeball" your sentences, and the run-ons will stick out like a sore thumb.

Here is a review of the technique to use when checking for run-ons that include coordinating conjunctions:

1. To avoid this type of run-on, circle or underline the words **and**, **or**, **but**, **yet**, **as**, **so**, **since**, and **for** in your sentences, since they *may* be functioning as coordinating conjunctions in the sentence. These words can sometimes have other functions as well.

2. Next, read the words that precede that conjunction. Do they make a complete sentence?

3. Then, read everything that comes after that conjunction. Do those words make a complete sentence?

4. If the answer is "yes" *to both* questions, then that conjunction is connecting two sentences and *requires the placement of a comma before it* (except if the conjunction is the word "because," of course!).

Let's try it. Draw a circle around each of the possible conjunctions in this sentence:

Hector plays soccer so well but he stinks at basketball.

Did you draw a circle around "so" and "but?" Now, do the test.

1. Read everything that comes before "so." "Hector plays soccer" is a sentence. So far, so good.

2. Now, read what comes after the word "so." "Well but he stinks at basketball" is not a complete thought. Therefore, the word "so" is *not* connecting two sentences, and a comma should *not* be placed before it.

3. Next, apply the test with the word "but." What comes before it is a complete sentence (Hector plays soccer so well). What comes after it is also a complete sentence (he stinks at basketball). Therefore, a comma must be placed before the word "but." Otherwise, you have a *run-on*.

I think it's time to practice with a variety of sentences. Follow the directions carefully in this set of exercises.

BTW

There is another reason why you need to commit the second run-on rule to memory. Most proofreading programs do not underline or highlight it as an error! Therefore, you may not have realized it was a mistake.

EXERCISE 8-2: Run-on or Not?

DIRECTIONS:

- *Underline the words that **may be** functioning as coordinating conjunctions:* **and, or, but, yet, as, so, since, for, because**
- *Apply the "run-on test" that we practiced earlier.*
- *For each of the following sentences, you will **add** either **a period, a comma, a semicolon,** or **nothing at all.**

1. I studied so much for the vocabulary test yet I received a 72 as a test grade.

2. Max is a nice dog's name and Sparkle is a nice cat's name.

3. Try on those shoes they look comfortable.

4. Julia wears a retainer because her teeth are crooked.

5. Jenny will go to the mall later Millie loves to draw.

6. My grandmother and grandfather live in Florida but they visit me quite often.

7. He was as quick as a panther.

8. Please wear a suit and tie as you will be meeting the president of the company.

9. Student teachers are so vulnerable so students should be kind to them.

10. This run-on stuff is pretty easy and I think I am getting the hang of it!

Topic 3: Sentence Variety

Although you have been writing sentences for many years, you may not realize that you have a habit of sticking to the same sentence format. If you have had a teacher comment on the simplicity of your sentence structure or recommend varied sentence structure, this section of the chapter may be quite helpful for you. A sign of a good writer is the ability to engage a reader and spark interest. One of the best ways to achieve these is by changing the way you begin sentences—without compromising the meaning, of course.

When you were younger you may have learned the four types (purposes) of sentences: declarative, interrogative, imperative, and exclamatory. Do you remember these terms?

Here is a quick review, in case you forgot them:

- A **declarative sentence** *makes a statement* and concludes with a period (or semicolon if it is connected to a related sentence).

> **EXAMPLE**
>
> ▶ Brighton is an excellent skier.
>
> *This sentence states something about Brighton.*

- An **interrogative sentence** poses a question and always ends in a question mark.

> **EXAMPLE**
>
> ▶ Does Bridget know how to surf?
>
> *This sentence poses a question about Bridget.*

- An **imperative sentence** gives a command or issues a request, and it can end either in a period or in an exclamation point.

▶ Carry this to your bunk before the guests arrive.

This is a command for someone to carry something to the bunk.

- An **exclamatory sentence** expresses strong feeling and always ends with an exclamation point.

▶ You are so amazing!

This is a compliment that ends in an exclamation point.

In your writing piece, a combination of the aforementioned sentences helps to engage the reader. Another way to raise reader interest is to *avoid contiguous simple sentences* and replace some of them with more complicated versions.

In Chapter 7, we reviewed simple subjects and simple predicates. It is time to use this knowledge to differentiate between the three types of sentences: *simple, compound, and complex sentences.*

Here is a quick review:

- A **simple sentence** contains only *one subject and one verb* (sometimes only one verb in the case of the "understood you"). Of course, the sentence can include other types of words in it.

▶ Finn climbed the tree.

"Finn" is the subject, and "climbed" is the verb in this simple sentence.

■ A **compound sentence** is a sentence with *multiple subjects and verbs*. We practiced with compound sentences in our study of correcting run-ons (Chapter 2).

▶ On our vacation to Mexico, we woke up early every morning, since the sunrises were breathtaking.

There are two sentences connected by a comma and a coordinating conjunction (since).

■ A **complex sentence** is a sentence that contains an *independent clause* (a complete sentence) *attached to a dependent clause* (a group of words that has a noun and a verb but cannot serve as a full sentence by itself).

▶ If you have trouble completing the homework, refer to the notes in your binder.

The sentence begins with a subordinate clause (if you have trouble completing the homework). The second half of the sentence is a complete sentence, so the subordinate clause is connected to that complete sentence.

■ A **compound-complex sentence** contains both a *compound sentence* (two separate sentences combined with a conjunction) *and a subordinate clause*.

> Although the process was difficult, Perry was able to finish all his college applications, since he managed his time very well.
>
> *The sentence begins with a subordinate clause followed by a compound sentence. This combination is what makes it a complex sentence.*

Wow! There are so many sentence structures from which to choose. One of the most effective ways to keep a reader even more focused on what you have to say is by *varying the beginnings of your sentences.* Thus, the next portion of the chapter will elaborate on the importance of mastering assorted *sentence beginnings.*

Think about first impressions. They mean a lot, right? When you are choosing a book to read, the first thing you see is the cover. When you are researching colleges, the design of their websites causes you to pass an initial judgment. It is instinctive to do so.

Reading sentences is no different. If you want the reader of your writing to be impressed with what you have to say, you need to impress them with *how* you say it. That is why a variety of sentence starters is essential. They demonstrate your fluency and command of the written word.

Here are the most popular types of sentence starters with examples:

Begin with a Simple Subject

This is the type of sentence to which you are most accustomed. Usually, it has a noun and a verb. It may have some other words in the sentence but nothing too complicated.

> Lucia is a master hairdresser.
>
> *"Lucia" is the subject. The linking verb is "is," and "hairdresser" is the predicate noun. This is considered a simple sentence.*

Begin with a Prepositional Phrase

In Chapter 2 (The Comma), we learned all about **prepositional phrases** at the beginnings of sentences. At least one prepositional phrase appears at the beginning of a sentence to provide more information. A complete sentence follows the phrase(s).

> At the end of the corridor, make a right.
>
> *"At the end" and "of the corridor" are prepositional phrases that begin the sentence.*

Begin with a Participle or a Participial Phrase

In case you don't know these terms, here is a quick lesson:

A **participle** is a word *derived from a verb that ends in "ing" (present participle) or "ed" (past participle).*

A **participial phrase** is a group of words that *begins with a participle.*

When the participle or participial phrase begins a sentence, it needs to be connected to an additional full sentence.

> Gliding through the air in a hot air balloon, Marvin admired the beautiful Colorado Rockies.
>
> *"Gliding through the air in a hot air balloon" is a participial phrase that is connected to a full sentence.*
>
> Mesmerized by the acrobats in the circus, the toddler did not respond to his name despite repeated attempts by his mother to call him.
>
> *"Mesmerized by the acrobats in the circus" is a participial phrase connected to a full sentence.*

Begin with a Subordinate (Dependent) Clause

In Rule 15 of Chapter 2 (The Comma), you will find a list of *subordinate conjunctions*. These conjunctions begin a grouping of words called a **subordinate clause**. When a *subordinate clause* begins a sentence, it is **dependent** upon another complete thought to function. We learned that the comma belongs after the subordinate clause and before the independent clause (complete sentence) if the subordinate clause falls at the *beginning* of the sentence.

EXAMPLE

▶ If you want to be on time for the interview, prepare your clothes the night before the big day.

> *"If you want to be on time for the interview" is a subordinate clause. It is not a sentence by itself even though it contains a noun and a verb. It depends on the second half of the sentence in order to be a complete sentence.*

Begin with an Infinitive Phrase

Do you remember the meaning of the word **infinitive**? It is the word "to" followed by the *original form of a verb*. An infinitive is always written in the present tense, no matter the tense of the rest of the verbs in the sentence. One way to vary sentence structure is to begin a sentence with an infinitive phrase, which consists of an infinitive and other words associated with it.

Be careful, though. The word "to" can sometimes be a preposition. The way to tell is to look at the word that follows "to." If it is a *verb*, then "to" is serving as part of the *infinitive*.

> To master the French language, Soriya studied abroad for a semester and immersed herself in French culture.
>
> *"To master" is the infinitive at the beginning of the sentence, since the verb "master" immediately follows the word "to."*

Begin with an Inverted Appositive

This is a bit tricky. An **appositive** usually describes a noun or pronoun that *precedes* it. However, if you want to vary your sentence structure, you can create a sentence that has a traditional appositive and then *reverse the order*.

Example of a simple sentence that has an appositive: Bob, a well-respected New York editor, selected me as the author of an edition of a popular book series.

Example of an inverted appositive: A well-respected New York editor, Bob selected me as the author of an edition of a popular book series.

Here is another example of a sentence beginning with an inverted appositive.

> A versatile entertainer, Pete Davidson is feted for his roles in comedic and dramatic roles.
>
> *"A versatile entertainer" is the inverted appositive in this sentence. It is a phrase that further describes Pete Davidson, but instead of being placed after Davidson's name, it opens the sentence.*

Begin with an Adverb

This rule does not work for all adverbs, so choose wisely. If you would like to begin a sentence with an adverb, it can be an *adverb ending in "ly."* We also covered Rule 6 (Introductory Words) in Chapter 2 (The Comma).

EXAMPLE

▶ Skillfully, Lionel Messi dribbled the ball toward the goal.

"Skillfully" is one type of adverb that begins a sentence (in the role of an introductory word).

Other examples of adverbs that begin sentences are the words "yes" and "no." These two words do not always function as adverbs, so you need to be wary. If the words "yes" or "no" begin a sentence, are followed by a comma, and are connected to an independent clause, then they are serving as introductory adverbs.

EXAMPLE

▶ No, you may not have a third s'more!

The word "no" is an adverb (even though it does not end in "ly").

Other types of adverbs are the ones you might ordinarily call transitions. Words such as **thus**, **therefore**, **hence**, etc. fall under this category.

EXAMPLE

▶ Thus, knowing basic directions is important in case your GPS stops working.

"Thus" is an adverb that serves as a transition at the beginning of the sentence.

Begin with an Interjection

An interjection is a separate part of speech that expresses feeling. It is often the first word of a sentence, and when it is combined with other words to form a sentence, it is set apart with a comma.

> Oh, you finally made it!
>
> *"Oh" is an interjection that appears at the beginning of a sentence.*

The previous section of the chapter was meant to help you learn how to captivate a reader further by composing a variety of sentence types, sentence structures, and sentence beginners. I would also like to point out that the length of sentences matters as well. The best writers alternate between short and long sentences. These should all be considerations when your goal is to be a better writer.

EXERCISE 8-3: Identify the Type of Sentence Starter

DIRECTIONS: *Below, you will find a bank of the most popular types of sentence starters.*

- *As you read each sentence, determine the **type** of sentence starter being used.*
- *Write the letter of the type of sentence starter on the line provided.*

Sentence Variety	
A: Simple Subject	**E:** Infinitive Phrase
B: Prepositional Phrase	**F:** Inverted Appositive
C: Participle or Participial Phrase	**G:** Adverb
D: Subordinate Clause	**H:** Interjection

_____ 1. Thankfully, residents of the island were unharmed by the hurricane.

_____ 2. To succeed in life, one must set goals and work hard to achieve them.

_____ 3. Vivek visited his former teachers often.

_____ 4. On the precipice of the mountain, Mackenzie took a selfie.

_____ 5. No, you may not leave the dinner table.

_____ 6. Wow, you look fabulous!

_____ 7. Daunted by the amount of schooling necessary to be a medical doctor, Claire opted for a podiatric program instead.

_____ 8. A judge on *The Voice* for several years, Blake Shelton is respected highly by viewers.

_____ 9. If you are asked to identify the best writer of all time, Shakespeare is considered the most gifted.

_____ 10. Serving twelve tables at once, Olivia ran around the restaurant like a chicken without a head.

Topic 4: Varied Word Choice: Synonyms, Imagery, and Figurative Language

What are some other ways you can make your writing more interesting? Sure, varying sentence structure is a great start, but you must consider your word choice carefully if you want to elevate your writing. There are a number of ways to engage a reader through word choice. This section will focus on some practical ways to make your writing sound more interesting and unique.

Synonyms

Try to focus on reducing the repetition of words. If you are not certain whether you repeated a word in a writing piece, do you know how to check? I am sure you are familiar with function keys (*control* or *command* keys, depending on your device). Once you are finished with a typed writing piece, try to search for a word you think you have used often. While typing this chapter, I press *Control + F* and type a word in the blank space. Voila! The program does the work for me by identifying that word throughout the document. At that point, it is my job to find a substitute word or expression.

One way to vary word choice is to search for synonyms for the word at hand. Be careful, though. Sometimes, online dictionaries provide synonyms that are not so close in meaning to your intended thought. Narrowing it down to searching for a particular word according to its part of speech can help you identify the viable substitutions.

Searching for a word's synonym can also provide you with an opportunity to select a more sophisticated word than its original counterpart. You will probably even learn a few new words along the way, and who doesn't want to broaden their vocabulary?

EXAMPLE

▶ Example: The dog ran down the hill.

▶ Substitute: The dog scampered down the hill.

"Scamper" is close in meaning to "run" (in the sentence provided).

▶ Not a good substitute: The dog extended down the hill.

Although "extend" can be a synonym for one type of "run," it does not match the meaning of what the dog is doing (in the sample sentence).

Imagery

Think about the first time you visited a place. What do you remember about it? Most likely, your senses were heightened, and those details were etched in your memory. Perhaps it was the aroma of fresh bread at a bakery, the varied colors of blue in the ocean water, or the music that was playing when you entered an amusement park. In any case, *details related to the five senses (touch, smell, sight, sound, and taste)* are important to include in any descriptive piece. We call these sensory details **imagery.** Imagery helps to provoke the reader's imagination, and it leaves a lasting impact on their reading experience.

Imagery is not only for fictional genres such as poetry or short stories. It is helpful to include it in all types of writing, from personal narratives to inspirational speeches, from memoirs to science labs, from research papers to newspaper articles.

Our senses add so much to our lives. Don't we want to provide that experience for our readers? How dull the world would be without such description. My advice to you is to start small. You do not want to overdo it with the imagery. That is called sensory overload. Instead, try to include sensory imagery from time to time to draw in the reader without distracting them from the storyline.

▶ Basic sentence: Beachgoers heard the birds chirping as the sun set over the water.

▶ Sentence with sensory details: Seagulls serenaded the beachgoers while the burnt orange hue of the setting sun marked a gleaming contrast with the icy blue water below it.

Adding words such as "serenaded," "burnt," "orange," "gleaming," "icy," and "blue" provide not only visual details but those of sound (serenaded=sound) and of touch (icy=touch).

Figurative Language

What is meant by the term figurative language? Just like imagery, figurative language appeals to the senses. So, you are probably wondering how figurative language differs from sensory details. The difference is that *imagery* describes something literal in a more descriptive way, but **figurative language** is *composed of words or sounds that are different in meaning from their literal interpretation.*

By now, I am sure your teachers have discussed figurative language with you, and you have probably been asked to identify figurative language in your assigned readings. Perhaps you had to incorporate figurative language into a poem. Poetry is the perfect place for figurative language practice, since most poems utilize several of these *poetic devices* (another term for figurative language) in each stanza.

However, it is also essential to incorporate figurative language into other genres. First, let us review the most popular types of figurative language. Rather than simply memorizing the definitions of these terms, it is often easier to understand the concept of figurative language by examining examples of them, so I included examples below each term.

A **simile** is a comparison of two unlike things using the words like/as.

> Your love is like a burst of fresh air.
>
> *This is a simile because the word "like" is used to compare two otherwise unrelated things: love and air.*

A **metaphor** is a comparison of two unlike things (without the use of like/as) or an unrealistic description.

> Your smile is sunshine in my life.
>
> *This is a metaphor because "smile" and "sunshine" (two unrelated things) are being compared without the use of the words "like" or "as."*

Personification is the granting of human qualities to an object, animal, or idea.

> The breeze whispered its lullaby.
>
> *Since the breeze is inanimate but is given a human ability in this sentence (whispering), this sentence is an example of personification.*

Onomatopoeia is the use of words to imitate sounds.

> The basketball swished through the hoop.
>
> *The word "swish" is an example of onomatopoeia because that word emulates the sound of a basketball going through the hoop.*

An **idiom** a common expression that is not translatable literally.

Talk is cheap.

We call this sentence an idiom because it is an expression in English that is not translatable into other languages. It insinuates that words are not enough to prove a point and that actions are essential.

Hyperbole is an idea that is extremely exaggerated to produce an instant picture for the reader.

I'm dying of thirst.

This is a common exaggeration called a hyperbole. Most likely, the person is not dying at all but is just very thirsty.

An **oxymoron** is when contradictory words are used together.

A deafening silence filled the control tower.

This sentence is an example of an oxymoron since the word "deafening" implies that something is very loud, yet it is describing the silence (no noise) in the control tower.

Symbolism is when a word or words is used to represent a different person, place, thing, or idea.

> An author includes an owl in a scene where someone is exhibiting wisdom or offering sage advice.
>
> *This is an example of symbolism, since the owl represents wisdom.*

A **synecdoche** is when one part of something is used to describe the whole, many, or more of something.

> The dinner costs fifty dollars a plate.
>
> *The word "plate" refers to the cost of one person's meal at an event or restaurant, which will probably be served on several plates throughout the event.*

Topic 5: Additional Writing Techniques

There are other types of writing that are often classified as **figurative language** but have different purposes. Since they are not related to literal meaning versus figurative meaning, I chose to include them in a separate section. Some of these elements add to the meaning of a piece of writing. Others add to the rhythm or rhyme of a writing piece.

Let's begin with those that add to the meaning of a writing piece:

Irony is an *unexpected turn of events*. Many students think that irony is only used in works of fiction, but this is not the case. I am certain that there have been many events in your own life, in scientific studies, and even in history that have taken an unexpected turn. Why not design your writing to save that unexpected twist for later instead of providing a "spoiler" up front?

Have you ever read the famous poem "Casey at the Bat"? Casey was the star of his baseball team, and it was the ninth inning with bases loaded and two outs when he was at the plate. I am sure you can infer what happened, since this poem has one of the most famous examples of irony:

EXAMPLE

> Oh, somewhere in this favored land the sun is shining bright,
> The band is playing somewhere, and somewhere hearts are light;
> And somewhere men are laughing, and somewhere children shout,
> But there is no joy in Mudville—mighty Casey has struck out.
>
> *This is an example of irony because everyone in Mudville expected Casey to win the game, but he struck out instead.*

Allusion is *a reference to an unrelated famous person, place, thing, or event* that would be recognized by the reader or the audience.

EXAMPLE

> George and Martha Washington were the Adam and Eve of the New World.
>
> *This is an example of allusion. Readers are expected to know about Adam and Eve, so a reference is made to them when comparing them to George and Martha Washington, even though these pairs did not live in the same time period.*

Allegory is a term used to describe when a story, character, place, or piece of art is *named to represent something deeper, hidden, or symbolic.*

> Hope asked her campers to persevere as they descended the treacherous cliff.
>
> *This is an example of allegory, since a character named Hope has optimistic qualities.*

A **pun** or a **play on words** requires readers to recognize *two meanings of an identical word or phrase.* A **pun** is a word that is meant to be funny for its dual meaning. A **play on words** can be either funny or can provide a deeper meaning.

> Mike's girlfriend wanted a ring, so he bought her a bell.
>
> *Since the word "ring" has two meanings, this sentence includes a pun. Everybody (including Mike's girlfriend) anticipates that the type of ring he bought her was a piece of jewelry. It is a funny twist that he bought her a bell (that makes a ringing noise) instead.*
>
> The giant told his average-height girlfriend: "I'm crushing on you."
>
> *This is an example of a play on words. The word "crush" has two meanings. It can mean to compress strongly (which a large giant can do to a smaller person), or it can mean to like someone in a romantic way.*

Remember your favorite storybooks from your childhood? Besides relishing in the consistency of a rhyme scheme, you loved those books so much because of the way they sounded when an adult read them to you. In addition to onomatopoeia, there are several more literary devices employed by a writer to enhance the sound of a written piece. Authors, especially poets, take great care in selecting words that provide a certain cadence or rhythm, especially when their piece is meant to be read aloud.

Alliteration is the *repetition of consonant sounds at the beginnings of words*. Alliteration is used to add to the rhythm of a line of poetry or a sentence.

Alliteration is *not as easy* as it appears. There are several rules involved to test whether alliteration is being employed correctly.

- Most people think that alliteration must appear several times in one line of writing for that line to be considered alliterative.

- Others think that alliterative words must begin with the same letter.

- Still, others think that words that begin with the same vowels are also alliterative.

Guess what? Not one of these is true.

- An example of **alliteration** may have either *two words in a row* (consecutive) or three words on the same line.

- Just because words in a line of poetry begin with the same letter, it does not mean there is automatic alliteration. The words have to make the same initial consonant sound. For example, the word "shake" and the word "stiff" both begin with an "s," but one makes the "sh" sound, and the other makes the "st" sound. Therefore, they are not alliterative.

- Similarly, words that begin with different letters may be alliterative, as long as they begin with the same consonant sound. For example, the word "cookie" begins with the same consonant sound as the word "kite" even though they begin with different letters.

EXAMPLE

▶ Busy bees surrounded the hive.

This is considered alliteration even though there are only two "b" words; this is because "busy" and "bees" are two alliterative words in a row.

▶ Physical fitness is essential.

This is considered alliteration because the word "fitness" and the word "physical" begin with the same "f" sound, and they are two alliterative words in a row.

Do you know how many times I find errors regarding alliteration? From questions on popular game shows to online grammar-quiz platforms to noteworthy grammar websites, there are two common errors made with respect to alliteration:

Incorrect: Annie acts as if she is innocent in the matter.

There is no alliteration in this sentence, since there are no words that begin with the same consonant sound. Repeatedly, I have seen people (including one of my daughter's ELA teachers) identify words that begin with vowels as "alliterative." This is not accurate!

(Side note: My daughter said I was "soooo embarrassing" and that I could not, under any circumstances, write a note to her teacher informing her of her grammatical errors.)

Incorrect: The temple is in the center of town.

There is no alliteration in this sentence. Even though several words begin with "t," they do not all make the same consonant sound. Some make the "t" sound while others make the "th" sound. Even though "temple" and "town" make the same sound, they are not directly next to each other, and there is no third word with a "t" sound to complete the alliteration for that sentence.

So, be on the lookout for faulty websites and texts that are riddled with misinformation about alliteration!

Assonance is the *repetition of vowel sounds within a line or a sentence*. It may also be called **internal rhyme**, since it is not related to rhyming the ends of lines (as in certain poems). We apply the same rules for assonance that we do for alliteration.

For a line to have assonance, words need to make the same vowel sound (but that sound does not have to be at the beginning of the word). To be considered assonance, there either needs to be two words in a row or three on the line. However, we can consider it assonance even if only one syllable of a word rhymes (in vowel sound) with other words on the line. Finally, just like in alliteration, various letters can make the same vowel sound, so don't look at the letters; listen to the sounds they make.

Don't be fooled, though. Just because words contain the same vowels, they do not necessarily make the same vowel sounds. Look at the first sentence in this paragraph. The words "don't" and "fooled" both contain the vowel "o," yet they make very different sounds.

> ▶ Sh**e** sk**ie**d swiftl**y** down the mountain.
>
> *This sentence contains assonance. The "e" in "she" makes the same sound as the "y" in "swiftly" and the "ie" in skied. Even though the "ow" in "down" and the "ou" in "mountain" make the same vowel sound, there are only two words in this sentence that make that particular vowel sound, and the two words are not directly next to each other, so we do not consider it assonance.*

Repetition is the purposeful use of the same word or phrase to add emphasis or grab a reader's attention. I know. I know. I spent an entire section of this chapter telling you to vary your word choice and to avoid using the same words.

It wouldn't be English without an exception, though. The intentional repetition of words can be an effective device if it is employed to emphasize a point or engage the reader. Those repeated words or phrases are most often used in proximity to each other for added effect. However, we do not usually consider repeated ending words of a line of poetry to count as the element of repetition. The repeated words need to appear either at the beginning or somewhere in the middle of the line of poetry for them to be considered a poetic element used for emphasis.

Did you notice the repetition I used two paragraphs up from here? I utilized "I know. I know." as a humorous way of letting you know that I recognized that what I was saying seemed contradictory. Those two sentences together created a cue for you, the reader, to anticipate that I was going to present a contradiction to you.

> ▶ Fair is foul and foul is fair.
>
> *This is a famous line from* Macbeth *in which repetition is the same words are utilized both as a form of repetition and as foreshadowing that things will not always be what they appear to be.*

EXERCISE 8-4: Identify the Literary Element

DIRECTIONS: Read each of the sentences below.

- *Choose a term from the word bank to identify each sentence's literary element.*
- *Write it on the line provided.*

Simile	Metaphor	Personification	Idiom
Allusion	Oxymoron	Pun/Play on words	Allegory
Irony	Assonance	Alliteration	Repetition
Symbolism	Hyperbole	Onomatopoeia	Synecdoche

_____ 1. Let's have some jumbo shrimp for dinner tonight.

_____ 2. Pharrell wore a fox coat to the fashion show.

_____ 3. Braveheart was a courageous advocate for Scottish independence.

_____ 4. It's supposed to rain cats and dogs tonight!

_____ 5. When I asked Rebecca if she would split the money, she tore the dollar in half.

_____ 6. Stop looking at me with that devious Joker smirk!

_____ 7. Never, never, never did I say that!

_____ 8. As quickly as a cheetah, Malachi finished the final lap of the race.

_____ 9. I am so hungry that I could eat a cow!

_____ 10. At the picnic, the fly buzzed near my ear.

EXERCISE 8-5: Writing Practice with Sentence Variety

DIRECTIONS: Use the prompt below to write an original short story that showcases your knowledge of sentence structure and sophisticated word choice.

- *Attempt to use a combination of simple, compound, and complex sentences. Vary your sentence length, sentence beginnings, and word choices. Avoid repetition. Attempt to include sophisticated vocabulary, sensory details, and figurative language.*

PROMPT: Pretend that, for just one day, you were given a superpower. Describe that day's events.

_____

_____

_____

_____

_____

_____

_____

_____

_____

_____

_____

_____

_____

_____

Flashcard App

The Writing Process

hy are students often intimidated by writing essays or research papers? As you know, essays and research papers are common tasks in college. However, the concept of developing one's writing into extensive pieces often seems like a daunting task to high schoolers.

In my opinion, this skittishness is rooted in two factors. One is the lack of adequate exposure to having read nonfiction writing pieces. From the time you were little, wouldn't you agree that your parents and teachers gravitated toward fiction and literature? For years, adults read fictional story books to you, and you, in turn, chose fiction books to read over nonfiction books. Over the years, you learned many important lessons from these stories, identified with characters, and grasped techniques of fiction writers—all very fulfilling ventures. As a result, when it comes to writing fiction such as short stories or even poetry, most secondary students understand the employment of figurative language and poetic elements, thus, finding it easier to emulate these devices in their own writing.

This is not to say that teachers have not provided you with opportunities to read nonfiction. You simply have not had to read nonfiction as often as fiction. Furthermore, most nonfiction read by youngsters includes biographies, autobiographies, or memoirs. In a sense, these are also stories, and they include conflicts and themes found in fiction books. Often, it is not until the secondary level that many students read published essays and articles more regularly. When we practice reading these genres, we develop a better understanding of what it takes to compose them ourselves.

The second reason why students shy away from extended writing pieces is due to lack of practice. You can probably count on one or two hands the number of essays you have completed since you began high school. Most times, these extended responses are assigned in the English or social studies classrooms, though, if you take college-level courses, you may be writing them for other disciplines as well. Contrast the number of essays you have written with the number of tests or quizzes you have taken while in school. There is no comparison. Therefore, your lack of experience in completing this task may make you feel inadequate.

Right about now, questions are probably swirling around in your head. Where do I begin? How will I be able to come up with that much to write about?

That is why I am here. We will be covering the steps of the writing process in this chapter, but the most important step is the first step: motivation. Think about essay writing as a new hobby. You are excited about it and want to do well. You may be rusty at first, but if you take the time to practice often, your performance will improve tremendously. Convince yourself that you can do this! I, for one, am confident that you can write a fabulous extended response if you have the drive to succeed and if you utilize the methods delineated in this chapter.

Initially, you will be given an essay question. As you navigate each topic that follows, there will be exercises for you to implement in several target areas, so that, in the end, you will come out with a complete essay. Each student's essay, naturally, will have a different outcome, so there will not be a sample essay at the end of this chapter.

Topic 1: Gathering Information

Once you are assigned an essay or research paper, your teacher will provide guidelines for you. Besides informing you of the topic and of the type of composition you will be expected to produce, teachers often give you a paragraph range or a page range (for example, two body paragraphs or three-five typed pages, double-spaced). Pay close attention to these requirements, as they will impact the amount of resources you will need to compile before getting started.

Imagine you decide to bake a cake. It is easier to have all the ingredients before beginning the baking process. It would be so inconvenient if you began mixing the ingredients only to discover that you forgot to buy one. Think about writing in the same way.

It is important to plan for this writing piece. You cannot simply sit down and begin to write, hoping that you have everything you need to meet the page/information requirement. Writing requires some preliminary steps, and the first one is to *gather your information.*

Naturally, the type of essay or paper you are writing will require different materials. Is it an essay based on an assigned reading? Must it include published sources? Does it involve your opinion or the opinions of experts? All these play into the development of your writing piece.

Fortunately, with the accessibility of the internet, you will have most *resources* at your fingertips, but it is important to *locate them before you write* rather than *as* you write. You want to *manage your time efficiently*, right?

Begin by creating a blank document called **sources**. Onto this doc, paste *links to any reference material* you will be using in your essay or research paper. To take it a step further, *organize these links* according to the section of the essay where you will include them. I know it might seem like this is an extra step that might be more time-consuming, but I promise you that this is a time-saver. You will leave this tab open while you write, and it will help you avoid something many writers face: writer's block. You will never be at a loss for what to write next. Furthermore, if you organize your source links according to topic, it will be glaringly obvious if you are deficient of information in a particular area. It is better to know this *before* you begin than to find out the hard way when the due date is near.

Remember, the best way to learn something is to practice.

Since this chapter is all about learning the necessary steps of essay composition, you will be applying these steps as you progress through the chapter.

Here is the essay question you will be answering. Note the requirements specified below the prompt:

PROMPT: Many high school students begin to consider possible career paths. After choosing one career path that interests you, write a three-to-four-page essay that covers the following information:

- The name of the career and why it appeals to you

- The education/training required to achieve this career

- The skills needed to be successful at this career

- The names of famous or well-respected people who hold this career and an explanation of why/how they have been successful at it

- The steps you will take to achieve this goal

REQUIREMENTS: Use *at least four different sources* in your essay. Be sure to use parenthetical citation according to the APA style guide.

It is never too soon to think about the future. Hence, it is no accident that I decided to give you this writing prompt, knowing that you will need to make some important decisions in the upcoming months and years. But let's not get ahead of ourselves.

First, you will need to make a choice of career. For some of you, this will be the most difficult part of the assignment. Do not worry. This choice is not a lifelong commitment. Although it would be nice for every junior or senior to have a definitive decision of a career, it is certainly not the norm. Consider this activity one that helps you explore one career in which you might have interest—no signed contract required.

EXERCISE 9-1: Gathering Information

You have a choice. You may either write down some of the information you gathered on the next two blank pages, or, if you prefer, you may create a blank document on your computer, so you can paste links there as well.

As you are **gathering information from the internet and/or from other reliable sources** *(people, books, etc.), remember to consider education required, skills necessary, accomplished people in that career, and steps necessary to reach that career goal. Try not to forget any of these "ingredients."*

Here is some space for the information you gathered. Remember to cite at least **four** *different sources.*

Information Gathered

_____

_____

_____

_____

_____

_____

_____

_____

_____

_____

_____

_____

_____

_____

_____

_____

_____

_____

_____

_____

_____

_____

Topic 2: Graphic Organizers

Would you be able to identify for me a **Venn diagram, a web,** or **a T-Chart**? Many of you may be familiar with these **graphic organizers** and others, as they are an integral part of the writing process in elementary and middle-level classrooms. Some graphic organizers are specific to a certain type of question, so graphic organizers cannot always be used interchangeably.

For example, a **Venn diagram** is used to *depict similarities and differences,* so it would be perfect to use for a *Compare-Contrast* activity but not applicable to the type of essay you are writing in this chapter.

Since many of you are visual learners, it may benefit you to utilize one or more of these diagrams to organize your ideas in a tangible way.

Most students think a particular graphic organizer must be used to organize an entire writing piece, but I want you to consider a different approach.

Sometimes, a particular diagram is helpful in organizing a *portion* or element of your writing piece.

A **KWL chart** (know, want to know, learned) might be good when you are beginning to delve into a topic that is somewhat new.

Cause-and-effect charts usually have two columns with an arrow from the set on the left to the set on the right.

Ladder charts show a progression from beginning to end.

Timelines may not seem like graphic organizers, but they are certainly a visual way to observe sequential items chronologically.

EXERCISE 9-2: Completing a Web Based on Skills Necessary to Be Successful in Your Career

*Let's try a graphic organizer that aligns well to one portion of your essay. Consider the task of listing all the skills needed to be good at your chosen career. Now, complete the **web** below by writing the name of the career in the center and filling in the extensions with various skills. This exercise will also prompt you to come up with several skills, not just one or two.*

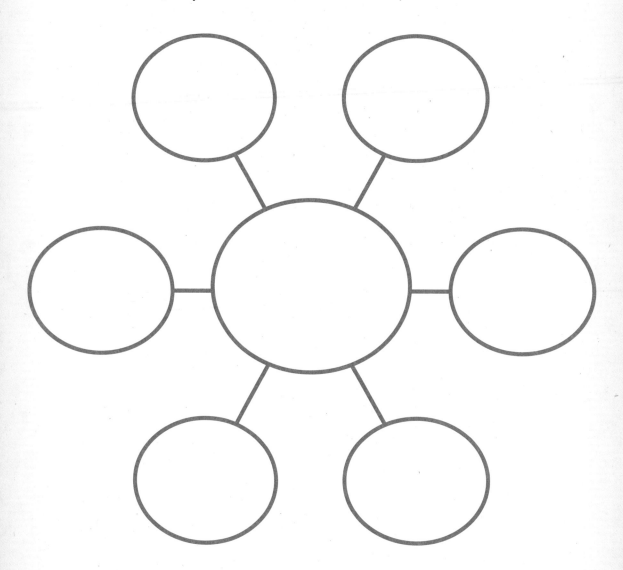

Did you leave any blanks? Are any of your answers repetitive? A web helps a writer develop an initial sense of whether they have enough varied details.

I hope this helped you process the variety and number of skills necessary to achieve your goal. Believe it or not, as you complete these activities, you are beginning to compose your essay mentally. Your mind begins to formulate ways to explain each of these concepts. This experience will help you develop details surrounding the information you wrote on the graphic organizer.

So far, you completed a graphic organizer based on one portion of your essay, which is a great start. What if you wanted to use a graphic organizer to plan the entire essay? The *T-Chart* works best for most types of essays.

Your **T-Chart** will vary based on the number of tasks required in your essay. It can be skeletal or detailed, depending upon how much time you want to spend completing it. I usually tell my students that a T-Chart is meant to help you organize and brainstorm. It should not contain complete sentences but, instead, a bulleted list of concepts. After all, you need to save your energy for the essay, don't you?

EXERCISE 9-3: T-Chart Based on Career Essay Tasks

On the next page are the bulleted tasks from the essay question. In the blank box of each row, list some items you will include in those sections. Although the first bullet (naming the career choice and why it appeals to you) will be part of your introduction, the other bullets will cover the information in your body paragraphs and will require more bulleted information.

	Task	Information
I N T R O	My Career Choice and Why It Appeals to Me	
B O D Y P A R A G R A P H S	Education/ Training Required	
	Skills Needed for This Job	
	Famous/Respected People in This Profession	
	Steps I Will Take to Reach This Goal	

Graphic organizers are very helpful for most learners, but there are other options available for planning your writing. The next section will delve into the most popular form of planning, both for writing and for presentations: the Harvard outline.

Topic 3: Outlines

Though there are many versions of essay outlines, none is more reputed than the **Harvard outline**. The purpose of the Harvard outline is to provide *headings for main topics* or paragraphs. Below each of these headings are *subheadings* and, sometimes, subheadings for those.

Overall, Harvard outlines or any outlines, for that matter, *help writers organize their thoughts into paragraphs*. Think of the headings as the **topic sentences** and the subheadings as the **supportive details**.

To create a Harvard outline, there are a few rules:

- Never write full sentences.

- Never type a 1 if there is not a 2. Never type an A if there is no B.

- Begin with Roman numerals, then capital letters, then Arabic numerals (what we consider *regular* numbers), then lowercase letters, then lowercase Roman numerals, then double lowercase letters. In other words, you will be alternating between numbers and letters (but each number/letter subheading will have a different form).

- Align spacing of like letters or numbers. When typing, use automatic list formatting or the tab key to establish this spacing.

- It is not necessary to have subheadings, but it is common to have them.

While some writers prefer to organize their writing by using graphic organizers, others prefer the more formal style of the Harvard outline. It is usually a matter of taste, though, occasionally, teachers or professors may require a Harvard outline to be submitted for approval before you begin the writing process. This is why it is important to know how to produce either one.

Sample Harvard Outline

How to Bake a Cake

I. Reason for baking a cake
  A. Friend's Birthday
  B. Homemade cake = shows effort
  C. Thesis – baking a cake = more thoughtful and can be easy by following recipe
II. Ingredients for cake/frosting
  A. Find recipe
  B. Check cabinets
  C. Shopping list
  D. Buy what I still need + candles!
III. Preparing batter
  A. Preheat oven
  B. Grease pan
  C. Wash hands
  D. Combine ingredients
    1. Liquids in one bowl
    2. Dry ingredients in second bowl
    3. Combine
    4. Pour into cake pan
IV. Baking the cake
  A. Center rack of oven
  B. Keep door closed
  C. Set timer – 40 minutes
  D. Toothpick test
    1. Toothpick in center of cake
    2. Comes out clean – cake is done
    3. If not, try again – new toothpick every 5 min. until clean
V. Making frosting while cake bakes
  A. Combine conf. sugar w/ water
  B. Food coloring
VI. Cooling the cake
  A. Oven off
  B. Remove cake (mitts)
  C. Cool on rack—20 minutes
VII. Decorating the cake
  A. Frost cake
  B. Write "Happy Birthday"
  C. Sprinkles
  D. Candles

EXERCISE 9-4: Creating a Harvard Outline

In the space below, take the information you included in your T-Chart in Exercise 9-3 and transcribe it onto the Harvard outline below. In this way, you will understand the benefits of the Harvard outline, as it requires further development of chronological details.

- *Remember to include a topic at the top.*
- *Follow the numbering and lettering system as provided in the sample above.*

Harvard Outline

_____

_____

_____

_____

_____

_____

_____

_____

_____

_____

_____

Topic 4: Organization of an Essay

Now that you have your outline completed and before you begin writing your first draft, it is important to review the main parts of each type of paragraph in an essay: the introduction, the body, and the conclusion.

An **introduction** is an important part of the essay. It influences the reader's first impression. Most introductions begin one of three ways: *with a general sentence, with a rhetorical question, or with a famous quote.*

The follow-up sentences in an introductory paragraph, especially one that relies on research, includes book information or author information. A narrative introduction provides more background information without delving deeply into details.

In any case, the most important sentence in any essay is called the **thesis statement**. This sentence is the *last sentence of the introductory paragraph*. The thesis lets the reader know *what the essay is about*. Sometimes, it also clarifies *how the essay will be organized*.

Here is a sample introduction for you to peruse.

▶ "What do you want to be when you grow up?" This question is asked of children frequently, but now that I am approaching adulthood, it is a question that has caused me many sleepless nights. How does one go about making that choice? Most people advised me to follow my passion or to choose something that I am good at doing, but that still did not provide enough clarity for me. Fortunately, what made it easier to make my decision was the fact that I have a role model who works in this field of interest: Mr. O'Toole, my ELA teacher. Because of Mr. O'Toole's positive influence on me and on others, I have made the decision to pursue a career in education.

The essay begins with a quote. The follow-up sentences explain how the writer was floundering for a career. A rhetorical question was also raised. The thesis states the career choice of the writer: education.

Body paragraphs are the paragraphs located in the *middle* of the essay. These will be longer than your introduction and your conclusion. It is in the body paragraphs where you will *provide all the important* **details** *in the essays.* For each of your details, you will incorporate **evidence**, **explanations**, and **analysis**.

The first sentence of a body paragraph is called a **topic sentence**. It is an important sentence, for it mentions *the main points that will be covered in that paragraph.* Although I will not provide an entire body paragraph as an example, here is an example of a topic sentence based on the T-Chart's first body paragraph topic.

EXAMPLE

> Becoming a teacher requires a great deal of education, including a four-year college degree and a master's degree either in education or in a particular field of study.
>
> *Since the first body paragraph is supposed to include the training needed to become a teacher, the topic sentence of this paragraph summarizes the degrees necessary to become an educator.*

The follow-up sentences in the body paragraphs are organized to explain the topic sentence more fully.

Multiple details are included in each body paragraph. If it is a research essay, excerpts from sources must be included. When incorporating a source, it is important to follow these steps:

- Use an **explanatory phrase** *before the excerpt.*

- Place the **direct excerpt** in *quotation marks* (copying it exactly as it appears).

- *Explain the excerpt* you included, delving into *why it is important to cite* in this writing piece.

> ▶ According to May Showwell, the Director of Educational Studies at Pedagogy University, "Taking introductory courses in the areas of classroom management, questioning techniques, and cooperative learning are all helpful in developing a well-rounded course of study for the next season of educators in our communities" (Showell, 2019, p. 19). Showell goes on to emphasize the importance of foundational courses in building both confidence and knowledge in fledgling educators.
>
> *This is the proper way to incorporate an excerpt into a research paper or essay. Notice that there is an explanatory phrase before the excerpt. The direct excerpt is in quotation marks. The citation information is in parentheses. It is followed by a further explanation of the source.*

When you are ready to write the **conclusion**, a transition is a nice way to begin (but never say "In conclusion"—it is too informal). The conclusion is meant *to summarize* what you have said. It is also meant *to draw conclusions* and *state the theme* of the essay.

Topic 5: First Draft

A **first draft** is a luxury that you may not always have. Understandably, some essays will be written in person, on the spot, and in a limited amount of time, especially when they are tests in high school or college.

However, if you have the time to write a first draft of a piece, I recommend it highly. I have heard teachers call first drafts *free writing*. **First draft** and **free writing** are *not* interchangeable terms. **Free writing** insinuates encouragement to write anything on one's mind. Writing a *first draft requires more depth* than that.

There are very few professional writers who write perfectly the first time around. Usually, a writer will create an outline or a bulleted list (at the least) and proceed to compose a first draft. A primary draft is a way for the author to *organize thoughts in the form of sentences*, bearing in mind that there will be an opportunity to revise and perfect a piece.

Let's assume, for the remainder of this section of the chapter, that you can spend some quality time on your essay or paper. Follow *these four steps* to remain focused on the task at hand:

- Use the materials you gathered. A first draft does not mean that you cannot use reference materials. Those will provide a springboard for your ideas.

- Do not set too many restrictions on yourself when writing a first draft. Although it is more focused than *free writing*, to avoid writer's block, remind yourself that, later, there will be time to edit.

- Consider your purpose in writing the piece. Are you trying to persuade, entertain, inform, describe, or instruct? Bear in mind your focus before beginning the first draft.

- Consider your audience. If I were writing this book for middle schoolers, the language and examples would be tailored for preteens. In the same way, you need to consider the interest level and intellectual level of your readers. Is this a piece for which you are being graded or judged? That should influence your tone and word choice as well.

EXERCISE 9-5: Writing a First Draft

DIRECTIONS: Imagine that your prospective college asked you to send your career-choice essay to them as a writing sample. In the space below, complete the following steps:

- *Write a first draft of your career-choice essay.*

- *Use the information in your T-Chart from Exercise 9-3 to organize your ideas into paragraphs (the first row will provide the information for the introduction or first paragraph, the second row will provide the information for the first body paragraph, etc.).*

- *Refer to the web you completed in Exercise 9-2 to help you with the skills paragraph.*

- *Even though you do not have a draft of the conclusion, jot down an overview of the lesson that came through in this essay. Don't mention the word "lesson."*

If you prefer to type the first draft, feel free. If you prefer to handwrite it, I am providing some blank pages for you.

First Draft

_____

_____

_____

_____

_____

_____

_____

_____

Topic 6: Editing

How does it feel to be finished with your first draft? I hope you feel accomplished.

When I ask my students if they know *the difference between editing and proofreading*, they often think these terms mean the same thing. Both terms fall under the umbrella of *revising*, but they are revisions for a different purpose.

Editing refers to the *revision of content* in your writing and in the *organization* of your writing.

The reason I recommended that you use paragraphing in your first draft is that it often informs the writer of gaps in particular places. For example, if you notice that you have hardly any information in your skills paragraph, now would be the time to gather some more information.

Once the first draft is written, good writers revisit their writing to add details and sources. They also tend to move things around to make the piece more cohesive, especially in cases where details should be chronological. This is all part of the writing process.

Here are some useful questions to ask yourself once your first draft is complete and you are ready to edit for content and organization:

Editing Checklist
• Does my writing seem focused?
• Will the reader understand my purpose in writing the piece?
• Have I left out any necessary information?
• Have I explained my details?
• Should I be more specific?
• Have I included irrelevant information?
• Have I repeated myself?
• Are my details chronological/arranged in the proper order?
• Is my level of sophistication apparent?
• Will my essay appeal to the intended readers?

Another step in the editing process is to add **transitional words and phrases**. Between details, sophisticated writers include certain words and phrases to help the details sound less like a list. Transitions *help the essay flow* better.

Below you will find a list of transitions that can help you in making your essays sound seamless and more formal.

Warning: Overuse of transitions can be distracting. Use them moderately.

Transitional Words and Phrases	
Sequencing transitions • First, • Next, • Then, • Finally, • Furthermore, • In addition,	**Contrasting transitions** (Never use "*differently*" or "*whereas*" at the beginning of a sentence!) • In contrast, • On the other hand, • Unlike • Conversely,
Supportive detail transitions • For example, • One example of this • This is/was evident when • Evidence of this can be found when • As is/was evident in	**Concluding transitions** (Never begin the sentence with "In conclusion.") • Clearly, • Hence, • Therefore, • Thus, • It is clear that • It is obvious that (but NOT *obviously*) • It is evident that (but NOT *evidently*)
Comparative transitions (Never use "as well as" at the beginning of a sentence!) • Similarly, • Just as • In the same way, • Comparatively, • Also, • Likewise,	

EXERCISE 9-6: Editing a First Draft

Now that you know the steps in the editing process, rewrite your first draft. Remember to follow these steps:

- *Consider the answers to the questions of your Editing Checklist.*
- *Add more relevant details.*
- *Develop your analysis.*
- *Make clear connections by inserting appropriate transitional words and phrases.*
- *Make any necessary changes in sentence or paragraph organization.*

If you prefer to type the edited draft, feel free. If you prefer to handwrite it, I am providing some blank pages for you.

Editing a First Draft

_____

_____

_____

_____

_____

_____

_____

_____

_____

_____

_____

IRL Nowadays, students turn to online sources to assist them with many aspects of their education. Often, they ask questions in chat rooms, expecting the responses of experts.

WARNING: Many people in chat rooms are amateurs whose advice or feedback could, in fact, provide you with misinformation.

Rather than online chat rooms, there are two ways I like to get feedback regarding my writing:

- Have someone you trust read the first draft. Ask them for constructive feedback, and consider that feedback when adjusting your writing piece.

- Record yourself reading the essay (as if it were a speech). Without having the essay in front of you to read, simply listen to the recording. Jot down any questions you might have for *the speaker* (i.e., you), as if that person were presenting a speech to you and you were a journalist asking them questions afterward. This skill will help you understand what you may have left out of the essay.

Topic 7: Proofreading

Remember when I explained that editing and proofreading were different methods of revision? When most students think they are proofreading, they, instead, are simply rereading, expecting mistakes to jump out at them.

Proofreading involves checking the *grammar, mechanics, word choice, and sentence structure*. Proofreading is so much *more than just rereading*.

Standard **Proofreaders' Marks** have been around for years. Perhaps your teachers or professors use them. If your current teachers do not use them, you will probably come across a teacher or professor who utilizes a series of codes and abbreviations to correct your grammar. It is helpful for you to learn them.

These are the same abbreviations and codes that are used in the publishing world. Once you commit them to memory, you will know the secret to breaking the code. (I tried to make it sound more exciting. It did not work, did it?)

In any case, here is a list of the most common Proofreaders' Marks:

Common Proofreaders' Marks			
vt	shift in verb tense	<u>a</u>≡	three lines beneath a lowercase letter means it should be capitalized
ww	wrong word		
sp	spelling	/	slash through a letter means it should be lowercase
hom	homonym		
s/v	subject/verb agreement	a/lot	slash between letters means the word should be split into two words
s/pl	singular/plural agreement		
RO	run-on	^	a letter/word/punctuation mark should be inserted
FRAG	fragment		
		♂	this letter/punctuation mark doesn't belong there
awk	awkward word choice/ placement	X	omit this word/letter
rep	repetition	∼	the words should be switched
¶	begin a new paragraph	⌣	the words should be connected
		ab	abbreviation

The best way to utilize the Proofreading Checklist is to check for *one skill at a time*. I know that sounds tedious and, admittedly, it takes a long time, but it is *so much more effective* than just rereading.

EXERCISE 9-7: Utilizing Proofreaders' Marks

DIRECTIONS: Use the Proofreaders' Marks to correct errors in your first draft, one skill at a time! Read the entire piece for verb tense shifts; then, read it for wrong words, then, for spelling, etc. Believe me, if you are isolating each skill, it will be easier for you to discover a mistake in that skill. If you are proofreading a handwritten draft, try to use a different color than the color you used for editing, so it stands out to you.

BTW

Beware! I know many of you have built-in proofreading programs that underline or highlight grammatical errors for you.

These programs are not foolproof!

As a matter of fact, to prove this, I gave my students the task of typing a piece in which they broke grammatical rules such as writing sentences with the comma splice and typing numbers below eleven in numerals.

*You guessed it! None of these errors were identified by their **very popular** proofreading programs. There is nothing that replaces your knowledge!*

*Now that you know the rules, **you** need to be the ultimate proofreader. All you need is one stickler to notice that you made grammatical errors on a piece that should have been error-free. You do not want to take that risk.*

EXERCISE 9-8: Writing the Final Essay

DIRECTIONS: Now that you have applied all the editing and proofreading skills to your first draft, it is time to write the final copy of your "Career Choice" essay.

- *Before completing the final copy, utilize the prescribed editing and proofreading skills.*

- *Of course, even though we are calling it "final," you can always revisit it for minor adjustments.*

Below is the space to handwrite your Final Essay. If you prefer to type it, then do so.

Final Essay

_____

_____

_____

_____

_____

_____

_____

_____

_____

_____

_____

_____

_____

_____

_____

_____

_____

_____

_____

_____

_____

_____

_____

_____

_____

I hope this topic of choosing a prospective career was helpful to you, as I know many of you will be writing college application essays soon (if you have not done so already). As this essay was your final activity in the book, I want to tell you that I admire you for putting forth so much effort to make yourself a better writer.

Continue to do your personal best, and be proud of everything you have achieved!

Answer Key

1
Capitalization

EXERCISE 1-1: Capitalization Rules 1–3

1. I can't tell you why i am not going on our spring field trip out west to disney world in anaheim, california.

   The word "I" requires a capital letter, as do proper nouns such as Disney World and Anaheim, California.

2. The newly elected President, abdullah shahid, addressed the united nations congregants in new york city.

   Specific people and places are capitalized. The word "president" should be lowercase, since it does not precede a name.

3. do you know how quickly mars and venus rotate around the Sun?

   Since "do" is the first word of the sentence, it must be capitalized. Planets need to be capitalized. The sun should not be capitalized.

4. The Dublin merchant was a ship that transported Irish emigrants from the city of cobh to Ellis island via the Atlantic ocean.

   Since Dublin Merchant is the name of the ship, the word "merchant" must be capitalized. Cobh is a city and must be capitalized. Since Ellis Island and Atlantic Ocean are the names of specific places, they must be capitalized.

5. Does jivan celebrate hanukkah, kwanzaa, or Christmas?

   Jivan must be capitalized because it is a person's name. Hanukkah and Kwanzaa are holidays, so they must be capitalized.

6. calendars were developed in the bronze age by sumerians in Mesopotamia.

    "Calendars" is the first word of the sentence, so it needs to be capitalized. Since Bronze Age is a particular time period, and Sumerians are a specific group of people, they must be capitalized as well.

7. Do you prefer Band-aid bandages or Curad Bandages?

    Since Band-Aid is the name of a brand, both words must be capitalized. However, "bandages" should be lowercase, since the word "bandages" is not part of the brand name.

8. Early settlers in north America traveled West to explore the frontier.

    Since North America is the name of a continent, the word "North" must be capitalized. However, general directions such as "west" are not capitalized.

9. The guest speaker shook the hand of principal Tomkins upon receiving the Most-valued Speaker award.

    Since the word "principal" precedes a name, it is considered part of a proper noun and must be capitalized. The same holds true of "valued" and "award" since they are part of a specific award's title.

10. Fluffy, the siamese cat, runs faster than moxie, my german shepherd.

    Siamese and German show places of origin and must be capitalized. Moxie is a name, so it must be capitalized as well.

EXERCISE 1-2: Capitalization Rules 4–6

___E___   1. Dale decided to take **M**ath 202 in college even though he had never taken that course in high school.

    Math 202 is the name of a specific course, so it must be capitalized.

___D___   2. Mr. Jones caught Bilal reading *The Fall **of t**he Roman Empire* in the hall right before the quiz.

    Small words in book titles do not get capitalized unless they are the first word.

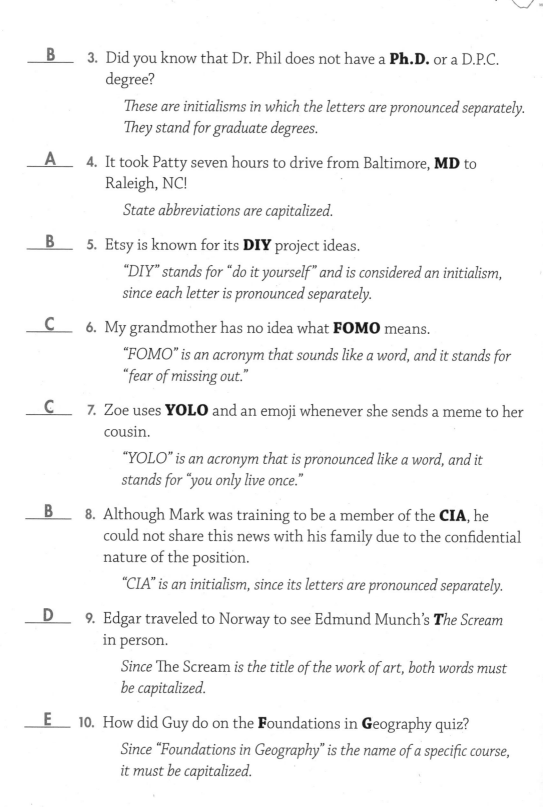

B   3. Did you know that Dr. Phil does not have a **Ph.D.** or a D.P.C. degree?

> *These are initialisms in which the letters are pronounced separately. They stand for graduate degrees.*

A   4. It took Patty seven hours to drive from Baltimore, **MD** to Raleigh, NC!

> *State abbreviations are capitalized.*

B   5. Etsy is known for its **DIY** project ideas.

> *"DIY" stands for "do it yourself" and is considered an initialism, since each letter is pronounced separately.*

C   6. My grandmother has no idea what **FOMO** means.

> *"FOMO" is an acronym that sounds like a word, and it stands for "fear of missing out."*

C   7. Zoe uses **YOLO** and an emoji whenever she sends a meme to her cousin.

> *"YOLO" is an acronym that is pronounced like a word, and it stands for "you only live once."*

B   8. Although Mark was training to be a member of the **CIA**, he could not share this news with his family due to the confidential nature of the position.

> *"CIA" is an initialism, since its letters are pronounced separately.*

D   9. Edgar traveled to Norway to see Edmund Munch's **T**he Scream in person.

> *Since* The Scream *is the title of the work of art, both words must be capitalized.*

E   10. How did Guy do on the **F**oundations in **G**eography quiz?

> *Since "Foundations in Geography" is the name of a specific course, it must be capitalized.*

SAMPLE EXERCISE 1-3: Writing with Capitalization

Dear Mr. Wu, **(1, 3, 4)**

I am writing to request that I be considered for AP Art History next year. **(1, 2, 4, 5)** As you know, I will be a senior this fall, and art is one of my favorite subjects. **(1, 2)**

One of the reasons why I should be considered is because I am fascinated by all types of history. **(1, 2)** Artists have been depicting historic events from the War of the Roses to the War of 1812. **(1, 3)** They have provided us with portraits of famous people from Dr. Martin Luther King Jr. to Mother Teresa. **(1, 3, 4)** They have even portrayed beautiful landscapes from the glaciers of Iceland to the eruption of Mt. Vesuvius. **(3, 4)** I have learned so much history through artists, and I am eager to follow in the footsteps of Uncle Mike, my father's brother, who has a Ph.D. in Art History from Oxford University in Great Britain. **(1, 2, 3, 4, 5)**

In addition, I love to spend hours reading books such as *Art That Changed the World* and *The Short Story of Art*. **(1, 2, 5)** I have also studied famous artists' works, especially John Berkey's paintings of Mars and Venus, as well his paintings that show the beauty of the earth, the sun, and the moon through vivid colors and unique perspectives. **(1, 2, 3)**

I understand that this course sponsors a field trip to the Met as well as to MOMA, two of my favorite museums in New York City. **(1, 3, 4)** A visit to these museums accompanied by Mrs. Manet and my classmates (not to mention a lunch break in beautiful Central Park) would provide such a memorable and valuable experience for me. **(1, 3)** I would even be willing to invite my uncle to conduct a Google Meet with our classmates, just to give them an insider's view of the art world. **(1, 3)**

For these reasons, I hope that you select me to be a member of the prestigious group of students enrolled in this course. **(1, 2)**

Sincerely, **(1)**

Peter Pallette **(3)**

2

The Comma

EXERCISE 2-1: Comma Rules 1–9

___3___ 1. Please forward the books to Sheila Royden, 684 Main Street, Roslyn, NY 11545.

  Using the envelope rule, a comma belongs after the person's name, after the street address, and between the city and state.

___8___ 2. Jody wrote a letter to Marissa, her best friend from camp.

  The phrase "her best friend from camp" is an appositive that further describes Marissa.

___9___ 3. Patrick decided to study for his quiz, since his grades in math were plummeting lately.

  The conjunction "since" is connecting two complete sentences.

___NC___ 4. Jason said that he forgot his lunch today.

  The word "that" suggests that something is being paraphrased. Hence, there is no explanatory phrase followed by a direct quotation, so no comma is needed.

___3___ 5. The French students did not have the opportunity to travel to Quebec, Canada.

  A comma belongs between a city and a country.

___1___ 6. Nicole went to the bank, to the post office, and to CVS before returning home.

  Use commas when more than two phrases are being listed.

___6___ 7. Incidentally, you are wearing two different sneakers.

  "Incidentally" is an introductory word at the beginning of the sentence.

5   **8.** The grades, therefore, were lower than expected.

> *"Therefore" is an interruption in the middle of this sentence and must be surrounded by commas.*

NC   **9.** Poppy enjoys going to the gym but hates working out.

> *The conjunction "but" is not connecting two complete sentences, so no comma is required.*

7   **10.** Go over to the door, Matt.

> *Matt is being addressed directly, so Matt's name must be set apart from the rest of the sentence.*

2   **11.** Catch the ball. Then, run down the court. Next, aim for the hoop. Finally, shoot.

> *Since these sentences must appear in this order, commas must follow the introductory words in the second, third, and fourth sentences, but the sequencing causes them to fall under Rule 2 rather than Rule 6.*

4   **12.** "I have no more patience for you," said Nurse Monroe.

> *This is a direct quotation with the explanatory phrase at the end of the sentence. In this instance, the comma belongs before the closing quotation mark.*

6   **13.** Carefully and skillfully, the spider crafted its web.

> *When two introductory words appear at the beginning of the sentence and are connected by the word "and," the comma is placed after the second introductory word.*

8   **14.** Ms. Ramirez, the most patient teacher, accepts late assignments.

> *The phrase "the most patient teacher" further describes Ms. Ramirez. Because this appositive falls in the middle of the sentence, it must be surrounded by commas.*

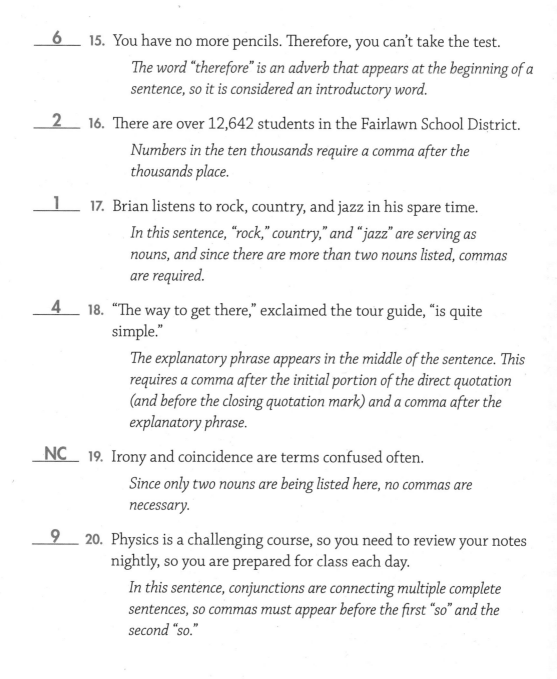

___6___ **15.** You have no more pencils. Therefore, you can't take the test.

The word "therefore" is an adverb that appears at the beginning of a sentence, so it is considered an introductory word.

___2___ **16.** There are over 12,642 students in the Fairlawn School District.

Numbers in the ten thousands require a comma after the thousands place.

___1___ **17.** Brian listens to rock, country, and jazz in his spare time.

In this sentence, "rock," "country," and "jazz" are serving as nouns, and since there are more than two nouns listed, commas are required.

___4___ **18.** "The way to get there," exclaimed the tour guide, "is quite simple."

The explanatory phrase appears in the middle of the sentence. This requires a comma after the initial portion of the direct quotation (and before the closing quotation mark) and a comma after the explanatory phrase.

___NC___ **19.** Irony and coincidence are terms confused often.

Since only two nouns are being listed here, no commas are necessary.

___9___ **20.** Physics is a challenging course, so you need to review your notes nightly, so you are prepared for class each day.

In this sentence, conjunctions are connecting multiple complete sentences, so commas must appear before the first "so" and the second "so."

EXERCISE 2-2: Comma Rules 10 and 11

__10__   1. By the way, the pollen index is 10 today.

> *Since "by" begins a three-word prepositional phrase at the beginning of a sentence, a comma is required after "way," which is the object of the preposition.*

__NC__   2. Two big brown bears approached the campsite.

> *Although "two," "big," and "brown," are adjectives, their order in the sentence cannot be switched. Therefore, no comma is necessary between these adjectives.*

__NC__   3. Under desks there are footrests.

> *Although "under" is a preposition that begins a sentence, no comma is required after the object of the preposition (desks), since the prepositional phrase is only two words in length.*

__11__   4. The animals in the petting zoo were gentle, friendly, and playful.

> *Since "gentle," "friendly," and "playful" are adjectives that can be switched in order, they require commas between them.*

__10__   5. On top of mountains, there is a lot of snow.

> *Even though "on top" and "of mountains" are two-word prepositional phrases, because they appear at the beginning of a sentence and are in consecutive order, a comma must be placed at the end of the second phrase (after "mountains").*

__11__   6. Tennis players get a good night's sleep before participating in competitive, arduous British tournaments such as Wimbledon.

> *A comma must be placed between "competitive" and "arduous," since they are adjectives that modify equally. However, no comma is required between "arduous" and "British," since their order in the sentence cannot be reversed.*

NC   7. Environmentalists are determined to save the environment by recycling old plastic water bottles.

> *Even though "old," "plastic," and "water" are adjectives, they do not modify equally and do not require commas.*

10   8. After the prom and before graduation, seniors take final exams.

> *"After the prom" and "before graduation" are prepositional phrases at the beginning of a sentence that are connected by the word "and." When this occurs, the comma belongs after the object of the preposition of the final phrase (after "graduation").*

11   9. The talented, attractive actress received a bit part in the new *Star Wars* movie.

> *"The" is an article (a type of adjective), but it cannot be switched with "talented," so no comma should be placed between them. "Talented" and "attractive" are adjectives that modify equally, and their order can be switched, so a comma is required between them.*

11   10. The blue, white, and red French flag could be seen all over Paris on Bastille Day.

> *"The" is an article (a type of adjective), but it cannot be switched with "blue," so no comma should be placed between them. The order of the colors blue, white, and red can be switched, which means that they are adjectives that modify equally, so commas are required between them. However, no comma should be placed between "red" and "French," since these adjectives do not modify equally.*

EXERCISE 2-3: Comma Rules 12–15

13   1. Dear Dr. Wilburt:

Please consider me for the summer internship. I look forward to meeting you in the near future.

Sincerely,
Tobias Gordon

A colon is required after "Dear Dr. Wilburt" because it is a salutation in a business letter. A comma is required after the closing "Sincerely."

NC   2. Remember not to place a comma before "because" when practicing Comma Rule 9.

This sentence does not require a comma.

15   3. When your tights have a run, run to the mall to buy a new pair.

The word "when" is a subordinate conjunction that begins a sentence. A comma must be placed after the last word of the subordinate clause, which, in this sentence, is the first "run."

14   4. The spider that the bird ate, ate two flies earlier that morning.

This sentence does not begin with a subordinate conjunction. To avoid confusion between two identical words (ate), a comma must be placed between them.

13   5. Dear Patrice,

I can't wait to have a sleepover once the school year ends!

Your friend,
Mannat

The salutation "Dear Patrice" is one for a friendly letter. Therefore, it must be followed by a comma. A comma must also be placed after the closing "Your friend."

___15___ 6. As the roller coaster picked up speed, the riders screamed loudly.

The word "As" is a subordinate conjunction that begins a sentence. A comma must be placed after the last word of the subordinate clause, which, in this sentence, is "speed."

___15___ 7. If you want to follow the speed limit, limit the amount of pressure you place on your brakes.

The word "if" is a subordinate conjunction that falls at the beginning of a sentence. A comma must be placed after the last word of the subordinate clause, which, in this sentence, is the first "limit."

___NC___ 8. My dearest Matthew thanked his friend sincerely.

Even though the words "dearest" and "sincerely" appear in this sentence, they are not part of a friendly or a business letter and do not require a comma.

SAMPLE EXERCISE 2-4: Writing with Commas

May 19, 2021, was the most embarrassing day of my life. **(3)** Giovanni, the boy next door, was a senior at Scholastic Prep, and he asked me to go to the prom with him, since he wasn't dating anyone seriously. **(8, 9)**

"Crystal, I know this is weird, but I really need a prom date. What do you think?" **(7, 9)**

"Yes, I would be happy to go with you," I replied in a confident, enthusiastic manner. "By the way, when is the prom? **(6, 4, 10, 11)**

Giovanni was barely audible, "Tomorrow." **(4)**

"Tomorrow?" I retorted, as I wondered how I would ever pull off the dress, the nails, and the hair in time. **(9, 1)**

"Yeah, sorry about that," he added, as he held his adorable dog, Fluffy, which was a white, tan, and black Cavanese. **(4, 12, 8, 11)**

"You're lucky your dog is cute!" I answered. "I'd better get going, since I have fewer than 24 hours to pull this off." **(4)**

If you can't guess what went wrong, I'll tell you: everything! (15) I had little time to shop, so my mother suggested I borrow something from my cousin. (9) Let's just say Priscilla has "eclectic" taste and leave it at that. After two hours and many ill-fitting dresses, I surrendered to an animal-print gown that was snug at best. (10) Because I had no time to have my nails done professionally, Priscilla promised that she would step in as my manicurist. (15) Horror crept over my face, as she filed them into such sharp points that they resembled claws rather than delicate fingertips. (9) There was no point in even polishing them at that point. Graciously, I thanked her and began sobbing as I entered my mother's car for the ride home. (6, 9)

My mother, the amateur therapist, knew what would make me feel better. Thankfully, she told me she made a hair appointment at the chichi salon in town for the next morning. (6) I knew a good hairstyle could salvage the rest of my mishaps.

When I arrived at the salon, I was introduced to Enzo, who seemed nice enough. (15, 12) I explained that I was limited in time and described precisely how I wanted my hairstyle: sleek, shiny, and modern. (11) I walked out with the complete opposite. My hair looked frizzy, puffy, and utterly ridiculous. (11) On top of that, Enzo, the "genius" that he was, said he couldn't be rushed when crafting his masterpiece! (10, 8) This meant I had only an hour to rush home and get dressed before Gio picked me up!

It was, in fact, thirty-five minutes later when the doorbell rang. (5) As I walked down the stairs in my leopard dress and my poofy hair, tears streamed down my face. I didn't want to let Gio down, but the entire ensemble was absurd, and I knew it. (9)

His reaction, however, was quite unexpected. (5)

"Don't cry, Fluffy," he said. 'I have a thing for girls who try to compete with my Cavanese for my affection." (7, 4)

My most embarrassing moment turned into the night I fell in love with my goofy neighbor, who knew how to make me laugh even when I looked like a canine in a snowstorm. (12) What could be better than that?

3
Colons and Semicolons

EXERCISE 3-1: Colon Rules

__2__ 1. Here are the steps you should take when writing a paragraph**:**
- Read the question carefully.
- Highlight key points in the essay question.
- Write an outline or complete a graphic organizer.
- Begin with a topic sentence.
- Incorporate relevant details and excerpts (if applicable).
- Write a closing sentence.

A complete sentence preceding a vertical list requires a colon.

__7__ 2. The sun will rise at 5:45 tomorrow morning.

A colon is required between the hour and the minutes.

__3__ 3. WARNING**:** Swim at your own risk!

The word "WARNING" is a key word, and instructions follow that word, so a colon is required.

__NC__ 4. "Don't forget to pay your cable bill," Steven's mother reminded.

Since the explanatory phrase ends the sentence, no colon is required.

__7__ 5. Pastor Jim read the Golden Rule from Matthew 7:12.

This is an excerpt from the Bible, so there must be a colon between the chapter and the verse.

__NC__ 6. *Are You There God? It's Me, Margaret* is a classic for young adults by Judy Blume.

No colon is needed in this title, since the first part of the title ends in a question mark.

   5   7. Dear Governor Brooks:

Thank you for considering me for the Distinguished Students of America internship. It would be my pleasure to serve as your intern this summer, as I am interested in pursuing a career in public service, and I am motivated to learn from one of our country's most respected leaders.

Sincerely,
Tabatha Marcus

This is a business letter requiring a colon after the salutation.

  NC   8. Becoming a successful politician requires good public speaking skills, knowledge of the jurisdiction, corroboration with residents and fellow leaders, and the ability to remain composed under pressure.

This is simply a list within a sentence that does not require a colon or a semicolon.

   7   9. When you want to express a ratio of 2 to 1, you may write it as 2/1 or 2:1.

Ratios have colons between the numbers.

   4   10. Principal Stringer reminded us of the most important school rule: "Be kind to each other."

A complete sentence precedes a direct quotation here.

EXERCISE 3-2: Semicolon Rules

  2A   1. Jose is a very attentive listener when Malcolm needs a good friend; likewise, Malcolm depends on Jose for advice.

Since "likewise" is a conjunctive adverb, and this adverb is at the beginning of a sentence that is directly related to its preceding sentence, a semicolon is needed.

_NS_ 2. Anne is a wonderful cook, yet she prefers to eat at restaurants.

Since there is a coordinating conjunction (yet) and a comma connecting two complete sentences, a semicolon is unnecessary.

_3_ 3. Because she comes from a military family, Natasha has lived in several places including San Diego, California; Cherry Point, North Carolina; and Blount Island, Florida.

Since there are several commas separating cities and states, the semicolon is used after the names of states to provide clarity for the reader.

_2C_ 4. Reggie received a 99 on his last chemistry exam; of course, three points of extra credit helped bring his score from an A to an A+.

Since "of course" is a prepositional phrase that appears at the beginning of a sentence that is directly related to its preceding sentence, a semicolon is needed.

_NS_ 5. In case of emergency, dial 911.

There is only one sentence here, and nothing is being listed or is unclear, so a semicolon does not belong in this sentence.

_NS_ 6. Jonathan plays soccer, football, and lacrosse, so he has hardly any time for socializing.

Since there is a coordinating conjunction (so) and a comma connecting two complete sentences, a semicolon is unnecessary.

_2B_ 7. Blaze has had two injuries in the past year; so far, he seems to have made a full recovery.

Since "so far" is a transitional expression, and this transition is at the beginning of a sentence that is directly related to its preceding sentence, a semicolon is needed.

_____1_____ 8. Patricia took the ACT three times; she is hoping that her score will improve enough for her to be considered by her top-choice college.

> *These two sentences directly correspond with each other. A semicolon is the appropriate punctuation mark to use between them.*

_____NS_____ 9. Niran purchased the largest backpack available, but his books and laptop barely fit in it!

> *Since there is a coordinating conjunction (but) and a comma connecting two complete sentences, a semicolon is unnecessary.*

_____NS_____ 10. Coincidentally, two of the young ladies nominated for Prom Queen were wearing the same dress.

> *There is only one sentence here, and nothing is being listed or is unclear, so a semicolon does not belong in this sentence.*

EXERCISE 3-3: Colon or Semicolon?

_____S_____ 1. Jeannie showed up for the audition without her sheet music; thus, she was unable to try out for the musical.

> *These two sentences directly correspond with each other. A semicolon is the appropriate punctuation mark to use between them.*

_____C_____ 2. Winter is a season that can be treacherous for the following reasons: slippery roads, icy sidewalks, and frigid temperatures.

> *A complete sentence is followed by a corresponding list, so a colon is the correct punctuation mark.*

N   3. Dear Cathy,

    I miss you so much! The summer has been so lonely without you. I can't want until you return, so we can go hiking on some new trails I discovered.

Your friend,

Louise

    Since this salutation opens a friendly letter, a comma (rather than a colon) is the appropriate punctuation mark to end the salutation.

N   4. Calvin ate four tacos at lunchtime, so he had no appetite for dinner.

    Since there is a coordinating conjunction (so) and a comma connecting two complete sentences, a semicolon is unnecessary.

C   5. I asked the librarian to help me find *History of our Nation* 3:16–20 in the stacks.

    A colon is necessary between the chapter and the pages of this source.

S   6. I heard that Sara recently contracted Covid-19**;** until last week, she had been able to avoid it.

    These two sentences directly correspond with each other. A semicolon is the appropriate punctuation mark to use between them.

N   7. Remember to bring your bathing suit, towel, sunscreen, and sunglasses to the beach.

    There is no sentence or important word preceding this list of items, so a colon is not appropriate.

_____S_____ 8. Luciano's parents are opera singers**;** naturally, he has some innate ability to carry a tune.

> *These two sentences correspond directly with each other. A semicolon is the appropriate punctuation mark to use between them.*

_____C_____ 9. Have you read *Take Deep Breaths**:** An Insider's Guide to Managing Stress*?

> *Since the title of this book also has a subtitle (without a question mark or exclamation point), a colon should be used between the title and the subtitle.*

_____C_____ 10. The child screamed at the puppy in awe**:** "I want to take you home!"

> *Since the explanatory sentence is complete and it falls before the direct quotation sentence, it should be followed by a colon.*

SAMPLE EXERCISE 3-4: Writing with Colons and Semicolons

Dear Superintendent Waters: (**C5**)

I am a student in Mme. Monet's French 3 class. Having just returned from our trip to Quebec, I wanted to inform you about our adventures; most of them were harmless! (**S1**)

As you know, we departed at 5:00 a.m. from the school parking lot; naturally, we were all very sleepy as the bus pulled away from the school. (**C7, S2A**) After a few hours of rest, many of us woke up to see several animals out the window: cows, horses, and even goats! (**C1**) Before we knew it, it was lunchtime; Mme. Monet allotted 30 minutes for this break, so we could remain on schedule. (**S1**) As we boarded the bus, our teacher reminded all of us of the regulations we would have to follow at the border: "Have your passports in hand, ready to be checked." (**C4**)

Surprisingly, the border check went smoothly, and we were on our way in no time. Immediately, we noticed a change in the signage; for example, the stop signs said, "Arret." (**S2B**) Mme. Monet had us play a game of travel bingo.

She included many French words on our Bingo boards; le cheval, la bouche d'incendie, le feu de signalization, and la boulangerie were just a few of the words and phrases. (S1) In case you don't know French, these words mean the following: horse, fire hydrant, traffic light, and bakery. (C1)

After a long, twelve-hour drive, we finally arrived at our hotel, which was in Old Quebec; it was so beautiful! (S1) After all of the luggage was brought into the lobby, Mme. Monet went onto the bus to make sure no one left anything behind; naturally, she emerged from the bus with a pair of airpods and a cell phone. (S2A) Matthew was always losing things; it was no surprise that he left those items behind on the bus. (S1)

After settling into our rooms and getting a good night's rest, we were ready to explore! That week, we knew we would be seeing so many places: Old Quebec, Canada; Notre-Dame-du-Portege, Canada; Champlain, Canada, and Lake Placid, New York. (S3)

Though the week flew by, here is a list of some of the highlights:
- The funicular ride
- Walking on the glass bridge across the Montmorency Falls
- Visiting the beautiful Notre Dame Cathedral
- Taking selfies in front of Le Chateau Frontenac (C2)

I should post a few of those pictures on our school's Twitter page, right?

I would be remiss if I did not mention the incredible food; we ate our fair share of staples of the Quebecois diet: croissants, poutine, and crepes. (S2A, C1)

This trip was so phenomenal! By the end of the week, I found myself speaking so much French! On the way home, Matthew and I attempted to speak solely in French; that only lasted for an hour, since it was very tiring to Google all the words we had not yet learned! (S1) In any case, we laughed like crazy while pronouncing English words with a French accent; however, the students around us did not find it quite so funny. (S2B)

I want to thank you for allowing us to take this "bon voyage" to Quebec. It was immensely enjoyable and valuable; perhaps next year's trip can be to Paris? (lol) (S2B)

Yours truly,
Alec Francophile

Quotation Marks, Dialogue, and Punctuating Titles

EXERCISE 4-1: Direct Quotations

___Q___ 1. "May I borrow a pen?" asked Edward right before the quiz began.

> *These are exact words stated by Edward, so they need to be in quotation marks.*

___NQ___ 2. The manager reminded the customers that they needed to stand in line and wait to be called before approaching the cashier.

> *The word "that" indicates that the manager's words are being paraphrased. Therefore, no quotation marks are necessary.*

___Q___ 3. "The skills required for being a good server," explained the restaurant owner, "include knowing the ingredients of the food, noticing the needs of the diners, and refilling water glasses constantly."

> *These are exact words of the restaurant owner, as indicated by the explanatory phrase in the middle of the sentence. As such, the exact words need to be surrounded by quotation marks.*

___NQ___ 4. Ms. Steel conducted the orchestra class by raising her baton and explaining directions in a soft tone.

> *Since we do not know the exact words of Ms. Steel, there is no need for quotation marks.*

Q   5. Cynthia reviewed the day's schedule with her twin daughters: "When school ends, you will go to basketball practice and then attend Grandma's birthday dinner."

Since the exact words of Cynthia are provided after the initial explanatory sentence, quotation marks are required.

Q   6. "It isn't fair," said Antonio to his Chinese teacher, "that you did not provide exam directions in English."

These are exact words of Antonio to his Chinese teacher, as indicated by the explanatory phrase in the middle of the sentence. Thus, the exact words need to be surrounded by quotation marks.

Q   7. Ms. Zheng responded, "You should know better than that, Antonio. One of the first things I taught you at the beginning of the year was that you needed to be able to decipher directions in Chinese."

These are exact sentences spoken by Ms. Zheng to Antonio, and since Ms. Zheng's sentences are sequential and were stated at the same time, only one set of quotations marks is necessary.

Q   8. Antonio relented: "It was worth a try."

These are the exact words of Antonio following an explanatory phrase, so the exact words belong in quotation marks.

Q   9. "Bedtime is usually at 7:00 p.m.," Cecilia explained to the babysitter, "but because this is a special occasion, the babies should be put to bed by 8:30 at the latest."

These are exact words of Cecilia to the babysitter, as indicated by the explanatory phrase in the middle of the sentence. Hence, the exact words need to be surrounded by quotation marks.

___Q___ 10. "Your brother's new sneakers are so cool!" said Tyler to his friend, Nate.

These are Tyler's exact words, so they require quotation marks.

EXERCISE 4-2: Identifying Terms Related to Dialogue

___d___ 1. run-in quotation

___c___ 2. character directions

___g___ 3. excerpt

___j___ 4. fade in

___a___ 5. dialogue

___i___ 6. INT.

___e___ 7. teaser

___f___ 8. block quotation

___b___ 9. O.S.

___h___ 10. stage directions

EXERCISE 4-3: Formatting Titles

___I___   1. Rodin's sculpture: *The Thinker*

___Q___   2. Bruce Springsteen's song: "Born in the U.S.A."

___I___   3. Movie soundtrack: *Black Panther*

___I___   4. Ship: *Lusitania*

___CO___   5. Washington Monument

___I___   6. Play: *Hamlet*

___I___   7. Court case: *Brown v. Board of Education*

___Q___   8. Inaugural poem: "The Hill We Climb"

___CO___   9. The Lord's Prayer

___Q___   10. Newspaper article: "School Finally Opens"

___I___   11. Video game: *Minecraft*

___CO___   12. Nobel Prize

___Q___   13. Board game: "Guess Who?"

___I___   14. Newspaper: *The Washington Post*

___I___   15. Broadway show: *Hamilton*

EXERCISE 4-4: Culminating Review of Quotation Marks and Formatting

____I____ 1. Coach Morrow instructed the team, "Go to your locker; change into your uniform; gather all your equipment; board the bus within ten minutes."

This is incorrect because there should be a colon after "Coach Morrow instructed the team" because "Coach Morrow instructed the team" is a complete sentence.

____I____ 2. Let's play "Old Maid" when you get home from school!

This is incorrect because Old Maid is a traditional card game. Traditional card games should not be punctuated.

____C____ 3. One of Shakespeare's most famous sonnets begins, "Shall I compare thee to a summer's day?" (Randolph, 130).

This is correct because the question mark remains within the excerpt, and a period always follows run-in parenthetical citations.

____C____ 4. "You bought me a puppy!" Samantha shrieked with delight.

This is correct because the exclamation point is inside the closing quotation mark. There is also a period to end the closing explanatory phrase.

____I____ 5. As my physical education class gathered around the track for our final assessment of the season, I was distraught. I was out of breath after running around the track once, and next, we were supposed to run a mile. I thought to myself, "How am I ever going to pass this class if I can't run the mile?"

This is incorrect because the character's thoughts should not be set apart with an explanatory phrase and quotation marks. The explanatory phrase "I thought to myself" should be eliminated entirely. The character's thoughts should be placed in italics and not in quotation marks.

_____I_____ 6. Ms. Li's class was so excited to take a field trip to see the Empire State Building and to take a tour of the famous ship, the Intrepid, while visiting New York City.

Although the Empire State Building is a monument, which should not have special treatment, the Intrepid *is a famous ship, and its name should, therefore, be italicized.*

_____C_____ 7. My sister's "fancy" outfit included a pair of ripped jeans and a dirty pair of Converse sneakers.

The word "fancy" is punctuated correctly because it is depicting sarcasm, since ripped jeans and dirty sneakers are not ordinarily considered fancy clothing.

_____C_____ 8. Always capitalize "I" whether it is at the beginning of a sentence or not.

The word "I" needs to be placed in quotation marks in this sentence. If it is not set apart with quotation marks, the sentence could be unclear to the reader who might misinterpret the word "I" as a typographical error.

_____I_____ 9. Marvin explained to his group, "I think we should begin by highlighting important lines in "The Road Not Taken" before we write the analysis of the poem."

This error is based on the "quote within a quote" rule. When an item that requires quotation marks (in this case, the poem title) appears within a set of quotation marks of dialogue, single (nested) quotation marks should be utilized around the poem title.

___C___ 10. PIERRE: (thoughtfully) It's raining. Would you like to share my umbrella?

MARIE: (enthusiastically) That would be great!

The punctuation in this play is correct because the characters' names in a play are followed by colons, and the character directions are placed in parentheses.

SAMPLE EXERCISE 4-5: Writing with Dialogue

Personal Narrative

"There is no way I am ever going on a roller coaster. Don't even think about trying to convince me," asserted seven-year-old Julia from the backseat. She knew we were on our way to Six Flags, an amusement park that was well-known for its many rides and attractions, especially its roller coasters.

"We'll see," I replied with a knowing smile. I was determined to have her try even a small coaster before the day's end. Julia was a kid who was not afraid of much, but when it came to coasters, it was an entirely different story. I'm not sure if it was the noise of the rickety cars racing along the tracks, the shrieks of the terrified but gleeful passengers, or the steep drops of the cars from the clouds to the grass within a split second, but, most likely, it was all three.

Julia added, "Look! There's the entrance!"

It's always a special feeling when you enter an amusement park. After tickets and bags are checked, that first walk onto a path lined with beautiful flowers and bright colors seems to put everyone in a good mood. I studied Julia's face as we entered the park, and she seemed even more excited than me. *This might not be so bad after all. Where should we go first? Should I walk her straight to a coaster or warm her up with a few other rides?*

"Where do you want to go first, Mom?" Julia asked, curious to see if we agreed.

"Well, we always begin with bumper cars, right?" I reminded her, veering to the left once we passed the fountain.

After a few of the rides that made both of us happy, we stopped for a quick hot pretzel and filled our signature park cups with water. Sitting on a bench, it was time to plan our next move. *There is no time like the present.*

"Let's go down this way. It doesn't seem so crowded."

Julia conceded and followed behind me, staring at all the overpriced games that we never played. She watched as a child of three or four tried to carry a stuffed panda twice her size, smiling the entire time.

We "suddenly" found ourselves in front of Runaway Train. Of all the roller coasters in this park, Runaway Train was not as high as the others, and the ride didn't last more than a minute. The only issue was that it was a very fast ride, so that could be scary for a fledgling coaster rider. Still, I thought it was worth a try.

"Oh, what's this ride?" I asked, pretending not to know what was ahead.

"Runaway Train, Mom. It's a coaster. Let's walk down the hill. I think the Himalaya ride is this way."

"Wait a minute! Let's take a look at this one," I pleaded, trying to get her to consider the coaster.

Just then, a group of kids around Julia's age deboarded the Runaway Train ride. They were skipping toward the entrance again, exclaiming how they loved it so much and wanted to go on it again and again. Since Six Flags was a pay-one-price type of park, boarding the same ride for an entire day was a possibility, though not one I would recommend.

"Let's just watch how the ride goes," I prompted Julia, knowing that she paid close attention to those children, admiring their bravery and envying their exhilaration.

As we watched the ride take off and kept track of its ups and downs and swirls and whirls, it seemed like those riders were back in front of us in a split second, but it was more like a minute or two. *This is it—my opportunity!*

"Why don't you ask them how it was?

"Mom, that's dumb. You are so embarrassing."

"What's wrong with asking someone something?"

"Everything!"

As luck would have it, those same children climbed out of the coaster cars and walked directly toward us. One of the kids must have sensed Julia's tentativeness, as she ran up to Julia with enthusiasm: "You HAVE to try it. It's the best ride ever."

Another chimed in, "We used to be scared too. It's not so high, and it's really quick. You should try it."

Julia smiled at them. She wasn't exactly one to make conversation, especially with people whom she didn't know.

"Thanks," she said, barely audibly.

As they cantered away toward their next adventure, Julia looked at me for a long moment: "If I try it and don't like it, do you promise you won't keep pestering me to go on again?" she asked, wavering between a yes and a no.

"That seems reasonable," I replied, knowing how much she would love the experience.

Fortunately, we were placed somewhere in the middle of the set of cars so that we could not see the hills ahead of us so clearly. Buckled in and ready to go, Julia held on for dear life. There was no turning back now. As the ride dipped and curled over the hills, we careened left and right, leaning into each other unintentionally. Though the ride was brief, Julia's faced evolved from terrified to composed to ecstatic in a matter of seconds. Before we knew it, the Runaway Train reached the station.

"That was it?" Julia asked, shocked at the brevity of the ride.

"Yup," I replied.

"Not bad, Mom," she smiled, as she looked at me with pride in her eyes. "I did it!"

"You did! Now, let's make our way to Rolling Thunder. I think it's to the right."

"Don't push it, Mom."

Runaway Train was the only coaster we rode that day many years ago. As time has passed, Julia, now a teenager, is the one convincing all of her friends to go on every roller coaster in the park. It makes me smile, thinking of the first time she trusted me, stepped outside of her comfort zone, and enjoyed the experience.

Sample Stage Play

Author's Note: Because I included multiple scenes in this example, I differentiated between them by including information about the setting of each scene, so the reader could recognize the changes in time, place, and/or mood from scene to scene.

LIST OF CHARACTERS: Rose (the mother)
Julia (the daughter)
Ticket taker
Child #1
Child #2
A few teenagers

Scene One

SETTING: **TIME:** 11:00 a.m.
PLACE: Six Flags parking lot
MOOD: nervous

JULIA: (assertively) There is no way I am ever going on a roller coaster. Don't even think about trying to convince me.

ROSE: (knowingly) We'll see.

(The noise of the rickety cars racing along the tracks, the shrieks of the terrified but gleeful passengers, and the steep drops of the cars from the clouds to the grass within a split second fill the air.)

JULIA: Look! There's the entrance!

(They walk toward the ticket booth.)

TICKET TAKER: Tickets, please. Open your bag, please.

(TICKET TAKER waves them through as ROSE and JULIA
walk down the amusement park entrance path.)

JULIA: (curious) Where do you want to go first, Mom?

ROSE: Well, we always begin with bumper cars, right?

(They veer to the left after passing a fountain.)

Scene Two

SETTING: **TIME:** one hour later
                PLACE: park bench
                MOOD: excited

ROSE: That was fun, right?

JULIA: It's so nice today. Can I have more of the pretzel? Don't get mustard
on my side. You know I hate mustard.

ROSE: I know. I know.

(They sit for a while, sipping water and finishing
their snacks. Then, they rise, looking in different
directions, deciding where to go next.)

ROSE: Let's go down this way. It doesn't seem so crowded.

JULIA: Mom, look! The water guns! Basketball! Goldfish!

ROSE: You know those games cost a fortune, and we already spent so
much on the park admission. Let's take advantage of the rides. They are
included.

(JULIA walks past a small child with
an oversized stuffed animal.)

JULIA: Mom, look! Omg, she is soooo cute. She's going to tip over with that huge panda.

(ROSE and JULIA laugh as they pass the little girl, making their way toward the Runaway Train, unbeknownst to Julia.)

ROSE: (innocently) Oh, what's this ride?

JULIA: Runaway Train, Mom. It's a coaster. Let's walk down the hill. I think the Himalaya ride is this way.

ROSE: (pleading) Wait a minute! Let's take a look at this one.

(A group of kids around Julia's age deboard the Runaway Train, skipping toward the entrance again.)

CHILD #1: That was awesome!

CHILD #2: Let's do it again!

(The two children board the ride for a second time.)

ROSE: (prompting) Let's just watch how the ride goes.

(ROSE and JULIA watch the ride take off, their heads moving up and down to emulate the ups and downs, swirls, and whirls of the ride. The two children deboard the coaster.)

ROSE: Why don't you ask them how it was?

JULIA: (cringing) Mom, that's dumb. You are so embarrassing.

ROSE: What's wrong with asking someone something?

JULIA: (exasperated) Everything!

(The two children walk directly toward JULIA.)

CHILD #1: (to JULIA) You HAVE to try it. It's the best ride ever.

CHILD #2: We used to be scared too. It's not so high and really quick. You should try it!

JULIA: (smiling shyly and barely audible) Thanks.

(JULIA looks at ROSE for a long moment.)

JULIA: (wavering) If I try it and don't like it, do you promise you won't keep trying to make me go on again?

ROSE: (relieved) That seems reasonable.

(They enter the ride and are seated in the center of the train. The two simulate a coaster ride, leaning into each other. During the course of the ride, JULIA's face changes from scared to composed to ecstatic. The ride ends quickly, and they exit.)

JULIA: (in disbelief) That was it?

ROSE: Yup.

JULIA: (smiling) Not bad, Mom. I did it!

ROSE: You did! Now, let's make our way to Rolling Thunder. I think it's to the right.

JULIA: Don't push it, Mom.

(They walk away, content.)

Scene Three

SETTING: **TIME:** ten years later
                PLACE: Six Flags park
                MOOD: excited

JULIA: (to her group of teenage friends): Come on, guys! It will be amazing! Let's start with Runaway Train! It's so much fun!

5

Apostrophes

EXERCISE 5-1: Punctuating Singular and Plural Possessive Nouns

1. snacks of the children = children's snacks

   We add an apostrophe and an "s" to plural nouns to show possession.

2. shirts of the boys = boys' shirts

   More than one boy owns shirts, so an apostrophe is necessary after "boys." Another "s" is not required.

3. eggs of the quail = quail's eggs

   The eggs belong to the quail, so an apostrophe and an "s" are necessary after "quail."

4. frisbee of the dogs = dogs' frisbee

   More than one dog owns the same frisbee. Since "dogs" already ends in an "s," only an apostrophe needs to be added.

5. board of the Wounded Warriors = Wounded Warriors' board

   Since Wounded Warriors is the proper name of the organization, the apostrophe must be placed after the "s" in "Warriors" in order to show that the board is related to the organization.

6. medals of the athletes = athletes' medals

   More than one athlete received medals, so an apostrophe belongs after the plural word "athletes."

7. dishes of Grandmother Solis = Grandmother Solis' dishes

   Since Solis is a proper noun that ends in "s" and we need to show that Grandmother Solis owns the dishes, a simple apostrophe after the last name is sufficient.

8. oven of the chefs = chefs' oven

   Multiple chefs share an oven, so the word "chef" is plural, and the apostrophe belongs after the "s" to show that they share one oven.

9. office of the boss = boss' office

   Since the word "boss" already ends in an "s," we only need to add an apostrophe after the last "s" in "boss" to show that the office belongs to the boss.

10. prison cells of Alcatraz = Alcatraz's prison cells

    Since Alcatraz is a singular proper noun, the possessive is formed by adding an apostrophe and an "s."

EXERCISE 5-2: Correct or Incorrect Apostrophes to Indicate Possession

_____Incorrect_____ 1. The lobby's floor was slippery.

   The word "lobby" is a place, but it is not a proper noun. When a place is used to describe possession, it does not require an apostrophe. It should say "The lobby floor was slippery."

_____Correct_____ 2. Cally's mother and Raquel's daughter travel together.

   Two separate people are traveling together.

_____Incorrect_____ 3. Emme and I's favorite ice cream flavor is strawberry.

   Never use the word "I" in the possessive form. The word "my" should replace "I's" in this sentence.

_____Incorrect_____ 4. Isaac's and Howard's aunt lives next door to their house.

   We know that Isaac and Howard share the same aunt because the word "aunt" is singular. Therefore, only the apostrophe after "Howard" is necessary (not the apostrophe after Isaac).

___**Correct**___   5. Grandma Jo gave an heirloom to her son's wife.

To indicate the son's relationship with his wife, an apostrophe is required. Although Grandma Jo is related to her son, an apostrophe is not required after her name, since the word that follows her name is a verb.

___**Incorrect**___   6. The Empire State Building and the Pentagon's lobbies are huge!

Since the Empire State Building and the Pentagon do not share the same lobby, separate apostrophes are required (Empire State Building's and Pentagon's). Even though these are buildings and buildings don't normally require apostrophes, since these buildings are proper nouns, the apostrophes must be included.

___**Incorrect**___   7. Savannah and somebody's saddles were left behind in the stable.

Since both of these people left their individual saddles (not a shared saddle) in the stable, an apostrophe and an "s" must follow both "Savannah" and "somebody."

___**Correct**___   8. Their teacher placed a prize in Hillary's and Jackie's backpacks.

Don't be confused by "a prize." That just explains how many prizes the teacher placed in each of the backpacks. The word "backpacks" is the word that will help you determine apostrophe usage. Hillary and Jackie have separate backpacks; their names both require apostrophes.

___**Incorrect**___   9. The first-place medal was their's.

It is never appropriate to add an apostrophe to a possessive pronoun (theirs), as it already signifies possession.

_____Correct_____ 10. Quincy's and my vocal teacher won a Grammy Award.

> *Two people have the same vocal teacher, since the word "teacher" is singular. When a proper noun (Quincy) is combined with a determiner (my) to indicate joint ownership or relationship, only the proper noun requires the apostrophe.*

EXERCISE 5-3: Culminating Apostrophe Review

___2___ 1. In two decades' time, technology usage has quadrupled.

> *The time belongs to multiple decades. An apostrophe needs to be added to "decades."*

___8___ 2. Ruth Bader Ginsburg was appointed a Supreme Court justice in the '90s.

> *The apostrophe replaces the century of the year being named. Place the apostrophe before "90s."*

___NA___ 3. The Class of 2020 was unable to have a graduation ceremony due to the global pandemic.

> *No apostrophe is necessary in this sentence, since the entire year "2020" appears.*

___8___ 4. "Lo, How a Rose E'er Blooming" is a popular holiday hymn.

> *The word "ever" was shorted in the title of the poem. An apostrophe needs to be added to the word "E er."*

___4___ 5. Roberto's and her birthday are the same, since they are twins.

> *The proper noun "Roberto" requires an apostrophe to indicate the shared birthday with his twin. The word "her" does not require an "s" or an apostrophe, since "Roberto's" already indicates shared possession.*

___1___ 6. Since his arm is broken, someone needs to carry Chess**'** bookbag to his next class.

Only an apostrophe needs to be added after "Chess," since his names ends in an "s," and the sentence shows his ownership over the bookbag.

___2___ 7. The Gomez**es'** youngest son, Darren, is featured on a reality TV show.

Since the name Gomez ends in a "z" and there are two parents who have a relationship with the son, the letters "es" need to be added to Gomez before adding the apostrophe.

___7___ 8. "Can't you see that I am busy?" asked Sra. Placida when Milo interrupted her repeatedly.

The word "can't" is a contraction for "cannot."

___NA___ 9. Because Herminia received all Cs on her tests, she did not qualify for the honor society.

No apostrophe is necessary, since a simple "s" needs to be added to the grade of C in order to indicate that there is more than one "C" (plural).

___6___ 10. After Mr. Scribner checked the penmanship quizzes, he noticed that most students had difficulty writing q**'s** and a**'s** in cursive.

In order to avoid confusion by the reader, a special apostrophe is added to letters that need to be made plural for any reason (in this case, "q" and "a").

SAMPLE EXERCISE 5-4: Writing with Apostrophes

Memorial Day was supposed to be a day to relax. How often did I have a Monday off from school *and* from work? My part-time job at Gino's, the local pizza place, wasn't much, but it was only a stone's throw away from my high school, so convenience kept me there. It was no surprise, however, that my mother's voice made me cover my head with the pillow.

"Fred, it's time! Wake up! We need to set up for the family reunion!"

"Coming," I replied, barely audibly. *Ugh. How could we prepare for guests at this ungodly hour?*

"I can't hear you moving," my mother admonished, knowing full well I hadn't taken a step out of my bed.

Before long, the doorbell rang, and throngs of aunts, uncles, and cousins arrived, many whom I had never even met before. I knew it was time to get up when three little kids burst into my room.

"Hey, aren't you Aunt Aida's son?" they asked, almost simultaneously. *Why did these kids know me when I hadn't a clue who they were? They must have been prepped in advance.*

Not even awaiting a response from me, the smallest one climbed onto my bed and asked, "Will you read this to me? Time's a'wastin'!"

I have no idea where he learned that expression, but you know little kids. They pick up on everything they hear. He grabbed my childhood book from the shelf swiftly while I was wiping my eyes with my sweatshirt sleeve.

"'*Twas the Night Before Christmas*," I observed. "That *is* one of my favorites. But, it's only May, you know. You'll have to wait 'til December for this one."

Unaffected, he jumped on my bed until I could stand it no longer. Dragging me down the steps, the three boys presented me to their parents like I was their new pet.

"Here he is!" another one shouted, as the adults swarmed around me with hugs and kisses. I felt like I was in the Twilight Zone, as they all knew my name, but I was clueless as to their identity. Maybe I was working too many hours at the pizza joint, after all.

"The Foxes have arrived," my mother announced, providing a cue as to their identity.

"The Foxes, right . . . I remember now," I added, still having no idea who they were.

"I'm your cousin Lisa," one of them stepped forward, and "I'm Rich" the other added, as I shook their hands again.

"It was so nice of your mother to organize this event. Many of us haven't seen each other since the late '90s!"

"That makes sense," I replied. I've only seen you once, then, since I was born in '85."

"Yes, that was a very long time ago, Great Auntie Jean added. It looks like your mother dotted all her i's and crossed all her t's in order to make this gathering so lovely."

As I walked out the side door, the scene was very impressive, no thanks to me. My mother must've spent days setting up the yard with pictures, balloons, name tags, and decorations. The smell of barbeque wafted toward me as I decided to plop myself at a round table in the shade.

"Fred, won't you help out a little?" Great Auntie Jean requested, as she attempted to carry an aluminum tray of hot food toward the Sterno that was set up on the table.

"I've got that!" Rescuing the baked ziti was, after all, an important part of the day.

After an hour of eating and schmoozing, it was time for the games. Mom had set up all kinds of backyard activities—cornhole, badminton, frisbee, and even hopscotch for the little ones. Everyone seemed to be having a great time, including me!

I was getting the hang of identifying certain family members, since my mother had color-coded their name tags according to immediate family. Ted and Linda's parents were Sal and Joan. Rich and Lisa's parents were Jean and Tony. Lisa's daughters were Genevieve and Roma. Ted's wife was Karol, but wait, whose daughters were Gina and Diana? Well, most of it was making sense. The main problem was that they all looked very much alike. I could even see my own resemblance in them!

What was most interesting to me was our shared sense of humor. No one in my grade thinks I'm funny. I mean it. NO ONE! My jokes are constantly falling flat, as my friends continue to roll their eyes and groan at what I think is a perfect punchline.

Here I was, however, surrounded by people who "got" me. By the day's end, we were falling out of our chairs, happy tears rolling down the family's and my faces as we shared our ridiculous jokes and embarrassing moments with each other.

When it was time to go, there was n'er a dry eye in the crowd. The closeness we felt was indescribable, and I think we feared that it would be 20 years until we would see each other again.

"Don't worry," Mom reassured everyone. "Same time next year?"

Everyone nodded in agreement as the Foxes climbed into their cars. One year wasn't so far away.

As I helped clean up, I said to my mother," It's a good thing I was off today. I would've missed this whole thing!"

Smiling, she replied, "Family's the most important thing, isn't it?"

Nodding my head, I ascended the stairs to return to my safe haven, grateful for having an awesome story to tell my friends and eager to compile an entire setlist of corny jokes for the following year's event.

6

Hyphens and Dashes

6-1: Practicing Hyphen Usage

_____ 1. Twenty-two students from my school were named National Merit Semifinalists!

Words from twenty-one to ninety-nine require a hyphen.

_____ 2. I stopped dating Paul due to his ultra-strange belief that aliens from Mars live in our neighborhood.

The prefix "ultra" usually requires a hyphen after it.

_____ 3. For my Sweet-Sixteen invitation, I would like calligraphy-type lettering.

The words "Sweet" and "Sixteen" are compound adjectives in this sentence and require a hyphen. Also, a hyphen is required after the word "calligraphy" and before the suffix "type" because "calligraphy" has more than two syllables.

__NH__ 4. I considered having a coauthor for this book but decided that might be too difficult.

A hyphen is not required between the prefix "co" and the root word "author," because the vowel "o" in "co" does not make the same sound as the "au" in author.

_____ 5. After calling off their engagement twice, Elizabeth and Richard decided to get re-engaged last month.

The word "re-engaged" is automatically hyphenated (whether it is at the end of a line or not), since the prefix "re" ends with the same letter as the root word "engaged."

_____ **6.** To save money, Josephine self-designed her wedding gown and asked her sister to sew it.

> *"Self" is one of the prefixes that is always followed by a hyphen.*

_____ **7.** Have you noticed that most planets have a ball-like shape to them?

> *Because the word "ball" ends with a double "ll," and the word "like" begins with an "l," a hyphen is required.*

_____ **8.** Copy down the following phone number: 718-546-0239.

> *Separate the area code from the exchange and the exchange from the four-digit unique number when writing or typing a phone number.*

_____ **9.** "Join me for a once-in-a-lifetime safari," said the tour guide at Animal Kingdom.

> *In this sentence, "once-in-a-lifetime" is a compound adjective describing safari.*

__NH__ **10.** Dr. Denton gave me a threefold treatment plan to rehabilitate my sprained ankle.

> *When "fold" is the suffix, it is only preceded by a hyphen if the number is greater than ten. Since three is below ten, no suffix is required.*

EXERCISE 6-2: En Dash or Em Dash?

___em dash___   1. "Give me liberty or give me death."

—Patrick Henry

An em dash is required for a quote attribution.

___en dash___   2. 1920–1933 was the range of years when Prohibition was enforced in the United States.

An en dash is required between a range of years.

___em dash___   3. The three coaches—Andrew, Martin, and Ian— attended the swim meet to gather information for their teams.

The em dash helps the reader to distinguish clearly the number of swim-meet attendees (rather than using commas for the appositive).

___em dash___   4. Reading, writing, listening, speaking—all are essential elements of an English Language Arts Curriculum.

The last portion of the sentence summarizes its preceding list.

___en dash___   5. 1200–1500 calories per day is the goal for maintaining a healthy lifestyle.

The en dash is used between a range of numbers.

EXERCISE 6-3: Culminating Review of Hyphens, En Dashes, and Em Dashes

___7___ 1. I'm running so late—where is my left shoe?—that I may miss the bus!

> *This is the em dash rule for interruptions since "where is my left shoe?" interrupts the main sentence.*

___12___ 2. "Now is the time to make real the promises of democracy."
                                                —Martin Luther King Jr.

> *This is the em dash rule for quote attribution, since Martin Luther King Jr. said these words in his "I Have a Dream" speech.*

___1___ 3. Charles Lindbergh went from living a once-happy existence to a life of solitude and desolation.

> *This is the hyphen rule for compound adjectives, since once-happy serves as a compound adjective modifying "existence."*

___5___ 4. Can you believe the Vietnam War lasted for two decades: 1955–1975?

> *This is the en dash rule for ranges of numbers, since this is a range of years.*

___10___ 5. Cover letter, résumé, interview, background check, references— there are so many steps in securing a job nowadays.

> *This is the em dash rule for summarizing; a list begins the sentence, and the portion after the em dash summarizes the purpose of those items.*

___3___ 6. The Tate is my least favorite museum in London, since I do not favor ultra-modern art.

> *This is the hyphen rule for prefixes that require a hyphen, in this case, the prefix "ultra."*

___8___ 7. I cannot believe Chiara had the nerve to go to the party without me—especially since I was the one invited, and she was only attending as my guest!

> *This is the em dash rule for emphasis, since the latter part of the sentence shows emphatic surprise.*

___4___ 8. I learned many new words over the summer including circum-spect and infamy.

> *This is the hyphen rule for word breaks, since the word "circumspect" is split between two lines of text.*

___2___ 9. You might think it is overcautious and excessive of me, but I decided to apply to twenty-two colleges.

> *This is the hyphen rule for numbers between twenty-one and ninety-nine.*

___11___ 10. In *The Wizard of Oz*, the principal actors—Dorothy, Scarecrow, Tin Man, and Lion—were so talented.

> *This is the em dash rule for appositives that contain commas; the em dash provides clarity in separating the word "actors" from the rest of the list, so it would not be added mistakenly to the list that is set apart by commas.*

SAMPLE EXERCISE 6-4: Writing with Hyphens and Dashes

Sample Cover Letter

Dear Principal Klein:

   As a rising senior, I have spent three glorious—albeit quick—years at Jefferson High School. It seems like yesterday that I walked tentatively through the halls during Freshman Orientation, not sure if I would ever find my way around this enormous and squeaky-clean building. Even if my initial tour had lasted twenty-four hours instead of one-and-a-half hours, I don't think I could have anticipated how much there was to learn about our school. Fortunately, my tour guides that day—Camille, Tricia, and Kara—made us feel welcomed and comfortable. They knew the ins and outs of the building, and they imparted so much knowledge on us in such a short span of time.

   By now you must have ascertained that I am interested in applying for the position of Freshman Orientation Tour Guide at Jefferson High. A high-achieving, outgoing individual with an interest in preserving the splendor of such a significant and a state-renowned educational institution, I look forward to leading newcomers through the building and ensuring them that these will be the most transformative years of their lives. Naturally, since tour guides represent the school in a positive light, it is imperative that the guide be a role model. Conscientious and hardworking are traits that my teachers use to describe me. As an active participant in student activities, I think this job would be a great way for me to point out the location of many of the hubs where these activities are held as well as to describe the benefit of becoming involved in extracurricular activities.

   Often, I can be seen in the building after school between the hours of 3:00–7:30 p.m., since I stay either for extra help, clubs, or sports. National Honor Society, French Club, Wrestling, Student Council—I am a well-rounded individual who dabbles in many interests. Recently, I was named "Public Speaker of the Year" by my peers on the Debating Team. The ability to project my voice would certainly come in handy in the role of Freshman Orientation Tour Guide.

For all of the reasons aforementioned, I hope that you consider me for the position—and maybe even for valedictorian! All kidding aside, I would love to help new students begin their journey through high school on a positive note, and I am confident that I would provide an ultra-informative introduction to our building. Grateful that you have been at the helm of our educational ship from the start of my journey, I hope to serve on your "crew" in a more formal capacity this September.

Sincerely,
Ian Wordsworth

Usage

EXERCISE 7-1: Linking Verb or Action Verb?

_____action_____ 1. The science teacher sounded the fire alarm.

"Sound" is an action in this sentence meaning "to ring."

_____linking_____ 2. Jason looks so tired today.

Jason is not physically looking at something.

_____action_____ 3. Turn toward the front of the room.

The action of turning one's body or head is intended in this sentence.

_____action_____ 4. Let me feel your cashmere sweater!

"Feel" is an action verb in this sentence, as the person wants to feel the texture of a sweater.

_____action_____ 5. The kitten grew into a cat so quickly.

Kittens are baby cats. In this sentence, the kitten grew bigger physically.

_____linking_____ 6. This gum tastes like watermelon.

Gum can't taste things. It is not an animate being. The word "taste" implies flavor.

_____action_____ 7. Look at my new locker decorations!

Someone is being asked to look at something with their eyes.

_____action_____ 8. A rainbow appeared in the sky after the storm.

The rainbow was visible and was not there before.

_____linking_____   9. Heather feels upset about her Spanish grade this quarter.

> *Heather is not touching anything. The word "feel" describes her emotion.*

_____action_____   10. The lawyer proved that the defendant was not guilty by using evidence.

> *The lawyer used physical evidence as proof.*

EXERCISE 7-2: Subject/Verb Agreement with Indefinite Pronouns

1. More of the adults (<u>own</u>, owns) credit cards.

   Since "more" is one of the "it depends" indefinite pronouns, you need to look at the object of the preposition between the subject (more) and the verb. Since "adults" is plural, the verb form must match up as if the subject were plural. Therefore, the verb choice "own" is correct because it matches up with a plural subject.

2. Both of the clubs (<u>meet</u>, meets) on Wednesday.

   The indefinite pronoun "both" is always plural, so the verb form that matches with a plural subject is "meet."

3. Somebody in the crowd (smell, <u>smells</u>) horrible.

   The indefinite pronoun "somebody" is always singular, so the verb form that matches with a singular subject is "smells."

4. Everything in the dorms (need, <u>needs</u>) to be cleared out by May 10th.

   The indefinite pronoun "everything" is always singular, so the verb form that matches with a singular subject is "needs."

5. All of my hard work (pay, <u>pays</u>) off in the long run.

   Since "all" is one of the "it depends" indefinite pronouns, you need to look at the object of the preposition between the subject (all) and the verb. Since "work" is singular, the verb form must match up as if the subject were singular. Therefore, the verb choice "pays" is correct because it matches up with a singular subject.

6. Many of the seals (<u>swim</u>, swims) close to the shore.

   The indefinite pronoun "many" is always plural, so the verb form that matches with a plural subject is "swim."

7. None of my homework assignments (is, <u>are</u>) difficult to complete.

   Since "none" is one of the "it depends" indefinite pronouns, you need to look at the object of the preposition between the subject (none) and the verb. Since "assignments" is plural, the verb form must match up as if the subject were plural. Therefore, the verb choice "are" is correct because it matches up with a plural subject.

8. Each of my science labs (<u>is</u>, are) challenging.

   The indefinite pronoun "each" is always singular, so the verb form that matches with a singular subject is "is."

9. Some of the residue (remain, <u>remains</u>) on the desk.

   Since "some" is one of the "it depends" indefinite pronouns, you need to look at the object of the preposition between the subject (some) and the verb. Since "residue" is singular, the verb form must match up as if the subject were singular. Therefore, the verb choice "remains" is correct because it matches up with a singular subject.

10. All of the balls (<u>roll</u>, rolls) off the table when it is tilted.

    Since "all" is one of the "it depends" indefinite pronouns, you need to look at the object of the preposition between the subject (all) and the verb. Since "balls" is plural, the verb form must match up as if the subject were plural. Therefore, the verb choice "roll" is correct because it matches up with a plural subject.

EXERCISE 7-3: Predicate Adjective or Adverb?

1. Angeline sat (quiet, <u>quietly</u>) in the back of the auditorium.

   Since "sat" is an action verb, it is followed by an adverb: quietly.

2. My dog, Muffin, appears (<u>happy</u>, happily) when she wags her tail.

   In this sentence, the verb "appear" is serving as a linking verb (similar to "look"). Since it is a linking verb, it must be followed by an adjective: happy. Muffin is not appearing or showing up anywhere.

3. Will the protagonist in *To Kill a Mockingbird* prove (<u>loyal</u>, loyally) to her initial beliefs?

   In this sentence, the verb "prove" is serving as a linking verb similar to the verb "be." Since it is a linking verb, it must be followed by an adjective: loyal.

4. Grandma was sick last week, but this week, she is feeling (good, <u>well</u>).

   This is the exception to the rule! You are allowed to use "well" after the linking verb if it indicates that someone who was sick has recovered.

5. Robin remains (dutiful, <u>dutifully</u>) by Batman's side when they are fighting the villains.

   Since Robin often stands next to Batman when combatting villains, the word "remain" in this sentence is an action verb. Hence, it should be followed by an adverb: dutifully.

EXERCISE 7-4: Abbreviations

__Incorrect__ 1. Chloe needs to go to the bank, etc. after work today.

   The abbreviation "etc." cannot be used in this sentence, since at least two items need to be listed, and only one task of Chloe's is provided: going to the bank.

Correct   2. Do you prefer M&M's or Skittles?

> *The ampersand is correct because M&M's is the name of a brand, so the ampersand should not be changed to the word "and."*

Incorrect   3. "How do you like them [Sic] apples?" is a famous quote from *Good Will Hunting*.

> *The abbreviation "sic" is placed properly, and the brackets are correct, but "Sic" is capitalized, and it should be lowercase.*

Correct   4. Benjamin Franklin, Thomas Jefferson, James Wilson, et al. were famous men who authored and signed both the Declaration of Independence and the Constitution.

> *The abbreviation "et al." is used correctly because there is a long list of authors, and only a few are mentioned.*

Correct   5. Twelve players advanced to the next round.

> *Even though the number twelve is higher than ten, and numbers below ten are the only ones that need to be spelled out, there is an exception. Since the number twelve is the first word of the sentence, it needs to be spelled out, so it is correct in this sentence.*

Correct   6. *Roe v. Wade* was one of the most controversial Supreme Court cases.

> *Since this is a famous court case, the abbreviation "v." is acceptable.*

EXERCISE 7-5: Have You GOT a Better Word?

NOTE: These are suggested answers and may vary by student.

__received__   1. I got an A on my test.

(*other possible answers: earned, acquired, obtained, scored, achieved*)

__stepped__   2. Joe got out of the car.

(*other possible answers: exited the car, left the car, walked out of the car*)

__arrived__   3. Suzanne got there early.

(*other possible answers: went, reached*)

__was__   4. Jill got fired today!

(*other possible answers: lost her job, was let go, was terminated*)

__became__   5. Jack got tired of waiting.

(*other possible answers: grew, was*)

__grew__   6. You got so tall!

(*other possible answer: became*)

EXERCISE 7-6: Writing Practice—Correcting Common Errors

Sample Writing Prompt Without Errors

Regardless of what others think, I decided to take a gap year between my senior year of high school and freshman year of college. **Though,** this seems like a bad idea to most. **Who** is it who has to pay for college tuition, you ask? None other **than me**. You might think I did not consider asking my parents before making this decision, especially after they already **hung**

my graduation picture on the wall and paid for Parents' Weekend at two prospective colleges**. However,** that is simply not true.

When I explained my reasoning to my parents, they had **fewer** concerns **than** I thought they would. After all, they were the ones **who** planted the traveling bug in me: taking me to countries from Mexico to Spain, from Norway to Japan. "Enjoy your life while **you're** young," and "You only live once" were mantras in my family home. It only makes perfect sense that I **cannot** "**lay** my hat down in **one** place" for too long.

So, I secured a part-time job teaching English online **that** will help me pay my expenses, and I am looking forward to traveling across Europe. My favorite **countries** in Europe **are** Italy **and** France, so it will be interesting to see where I land **first**. There will be **many** opportunities to take selfies and videos in order gain viewers on social media. I know **that is** going to be fun! After all, **I am** the one **from whom** all my friends ask advice when it comes to posting. What **can** go **wrong**?

My parents said as long as I call them once a week, **separate** my money into savings **money** and spending money, and **do not** run off with a **wine connoisseur**, they are fine with the decision. I do not want to become a full-fledged adult and think back on my late teens as a time when I should **have** done more with my life. Now is the time, **right**?

Once I return from my jaunt in Europe, I will apply to colleges and follow the "traditional" path. **Afterward**, I plan to pursue a career in education, so teaching online will be great life experience to include in my application essay. Hopefully, colleges will like me better than **many** other applicants. **From whom else** will they get an application like this? **These are** the reasons why I am taking a gap year. I hope I **convinced** you that **it is** a good idea.

Sentence Structure and Variety

EXERCISE 8-1: Fragment or Sentence?

__F__ 1. To the game!

There is no subject or verb in this fragment. This is simply a prepositional phrase.

__S__ 2. Maxine walked away.

"Maxine" is the subject, and "walked" is the verb, so this is a complete sentence.

__S__ 3. Don't run!

The subject is an "understood you," and the verb is "do (not) run," so this is a complete sentence.

__F__ 4. Exhausted by it all.

The verb is "exhausted," but it is not preceded by a subject.

__F__ 5. I have been.

This is not a sentence. Even though "I" seems like the subject, and "have been" is the verb, "have been" is a linking verb and, therefore, must be followed by either a noun or an adjective in order to create a complete sentence.

__S__ 6. Ron sings.

Even though it is simple, "Ron" is the subject, and "sings" is the action verb, so this is a complete sentence.

    S   7. Round the bases!

> *Since "Round" is an action verb in this sentence, and it is a command, the subject is the "understood you." This is a complete sentence.*

    S   8. Do I annoy you?

> *This is an example where the helping verb ("do") comes before the subject ("I"). Following the subject is the main verb ("annoy,") and these form a question. This is a complete sentence.*

    F   9. Very, very scared.

> *There is no noun or verb in this example. "Very" is an adverb. In this example, "scared" is functioning as an adjective. Therefore, this is a fragment.*

    S   10. Stop!

> *This is a sentence, and it happens to be a command. The action verb is "stop." The subject is the "understood you."*

EXERCISE 8-2: Run-on or Not?

1. I studied <u>so</u> much for the vocabulary test**,** <u>yet</u> I received a 72 <u>as</u> a test grade.

> *Although "so," "yet," and "as" all appear in the sentence, the only one that is connecting two complete sentences is "yet"; that is why a comma is placed before "yet."*

2. Max is a nice dog's name**,** <u>and</u> Sparkle is a nice cat's name.

> *The conjunction "and" is connecting two complete sentences. That is why a comma needs to be placed before it.*

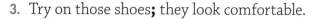

3. Try on those shoes**;** they look comfortable.

    There are no conjunctions in this sentence. However, it is still a run-on. You can place a period after the word "shoes" and before the word "they," but the more appropriate punctuation mark is the semicolon, since these sentences are related to each other. Note that if you place the semicolon, the word "they" should not be capitalized, but if you place the period, the word "they" must be capitalized.

4. Julia wears a retainer <u>because</u> her teeth are crooked.

    The word "because" is a coordinating conjunction, but even though it is connecting two sentences, it does not require a comma before it. It is the exception to the rule.

5. Jenny will go to the mall later**.** Millie loves to draw.

    This sentence has no coordinating conjunctions, but it is still a run-on. There are two completely unrelated sentences here. Therefore, the only punctuation mark that is appropriate is a period after "later" and before "Millie."

6. My grandmother <u>and</u> grandfather live in Florida**,** <u>but</u> they visit me quite often.

    Even though "and" and "but" are both conjunctions, the only conjunction that is connecting two sentences is "but." That is why there is a comma before the word "but."

7. He was <u>as</u> quick <u>as</u> a panther.

    Even though the word "as" appears twice in this sentence, neither "as" is connecting two sentences. Therefore, no comma is necessary.

8. Please wear a suit <u>and</u> tie**,** <u>as</u> you will be meeting the president of the company.

    The only conjunction that is connecting two sentences is "as." That is why a comma should precede it.

9. Student teachers are <u>so</u> vulnerable**,** <u>so</u> students should be kind to them.

> *Even though the word "so" appears twice in this sentence, each "so" is serving a different function. The first one is being used as an adverb (like the word "very"). It is not connecting sentences. However, the second "so" is connecting two sentences and requires a comma before it.*

10. This run-on stuff is pretty easy**,** <u>and</u> I think I am getting the hang of it!

> *The word "and" is connecting two sentences and requires a comma before it.*

EXERCISE 8-3: Identify the Type of Sentence Starter

__G__ **1.** Thankfully, residents of the island were unharmed by the hurricane.

> *"Thankfully" is an adverb at the beginning of the sentence.*

__E__ **2.** To succeed in life, one must set goals and work hard to achieve them.

> *The word "to" is followed directly by the verb "succeed," so it is an infinitive.*

__A__ **3.** Vivek visited his former teachers often.

> *This is a simple sentence where "Vivek" is the subject, and "visited" is the verb.*

__B__ **4.** On the precipice of the mountain, Mackenzie took a selfie.

> *In this sentence "On" is a preposition. There are two prepositional phrases in a row at the beginning of this sentence.*

__G__ **5.** No, you may not leave the dinner table.

> *The word "no" is functioning as an adverb in this sentence.*

__H__ **6.** Wow, you look fabulous!

> *"Wow" is an interjection at the beginning of this sentence.*

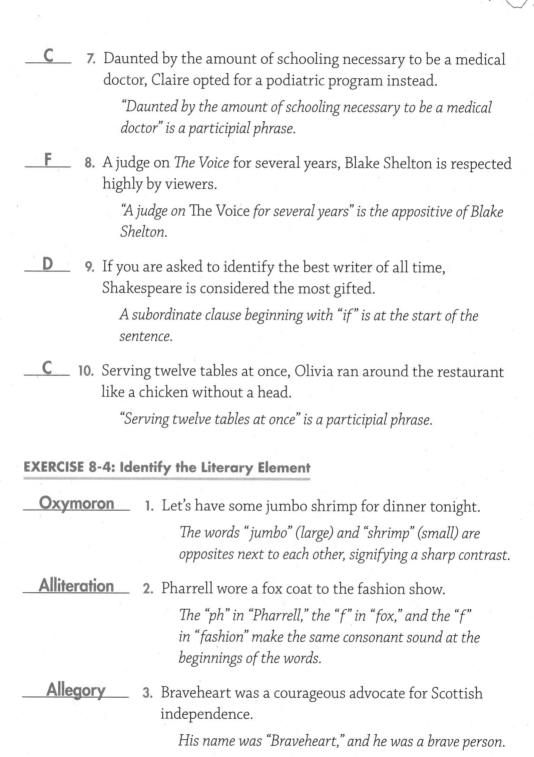

__C__ 7. Daunted by the amount of schooling necessary to be a medical doctor, Claire opted for a podiatric program instead.

> *"Daunted by the amount of schooling necessary to be a medical doctor" is a participial phrase.*

__F__ 8. A judge on *The Voice* for several years, Blake Shelton is respected highly by viewers.

> *"A judge on* The Voice *for several years" is the appositive of Blake Shelton.*

__D__ 9. If you are asked to identify the best writer of all time, Shakespeare is considered the most gifted.

> *A subordinate clause beginning with "if" is at the start of the sentence.*

__C__ 10. Serving twelve tables at once, Olivia ran around the restaurant like a chicken without a head.

> *"Serving twelve tables at once" is a participial phrase.*

EXERCISE 8-4: Identify the Literary Element

__Oxymoron__ 1. Let's have some jumbo shrimp for dinner tonight.

> *The words "jumbo" (large) and "shrimp" (small) are opposites next to each other, signifying a sharp contrast.*

__Alliteration__ 2. Pharrell wore a fox coat to the fashion show.

> *The "ph" in "Pharrell," the "f" in "fox," and the "f" in "fashion" make the same consonant sound at the beginnings of the words.*

__Allegory__ 3. Braveheart was a courageous advocate for Scottish independence.

> *His name was "Braveheart," and he was a brave person.*

Idiom   4. It's supposed to rain cats and dogs tonight!

It can't actually rain cats and dogs; it is an expression that is not translatable but is commonly understood to mean that it will rain a lot.

Pun   5. When I asked Rebecca if she would split the money, she tore the dollar in half.

The word "split" can mean to divide literally or figuratively.

Allusion   6. Stop looking at me with that devious Joker smirk!

Since the "Joker" is a famous character whom most people know, this is an allusion.

Repetition   7. Never, never, never did I say that!

The word "never" is used three times for emphasis.

Simile   8. As quickly as a cheetah, Malachi finished the final lap of the race.

The word "as" is used to make a comparison between a fast animal and a track runner.

Hyperbole   9. I am so hungry that I could eat a cow!

One cannot eat an entire cow in one sitting, so this is an exaggeration.

Onomatopoeia   10. At the picnic, the fly buzzed near my ear.

The word "buzz" imitates the sound of a fly.

SAMPLE EXERCISE 8-5: Writing Practice with Sentence Variety

Have you ever flown in an airplane? Perhaps you went parasailing? Even though I have done both activities, nothing compares to the day I learned to fly. Yes, you heard that correctly. Have I been reading too many fantasy novels? Probably, but that is beside the point. The truth is, I was granted a superpower one evening: the ability to fly. Unfortunately, I was grounded very shortly thereafter, but I am getting ahead of myself. Let me explain how it all began.

It was a blistery, cold day in late October, and I was all set to turn 18. Going to college in the Northeast does have some advantages. Leaves strewn across the path forming a sea of fall colors, chunky Irish sweaters peeking out from behind unbuttoned camel pea coats, and the smell of pumpkin spice invading every crevice of the campus made it that much more festive to celebrate a birthday. I mean, how often does one's birthday fall on the turn-back-the-clock Saturday? Magic was in the air, for sure, and I, for one, was ready for wherever the wind would whisk me.

A Halloween-themed mixer was on the agenda, and all I needed were a few tweaks to my costume. The local vintage shop sold me the perfect velvet-lapeled gray blazer along with a fire engine-red bowtie. Family Dollar helped me along without hurting my wallet, for I secured my black bowler hat, white gloves, oversized umbrella, and an assortment of artificial flowers (eagerly awaiting the hot-glue gun) for a mere ten dollars. After all, I was a freshman on a tight budget. The only thing I had left to do in finalizing my Mary Poppins costume was to borrow my roommate's floral tote bag (er, backpack) and fill it with a potpourri of surprises.

Time flew by, and before I knew it, the clock struck 9:00 p.m. My cronies and I departed the dorm and began to run across campus toward the student center. As you know, no respectable college student ever wears a coat over a costume, so my scantily clad sidekicks, Tinker Bell and Wonder Woman, were eager to get there in the blink of an eye. As we tore across the campus commons, mummies, witches, and pirates seemed to cyclone past us, but we remained steadfast in our determination to outrun any gale that came our way. Suddenly, without any notice at all, the heavens opened, and a deluge of rain, leaves, and snapping twigs befell us. Tinker Bell's fairy dust and Wonder Woman's lasso had nothing on my dollar-store umbrella, or so I thought.

They say that timing is everything, and that night was no exception. As I struggled with the fastener on the oversized parasol and snapped it open haphazardly with the strength of a Titan, a sudden gust crossed my path, lifting me vertically into the tree line like a runaway kite. One would think my sidekicks would have marveled at my agility at bobbing and weaving while dodging the illuminated lampposts, but no! They didn't even notice I was missing!

Covering their heads with their respective wings and belt, they continued their mad dash toward the sound of "Monster Mash" blaring from the opened veranda doors of the student center. Nice friends they were! At any rate, the wind picked up speed but, thankfully, transported me across campus in the right direction. Known for my driving prowess, I took the wheel . . . um . . . I mean . . . the umbrella handle . . . and shifted its course toward the party. Though it took all of one minute to glide across campus, all I could think about was what a perfect Instagram post this would have made if only I could have reached the phone at the bottom of my carpet bag-slash-backpack.

Seamlessly, the wind's final puff placed me gracefully aboard the balcony, adjacent to the open doors pulsing with music. Clapping my umbrella shut, I dusted off my attire and prepared to enter the mixer from the second floor but not before noticing someone peering down at me from the roof's gable. Knowing it was impolite to stare, I took one additional swift glance at the handsome young man hovering atop the roof like a tightrope walker, and I could not help but notice him holding a broom. As he tipped his hat to me, I stepped into the ballroom onto the dance floor with a smile from ear to ear. Magic was certainly in the air that night, and being "swept" off my feet took on a whole new meaning—in more ways than one.